DAUGHTERS *of the* DREAMING

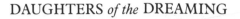

photograph: *Northern Territory News*

Diane Bell began her working life as a teacher. After the birth of her two children she returned to study, completed high school, a B.A.(hons) Monash University and a Ph.D. in anthropology at A.N.U. In 1981 she worked for the Aboriginal Sacred Sites Protection Authority in Darwin and in 1982 launched into private practice as a consulting anthropologist. In 1983 she became a Research Fellow at the A.N.U.

She is a full member of the Australian Institute of Aboriginal Studies and a board member of the journal *Aboriginal History*. On the basis of fieldwork spanning some eight years in Northern Australia, she has published widely. This is her second book.

During a *yungkurru* ceremony at Warrabri the women prepared this *kurduru* (ritual pole) which was displayed throughout the week-long celebration.

DAUGHTERS
of the
DREAMING

Diane Bell

McPHEE GRIBBLE/GEORGE ALLEN & UNWIN

McPhee Gribble Publishers, Melbourne

in association with

George Allen & Unwin Australia Pty Ltd
8 Napier Street
North Sydney, NSW 2060

Copyright © Diane Bell, 1983
First published 1983

Typeset in Plantin by Dovatype, Melbourne and
made and printed in Australia
by Globe Press, Melbourne

National Library of Australia
Cataloguing-in-Publication data
Bell, Diane, 1943-.
Bibliography.
Includes index.
ISBN 0 86861 464 5.
ISBN 0 86861 472 6 (pbk).
[1.] Aborigines, Australian — Northern Territory —
Women. 2. Ethnology — Northern Territory. I. Title.
306'.0899915

The photographs in this book were taken by the author,
unless otherwise credited.

CONTENTS

LIST OF MAPS AND DIAGRAMS   vi

FOREWORD   *1*

A NOTE ON ORTHOGRAPHY   *6*

I INTO THE FIELD   *7*

II CHANGE AND CONTINUITY   *41*

Reclaiming the Past/*41*
Fragments from the Frontier/*50*
The Present: Warrabri/*73*
The *Jukurrpa*/*90*
Bosses not Prisoners/*94*

III THE SUSTAINING IDEALS: LAND, LOVE AND WELL-BEING   *110*

The Kaytej *Jilimi* and 'Ring Place'/*110*
Yawulyu and Land/*128*
Health/*145*
Love/*162*

IV WE FOLLOW ONE LAW   *182*

'Sometimes We Dance Together'/*182*
Making Young Men/*205*

V THE PROBLEM OF WOMEN   *229*

APPENDIX 1   *255*

The Warlpiri Orthography/*255*
The Arrernte and Kaytej Orthographies/*255*

APPENDIX 2   *256*

Kinship/*256*
The Subsection System/*260*
Country Relations/*264*
Marriage/*267*
Ritual Reciprocity/*269*

BIBLIOGRAPHY   *273*

GLOSSARY   *283*

INDEX   *286*

LIST OF MAPS AND DIAGRAMS

Research Area and Field Locations   *4*
A Twentieth Century Landscape   *49*
Warrabri: A Schematic View (1977)   *75*
The Ancestral Landscape   *112*
The Kaytej *Jilimi* of 1977: A Fragment of a Genealogy   *117*

FOREWORD

'There is no life crisis, apart from the death of a loved one, as great as giving birth to a Ph.D. thesis,' a close friend of mine assured me, when in October 1980 with a month to go before the submission date, we sat at one end of my kitchen table and eyed the draft chapters stacked high at the other. In retrospect I agree. Rewriting for publication has not demanded the sustained creative effort and sheer hard work of producing a thesis. Rather it has been an opportunity to explore again, in a less frenetic fashion, the issues which I thought to be important when I first wrote of my experience of Aboriginal women's ritual life in Central Australia.

This book concerns my friends and teachers, their rituals and their models of social reality, but because women live as members of a wider society I also explore women's relation to men. In a sense then this book is a personal account of four years of my life, of the questions I posed and the answers I received.

Over the years many others have helped in the search for answers to my questions. Isobel (Sally) White, who was my teacher while I was an undergraduate at Monash University, first roused my curiosity about the problem of evaluating the status of Aboriginal women. The work of Annette Hamilton (Macquarie University) sustained my interest. A postgraduate scholarship to the Department of Prehistory and Anthropology, School of General Studies, Australian National University, allowed me to pursue my interest, and I am grateful to Nic Peterson and Caroline Ifeka for their supervision; to Anthony Forge and John Mulvaney for their forbearance during the four years I was a student in their Department; to the Australian Institute of Aboriginal Studies for fieldwork funds which provided for the eighteen months of fieldwork (September 1976 to January 1978 and December-January 1979-80) with my two children at Warrabri in the Northern Territory, and to the Department of Law, Research School of Social Sciences, which kindly gave me lodgings during the last stages of writing up. Participation in the Burg Wartenstein conference 'Development and the Sex Division of Labor' in Austria, 1980, allowed an exchange of ideas with women who had worked in vastly different fields from mine but who had pondered the same issues as I had.

My work as consultant anthropologist to the then Aboriginal Land Commissioner, the Hon. Mr Justice Toohey, permitted me extra time in the field (October 1978, October 1979, February and March 1980, December 1981) and my discussions with him regarding women's rights and responsibilities in land have been very helpful. Similarly, my work as consultant to the Central Land Council (July 1978, July 1979, November 1980, November-December 1982) and the Northern Land Council (September-October 1981, January-February and April 1982, January 1983) has also provided further fieldwork opportunities. From September 1979 till February 1980 I took a suspension of scholarship to work with the lawyer, Pam Ditton, on Aboriginal women's role in customary law. This cross-disciplinary research allowed me more time in the field and an opportunity to clarify and test ideas of women's status and role in Central Australia.

After completing the thesis I went on to work as anthropologist to the Aboriginal Sacred Sites Protection Authority in Darwin (N.T.). My specific task – to respond to requests from women for site protection and registration – enabled me to undertake fieldwork in many different communities in Northern Australia, a valuable experience in many ways. Then, in 1982, I launched into private practice as a consulting anthropologist, a lonely, challenging and bewildering year of endless demands from various groups and individuals. In those two years of working in the public domain I found the moral dilemma facing anthropologists who are entrusted with secret material was no longer academic.

In Aboriginal society there are certain matters which cannot be discussed in public: access to secret material concerning religious beliefs and practices is restricted to and by 'the old people'. But there are also matters of which it is inappropriate to speak in front of the opposite sex. Although women allow discussion of the structure of their ceremonies they will not permit the details of songs, certain designs, and ritual objects to be made public. On occasions this has meant that women appear to be ritually impoverished. They find this more acceptable than compromising their secrets. Following the instructions of the Aboriginal women with whom I worked, I have written only of those matters which they considered were open and could be read by both men and women.

In 1983 I joined the Anthropology Department of the Research School of Pacific Studies, A.N.U., for one year as a research fellow in the 'Gender, Ideology and Politics in the South Pacific' workshop. Once again the opportunity to set my ideas against those of anthropologists working in the area of gender relations is proving fascinating. It has been a time to pause – if momentarily – to reflect on past projects, to write, and to consider future work, which might include three years' comparative research in North America, following an invitation to join the Society of Fellows, Ann Arbor, Michigan, U.S.A.

In bringing this project on Central Australia to fruition, my deepest gratitude goes to the women who sat with me in the field and patiently explained their lives, values and beliefs to a raw southerner; to the women in Canberra and Alice Springs who always supported this project; and to my children who had never known their mother as anything other than a student. It is the warmth and care which these people have given me which is the greatest debt I have incurred over the past decade of being a student (secondary, undergraduate and post-graduate). I hope this book in some way vindicates their support.

In the field Sallie Kimarra Cartwright, Pam Ditton, Mary Laughren, Rita Napurrula Limbiari, Jane Lloyd, Diana Nakamarra, Rosie Nakamarra, Rosie Nampijinpa, Myrtle Napanangka, Alice Napurrula Nelson, Bunny and Annie Napurrula, Hilda Napurrula, Topsy Napurrula, Mollie Nungarrayi, Mona Nungarrayi, Elsie Kimarra Rex, Meredith Rowell, Pet Wafer and Barb Wigley were all part of my everyday survival as a person. Out of the field many of these women have continued to be part of my daily life and along with Diane Barwick, Sue Bennett, Maria Brandl, Marie Coleman, Marcia Langton, Jan Reid, Shelley Schreiner and Penny Tweedie, have kept me working. In transforming thesis to book I thank Marcia Langton who kept the all-night vigils necessary for the rebirth of Daughters; Margaret Lanigan who typed draft after draft; Jill Kitson for her inspired copy editing, Winifred Mumford for preparing the maps, Hilary McPhee and Di Gribble, whose patience is proverbial, and fellow members of the Anthropology Department for their all-round good humour. Lest it appear that women hold up 100 per cent of the world, I also acknowledge a debt to some men who have not only dis-

Research Area and Field Locations

cussed my work but have also been prepared to mind children, make coffee and collate papers. In the field Rod Hagen, Bob Kimarra Liddle, David Nash, Geoff Stead, Jim Wafer, Neil Westbury, Julian Wigley and Gary Jakamarra/Pitjarra Williams, and out of the field, Barney Cohn, Roger Keesing, John von Sturmer and Jack Waterford, have all provided such assistance.

Although my analysis and understanding of women's rituals is based on my own fieldwork and research, I owe the late W. E. H. Stanner a debt, which, because it may not be as obvious to the reader as it is to me, I wish to fully acknowledge here. It was his 1968 Boyer lectures, *After the Dreaming*, which set me thinking about the nature of changes in Aboriginal society; his monograph *On Aboriginal Religion* (1966) which directed my attention to the beauty, complexity and sheer poetry of Aboriginal belief systems; his portrait of 'Durmugam: a Nangiomeri' (1959) which brought to the arid wastelands of anthropological theory the intimacy and immediacy of the lives of the people who become the base of our studies. For reasons discussed below, I have chosen to locate my analysis within the framework of feminist thought, rather than in terms of a discussion of the nature of religious systems in general or of Aboriginal religion in particular. Obviously my analysis of women's rituals in Central Australia has ramifications for such studies, but the major issues raised in this work are not those which Stanner confronted in his study of religion.

I gratefully acknowledge the permission of The University of Chicago Press to quote from 'Women's Business is Hard Work: Central Australian Aboriginal Women's Love Rituals', *Signs* Vol 7, No 2: 314-337 and of University of Queensland Press to draw on material published in 'Aboriginal Women's Changing Role in Health Maintenance', Reid, Jan (Ed) *Body, Land and Spirit*, 1982: 197-224.

Diane Bell
Canberra
1983

A NOTE ON ORTHOGRAPHY

In various sources we find Aboriginal words rendered in markedly different ways – for example, Walbiri and Warlpiri. I have adopted the latter and throughout I have followed the practical orthography of the Yuendumu bilingual programme of the Northern Territory (see Appendix I). This orthography has the advantage of being widely known, of being the orthography of literate Warlpiri and it was the language in which I was given tuition by linguists and informants in the field. However, I worked with many who spoke the Arandic dialect of Kaytej (Kaititj) and Alyawarra for which the Warlpiri orthography was unsuitable. In cases where people, places and items were most commonly rendered in Kaytej or Aranda, I have used the Arrernte (Aranda) orthography of the Institute for Aboriginal Development, Alice Springs (see Appendix I).

I have not italicized Aboriginal place names or subsection terms. Where the same term applies to a place and a dreaming the latter only is italicized.

Chapter I
INTO THE FIELD

We were returning to the *jilimi* (women's camp) from the ceremonial ground where an initiation for a lad I had learnt to call 'son' was in progress. Several 'sisters' and 'aunts' were discussing a four year-old who had been present throughout the evening's proceedings. Although she had had no parental supervision or direction, the child had behaved and responded correctly throughout. As she trotted along beside us, one of the women asked, 'Who's boss for you?' 'No-one,' quipped the child, 'I'm boss for meself.' Her statement was greeted with general approval and mirth. The notion of being boss for oneself, of being in control of one's own life, so directly expressed by the child, does not diminish as women age, but rather is a central motif in the rich tapestry of desert women's lives.

My appreciation of the central position of Aboriginal women in the design and structure of desert society began in 1976 at Warrabri, a government settlement located 375 km north of Alice Springs in the Central region of the Northern Territory of Australia. At that time Warrabri was home to approximately 750 Aborigines and 70-80 whites. Not only was there a gulf between these segments of the population but the Aboriginal people themselves were divided according to language and land affiliation: Warlpiri constituted about 35 per cent of the Aboriginal population, Warumungu/Warlmanpa 20 per cent, Kaytej 10 per cent, Alyawarra 35 per cent.

At first glance the settlement appeared an unlikely scramble of structures: the water tower dominated the skyline, around it stood brick and prefabricated shelters, church and corrugated iron store, cool white hospital and the ruins of earlier single-men's quarters. A little further afield were tin humpies, bush shelters and broken discarded vehicles. Weaving in and out of these fixtures, dogs, children and the few serviceable vehicles moved rapidly, adults more slowly. Dirt, dusty heat and the throbbing of the power station filled all the remaining spaces.

There was of course an underlying order to the settlement and it was one which owed as much to Aboriginal preferences as to the presence of whites. Today people are cramped on settlements such as Warrabri, in daily intense interaction with whites and other Aborigines who a century ago were scattered across vast tracts of land in small mobile bands which congregated only in times of plenty, or in times of scarcity, when they clustered at the last of the permanent water. To ease the tensions of the population-intensive life-style of Warrabri and to preserve something of their old identity, Warlpiri and Warumungu oriented their camps to their traditional land west of the settlement, while Alyawarra and Kaytej oriented their camps to the east. Contact between east- and westsiders was minimal and occurred in the service core of the settlement where the whites lived and worked. Unemployment was chronic, health was poor. In many ways Warrabri resembled a refugee camp more than a small rural town.

With the passage of the *Aboriginal Land Rights (N.T.) Act* 1976[1] and the handing back of specified reserve lands, Warrabri became Aboriginal land, held by a Land Trust, administered by a local Aboriginal council and known as Ali-curang after a soakage associated with the travels of the ancestral dingoes. Some Aboriginal families (predominantly Warlpiri and Warumungu) have left Warrabri but the Kaytej, the traditional owners of the area, have remained strong. If anything the changes and shifts have strengthened the position of the Kaytej. In particular the Kaytej women had held firm in their resolve to live on their land and to celebrate in ritual the significance of the myths handed down from their forebears. It was Kaytej women who confidently instructed me in the far-reaching implications of women's ritual role in the maintenance of religious values in desert society.

My first lesson concerned appropriate behaviour for women research workers. In reply to my letter seeking permission to undertake fieldwork at Warrabri, the local council replied, 'Yes, but confine yourself to the women.' This was exactly what I had planned to do for I knew it was unproductive and even dangerous to work with members of the opposite sex. So, in my 1954 Holden panel van loaded with an improbable cargo of camping gear (most of which was never used), tools, a few books, children's toys and a flagon of wine, my two children and I set out from Canberra in August 1976 to drive to Port Augusta, where we boarded the old Ghan for a leisurely train ride to Alice Springs. We planned to arrive in time to take the intensive language course in Warlpiri which was offered at the Institute for Aboriginal Development, Alice Springs.

The course was gruelling. All the other students had some experience of Warlpiri from their work as teachers or advisers in Warlpiri communities. I made dreadful mistakes. 'Learn through the ear', our teachers repeated, 'try'. I did and unintentionally insulted all the adult Aboriginal males present by uttering a particularly crude sentence. I felt strangely out of my depth and no-one, it seemed, liked anthropologists. I was treated like a spy: 'Will you write down secrets and publish them? What will you contribute? Will you come back?' These challenges came from both white people and literate Aborigines. Twenty years ago fieldworkers would not have expected their work to be reviewed in this way, but the advent of Land Councils, Aboriginal Legal Aid Services and bilingual courses has provided new means by which people may voice their discontent. All fieldworkers in Central Australia now must face and answer such charges.

Before beginning my fieldwork at Warrabri I read all the available literature on Central Australia and discussed my project with other anthropologists but I had no real idea of what lay ahead. 'Don't drown in data' and 'Always carry your own water', I was advised by a colleague. The advice was reminiscent of that given to the young woman fieldworker of Laura Bohannan's novel *Return to Laughter*, 'Always walk in cheap sandshoes, the water runs out faster'.[2]

A mystique surrounds fieldwork: to the outsider it is an exotic endeavour undertaken in remote and sometimes dangerous corners of the unexplored tribal world; but I found there is also the insiders' mystique. At some universities prospective anthropologists may take courses in fieldwork method: usually one is shown how to operate a camera, rethread a reel-to-reel recorder and is advised to keep duplicate notes. Few are prepared to tell you what it was like and after the first trip you're a member of an exclusive club, one of the rules of which is not to tell it as it really was.

To admit to one's inadequacies, to how fumbling one was in the local language, to how socially inept, how angry and upset one became, is simply not the done thing. Instead, one speaks at an anecdotal level at anthropological gatherings, and in writing of the experience one constructs manuals which discuss establishing 'rapport', methodologies and coping with 'culture shock'. But it stands to reason that no amount of techniques or fieldwork strategies will induce an elderly person to divulge secret material to a young person of the opposite sex. Who we are, how we behave in the field, the resources (both personal and material) which we bring to bear, our research design, interests, skills and prejudices, are all elements in our field-work.[3]

After completing the language course, feeling thoroughly inadequate and despondent, I drove with my children directly to Warrabri to begin the 'real fieldwork'. Thus it was that late one Sunday afternoon we arrived and sought directions from several Warlpiri children. My speech in Warlpiri amused them and they followed us home. Excited children, touching everything, filled the house the council had allocated to us. My daughter immediately made friends with the girls and went off to ride horses but could not get a turn by standing in line. She returned somewhat amazed. My son offered some of his toys to share in a game with a few boys. They accepted and did not return them.

After several hours the children had shut themselves in a room to avoid being further touched and questioned. Within two hours of arrival I had been advised by the local headmaster not to allow children into my home. Fieldwork had begun. And in the months to come the whites who were confident that they knew 'these people', unhesitantly shared their insights and admonished me when I erred with comments such as, 'Remember Diane, you're a white woman'.

When I enrolled my children at the Warrabri school, I asked an Aboriginal woman working there if I could walk into the camps. She had heard I had arrived and gave me a long list of women to see and assured me I'd be welcome. I wandered around, was swept up by an argument between two young mothers trailing toddlers and shielded by a talkative Warlpiri woman. She asked what I was doing. I said I had come to Warrabri to learn about women's lives. Their only recent experience at Warrabri of fieldworkers had been a linguist and I was therefore immediately placed as a linguist. Professor Ken Hale, a brilliant field linguist, is a hard act to follow and any future linguist at Warrabri can only excel in the light of my poor example. 'Oh that Japanangka', people would say. 'He talks proper Warlpiri.'[4]

Later that day I sat chatting with the woman who had befriended me in the morning. She invited me to the 'women's business' which was to be held that day. I couldn't believe my good fortune. Each afternoon that week, Warlpiri women practised for the Education

Department trip to Melbourne and Canberra which they were undertaking later that year. I quickly saw that women's self-perceptions of being 'boss for themselves' were manifest in economic, social and ritual spheres.

Latish in the afternoon, shaded from the searing heat of the desert sun by a stunted eucalypt, several elderly Warlpiri women would gather. Inevitably their conversation turned to a consideration of 'women's business', to the ceremonies known as *yawulyu*, the organization and execution of which is women's responsibility. Men approached neither the ground where *yawulyu* was celebrated nor the camps where ritual items were stored, and although they might have been aware that a ceremony was in session, and have seen painted body designs when women returned to the married camps, men's opinions on staging *yawulyu* were neither sought nor required. The attitude of the older men was one of quiet respect and gratitude to the women who were assisting in the maintenance of their shared values. Younger men were more ambivalent: a mixture of bravado and apprehension masked their ignorance of the deeper meanings of *yawulyu*.

While a discussion of the structure, themes and imagery of *yawulyu* must wait until other strands of the social structure have been teased out, I would like here to describe a *yawulyu*, as I first witnessed this ceremony at Warrabri in 1976. I now know far more than I could have hoped to have learnt from that initial performance, and in a sense this book provides the context for understanding such ceremonies, but first impressions are important: they stimulate questions and mould one's frame of reference.

With the single word command of '*yawulyu*', the elderly ritual bosses summoned other women, young, old, single, married, widowed and divorced, to assist in the preparation and performance of the ceremony. Messengers and runners were despatched to the *jilimi* (single women's camps) to 'round up' participants and to collect fat and ochres for painting designs on the women's bodies and the sacred boards.

During the next two or three hours various women joined the group. Some wandered away to the nearby store and returned laden with provisions, but all the while the elderly bosses sat in a tight circle painting the bodies of the assembled women and the sacred boards. As they worked, they intoned songs which told of the exploits of the mythological ancestors who pioneered the country and gave form and meaning to their society and its institutions, thereby establishing the Law of the Dreamtime or *jukurrpa* as it is known in Warlpiri, an all-encompassing, all-pervasive force in the lives of desert people. In the dancing and display of boards which followed, the travels of these beings were re-enacted in song and action by the women who traced a direct relationship to these particular ancestors. Past and present were thus fused: the descendants became the ancestors and the Law was shown to be a living reality.

Just before sunset, the women paused to inspect their work. A group of about twenty women, elaborately painted with either black and white or red and white designs, sat facing the setting sun: the preparations were almost done. The assembled group had sung for the country where the ochres were quarried; they had sung for the ancestors who were to be celebrated in the dancing; they had provided ritual instruction for those women who were being groomed as future

Nangala, Nampijinpa, Nangala, Nakamarra and Nungarrayi, young Warlpiri girls display designs which tell of the travels of the willy-wagtail and the diamond dove. In the peaked design on Nakamarra's breast we see the tail feathers of the willy-wagtail. On the others the oval designs represent the grinding stones which the diamond dove carried in his journey to Pawurrinji. The oval design across the stomach promotes health and well being; it ensures that those who wear it will have an adequate covering of fat.

12

leaders, and had offered brief guidance regarding the structure of their activities to me. The mood was serious and serene. Their soft singing and plaintive harmonies calmed and soothed those present.

As the sun dropped lower on the horizon a group of seven women retreated some distance from the others, who continued to sing. The mood changed; the singers began to emphasize the rhythm of the songs with a hollow clap produced by cupped hand brought down sharply on cupped hand held low in the lap. The song was now a strong and decisive call for women of all groups from all 'countries' to 'muster up' for the performance. Once satisfied that all were present, the singers began to recount the travels of the ancestors who were depicted in the painted designs.

First to appear, dancing in a straight line from the north-west, were the women wearing the red and white designs. They represented the activities of the diamond dove who travelled from Kurinji country through desert lands (many miles to the north-west of Warrabri). As they neared the seated singers they held aloft the painted boards bearing ideational maps of the sites visited by the diamond dove in its trek south. The songs told of each site, of how the dove tired of travelling, of how the dove cried out for seed. On approaching a claypan known as Pawurrinji, the dove sighted the willy-wagtail, who was feasting on a small marsupial mouse. Women wearing the black and white designs of the wagtail danced forward to meet the travelling dove people; who then wove in and out of the wagtail ranks, flanking them before joining them in one circle. From where I sat I could see that the patterns traced in the red desert sand by the dancer's feet echoed those on the sacred boards.

Although the dancers were gasping for water and exhausted from the spirited dancing, the tracks of the ancestors, of the wagtail and diamond dove, had to be followed to their resting place. In a final sequence all the dancers united in a tight circle immediately before the seated singers to whom the painted boards were presented. The initial hostility and curiosity of the willy-wagtail to the newcomers were dispelled and the essence of the birds entered the ground: a stone arrangement on the claypan at Pawurrinji provides an enduring symbol of the long ago event.

After the 'going down' of the spirit of the birds – the climax of the performance – the mood changed abruptly to one of ribald joking and good-natured chaffing about the style of one's fellow performers.

The women who are the descendants of the diamond dove ancestor are responsible for the ritual maintenance of this stone arrangement at Pawurrinji. Too often such sites are taken to be evidence of male ritual activity. In this case the women explained that the arrangement pointed to the direction from which the diamond dove had approached the willy-wagtail and indeed there was a corresponding break in the scrub on the sandhill which backs the clay pan at Pawurrinji.

Singers were 'paid' for their work and the non-participants 'paid' for the privilege of seeing the ceremony. The payments were then redistributed amongst close kin. It was now completely dark and chilly. A fire was kindled and built up on the dancing ground. The women moved in closer, continued their soft singing of country and began the task of 'rubbing down' the boards. The designs had to be removed and the power with which they were infused during the dancing, absorbed and neutralized.

Clearly both exhilarated and exhausted, one of the bosses, a woman in her mid sixties, turned to me and said: 'It's hard work, you know, Diane! Drive us back to camp.' We began to stack the paraphernalia which the women had been using into my old Holden panel van. Befitting her status one elderly lady claimed the privilege of the front seat while the rest of the women clambered into the back of the van and perched precariously on spare tyres, jerry cans and tool boxes.

'*Nyarrpara?* [Which way?]', I asked. '*Karlarra* [West]', the old lady replied.

I had watched the sun set during the *yawulyu* so I set off on the first track I could locate in that direction. I set down two of the women who lived in the easily accessible brick houses built recently by the local Housing Association, but the other women lived in the makeshift camps of corrugated iron, bush materials and canvas which were located some hundred metres away.

The well-worn track divided into a myriad of paths and again I asked which way. My navigator indicated in the appropriate fashion by gesturing with her lower lip in the direction of the track I should follow. '*Kuja* [this way]', she said. I knew it was rude to point with one's finger but in the dark I could not read her gesture and she, like many of her generation, was half blind from trachoma and thus did not recognize immediately that I'd taken the wrong fork.

A loud groan from the back of the van soon alerted her to my error. 'Wrong way,' she said cheerfully. I couldn't back up because I couldn't see and I didn't have sufficient command of the language to ask about alternate tracks. From the light of a camp fire ahead I could see the track was clear; I edged forward in the hope of turning there. The old lady put her head down, in exasperation I thought, but then from the back of the van came the voice of a young girl, 'Diane, you can't go down there, too much *miyimi* [son-in-law], no room.' As at the mad hatter's tea party there was plenty of room, but I caught the urgency of her voice and managed to turn around and return to the fork. The younger girl leant over my shoulder and by curving her open palm indicated the correct path. Later she explained that a 'son-in-law' for the old woman was camped along the track I had been following. (Mothers and sons-in-law must totally avoid each other and therefore there was 'no room' on that road for us.)

My ensuing introduction to the women's camps was a nerve wracking fiasco. People were sleeping outside and to my untrained eye the ground was a chaotic entanglement of bodies, bedding, household goods, iron sheetings, water drums and dogs – everywhere dogs. I knew nothing of the structure of camps and I must have appeared quite ridiculous on that first foray as I wove in and out of people and property until I arrived at the *jilimi* in or near which the remaining women lived.

I listened to the greetings from husbands, children and other women and marvelled at the dignified and sprightly carriage of these women, all of whom were grandmothers, even great-grandmothers. One of the younger women recognized my distress and invited me to sit for a while in the *jilimi*. Other women emerged from the long, low snake-like building in which they slept and, swathed in blankets against the desert chill, they sat around a small camp fire talking about the *yawulyu*, joking and eating. The older women wrapped the ritual boards in an old blanket and placed them in a forty-four gallon drum where they were safe from dogs and children.

From the roof of the brush shade in which we now sat, some meat was brought down and shared around. A young girl fetched some damper and a billy can of sweet tea (which was hung on a four-inch nail driven into one of the supporting poles of the shade) and passed them to the older woman. It seemed that women of all ages were present in the *jilimi* and that like *yawulyu*, the structure and organization of the *jilimi* was the affair of senior women.

That evening I saw only the women who slept in the *jilimi*. These are the single girls who are reluctant or too young to go to their promised husbands; women who are seeking a safe environment while visiting Warrabri without their spouses or who, following a dispute, have temporarily vacated the swag of their spouse; women who are ill or

The Warlpiri *jilimi* at Warrabri, 1977.

in need of emotional support and those who are not yet through the final stages of mourning. Accompanying all these women are their dependent children and charges. During the day married women from nearby camps come into the *jilimi* to socialize but at night they return to their husband's camp. The atmosphere within the *jilimi* is usually pleasant and supportive: conversations centre on family, recent hunting expeditions, local scandal, ritual business and health. At initiation time there are discussions about the timing of the 'capture' of the boys and the maturity of the youths – these are matters which directly concern women – but otherwise male rituals are not discussed.

Forming the permanent core of the *jilimi* are those widows who have chosen not to remarry and other women who, although 'married', are not domiciled with their husbands. It is these women who today are the active ritual leaders and the repositories of religious knowledge. They are old enough to have reared children (not necessarily their own) to adulthood and to have acquired the necessary knowledge befitting the status of ritual leaders.

The *yawulyu* and the *jilimi* embody much that is dear to women: both provide visible proof in the wider society of women's separateness and independence. It is from the *jilimi* that women's ritual activity is initiated and controlled, and it is in the *jilimi* that women achieve a separation from men in their daily activities. A refuge, a focus of women's daily activities, an area taboo to men, a power base, an expression of women's solidarity, the home of the ritually important and respected women, the *jilimi* is all this and more. Throughout my stay at Warrabri the *jilimi* was my favourite work location. It was a safe place I could enter freely, where I could seek company or merely sit and contemplate.

Although my ability to understand conversational speech was limited, I had noted that in discussions during the *yawulyu*, and afterwards in the *jilimi*, certain terms recurred. Some, such as kinship and subsection terms, I knew from my background reading. Others, such as place and personal names, were unfamiliar. It seemed that in speaking to each other and of others, women drew on their intimate knowledge of family, personal life history, ceremonial status and relation to land. In different contexts women stressed different sorts of ties. If I was to understand the significance of events such as *yawulyu*, I obviously needed to know a great deal about how people were related to each other and to country. To understand the social organization of desert people, I needed to observe how these relations were played out over a period of time; I also needed to know how I should operate within the structure.

I could not ask for personal names because that is impolite and not always helpful (there were three Marys in one camp and two Rubies in another). Further, it is unnecessary for those inside the system to use personal names because reference to kin and country affiliation is sufficient to identify individuals. Instead, I adopted the strategy of asking what I should 'call' people in the various situations in which we found ourselves. In this way I came to understand how, in a system where place is fixed by birth, much remains open to negotiation.

I found children to be excellent informants: like me, they were learning and there was no loss of face if one of us erred. They taught me about the subsection system which divides the entire population into eight named categories called 'skins' in Aboriginal English. The skin system provides a sort of shorthand reference to the complex system of kinship and marriage, and to the appropriate behaviour for certain categories of kin. A person is born into their skin group and thus, in addition to a personal name, shares with other relatives who are similarly classified, a skin name. (The complexities of the skin and kinship systems are discussed in Appendix 2.)

Outsiders who intend to spend some time in desert communities need to be brought within the system so that Aboriginal people can interact and converse with them. During the language course in Alice Springs I had been given a 'skin' in order to participate in the activities of the group. I was the only unclassified member of the language class since everyone else had a 'skin' from their previous involvement in Aboriginal communities. I was given the skin name of Nakamarra, the remaining one of the eight 'skins' which did not place me in an avoidance relationship with my teachers. During the course I learnt kin terms and how to respond to the different members of that group as a Nakamarra.

As my comprehension of the system improved, the children quizzed me and tried to trick me with riddles concerning the identity of my potential spouses (all of whom fell into one skin group) and of my sons-in-law (who fell into another group). With the first skin group I could enjoy an open joking relationship: the latter had to be scrupulously avoided. These were important things for me to know and children were well disposed to teaching me.

Into the Field

At the slightest prompting women would lecture me on social structure, drawing in the sand to show the way in which their society was divided into various cross-cutting categories, enumerating the classes of person, and where appropriate, the individuals, included in each division. Warlpiri, in particular, are born structuralists and delight in demonstrating the logic of patrimoieties, matrimoieties, generation levels and marriage rules by reference to kin, subsection and land.

As a student I had learnt of the division of Aboriginal society into two groups, that is, moieties, but I had been directed to the importance of patrimoieties in matters concerning land and the Law. My female instructors were anxious to clarify and broaden my understanding of the interconnections of the divisions of their society. At times they would stress their mother's line and membership of a matrimoiety. At others they would speak of their siblings, cousins, grandparents and grandchildren as belonging to the same generation level.[5] In some ways my anthropological training was a hindrance and their attempts to clarify created confusion.

In this respect I was fortunate to have Warlpiri women as teachers

Photo Pam Ditton

My 'aunts', the Napurrula, watch as my 'mother's brother's daughter', a Napangardi, draws an aspect of the kinship system in the sand for me. Her blindness in no way inhibited her demonstration.

in the first months of fieldwork. All of the four language groups at Warrabri share similar systems of social classifications so I was able to apply the understandings I gleaned from Warlpiri across the board. Basic information was available to and from all Warrabri residents but to understand the nuances of the ritual vocabulary and land-based relations, it was necessary to seek tuition from the older women. Only they have the knowledge and authority to speak of such matters and in the final analysis it is they who decide which rules apply in ambiguous situations.

In the *jilimi* after the *yawulyu* I had asked why some women sang while others danced; I asked why some women wore one design and some another. Explanation revolved around the roles of *kirda* and *kurdungurlu*, words which I had heard during the performance. I was told that the *kirda* were the women who followed the dreaming from the father and grandfather: they had to dance for the country and wear the designs for the dreamings and places in the country. On the other hand, the *kurdungurlu* were the women who called the dreaming 'mother': they had to sing, paint the *kirda*, and ensure that the Law was correctly followed.

I drew a line in the sand for each of the women who had danced for the willy-wagtail dreaming. One of the senior women, with a sweep of her hand, encompassed my lines: 'This side, the *kirda* side, call the dreaming "father".' Then, sweeping her hand in the opposite direction: 'And this side, the *kurdungurlu* side, call the dreaming "mother".' With hands cupped before her like the weights of a scale, she balanced one side against the other: 'These two have to help each other,' she explained. Her daughter, who had participated in the *yawulyu* I had just seen, then joined in the lesson, to add: 'But for my dreaming, from my father, we turn around and I am *kirda* and they are *kurdungurlu* for me.' The underlying ritual reciprocity inherent in the conceptual division of the world into *kirda* and *kurdungurlu* was thus graphically expressed for me.[6]

Often after sessions like these the women would test me to see if I understood. 'You reckon you're Nakamarra.' 'I don't know about here,' I'd say. 'They called me that in Alice Springs.' 'We'll see,' the senior *kirda*, herself a Nakamarra, replied. During the *yawulyu*, I had realized that Nakamarra was a fortuitous choice in that it made me sister to one of the important *kirda*. Further, I could give a semblance of correct behaviour on the basis of my Alice Springs training. At the end of the week I was declared by these women to be a Nakamarra, the younger 'sister' of the willy-wagtail *kirda*. I was thereby related to all the Warlpiri camp, but I was also identified with a particular family to distinguish me from other Nakamarra. I learnt to be a woman as a Nakamarra. Had I been given a different classification it would probably have been equally profitable, but I would of course have established different friendships and relationships.

I soon learned that the allocation of a 'skin' is no haphazard business. When in 1977 a linguist came to Warrabri, I introduced him to one of my 'husbands' as a speaker of the Warlmanpa language. This 'husband' adopted the linguist as 'son', that is, as a joint 'owner' of his dreaming, in the same *kirda* set, but in a junior relationship which allowed tuition to occur. Similarly, my first teacher had adopted me as a younger sister, that is, as a member of the same *kirda* set, but as a junior. She could teach me, but the relationship was easy. The woman who became my closest friend and most serious teacher however, was of the upper generation level. I called her 'aunt'. She was a member of the same *kirda* set but, as my 'father's sister' (a structural equivalent to a father), an authority figure.

When my language proficiency enabled me to enter into women's discussion in the *jilimi* and of *yawulyu*, I could test my understandings in new situations and probe individual cases instead of relying on post mortems of ritual action. In this way I came to understand that in ritual women emphasize their role as nurturers of people, land and relationships. Through their *yawulyu* (land-based ceremonies) they nurture land; through their health and curing rituals they resolve conflict and restore social harmony, and through *yilpinji* (love rituals) they manage emotions. Thus in women's rituals their major responsibilities in the areas of love, land and health fuse in the nurturance motif with its twin themes of the 'growing up' of people and land and the maintenance of harmonious relations between people and country.

To understand this concept of nurturance, which is so different from that of Western culture, we must look to Aboriginal religious beliefs and practices. When women hold aloft the sacred boards for their country, when they dance hands cupped upward, they state their intention and responsibility to 'grow up' country and kin. This wide-ranging and broadly based concept of nurturance is modelled on the Dreamtime experience, itself one all-creative force. For Aboriginal women, as the living descendants of this time, the physical acts of giving birth and of lactation are important but are considered to be one individual moment in the much larger and total design of the *jukurrpa* (Dreamtime).

In learning of the way in which country is maintained, I came to know the names of places, flora and fauna, but it was through actual visits to country and participation in *yawulyu* that I learnt the significance of the women's world. I came to appreciate what country means. The land was rich in resources but it was also alive with meaning. The Central Desert is a land of contrasts and changes. Warrabri receives an annual rainfall of less than ten inches but in March 1977, when eight inches fell in eight days, the country was transformed. As the flood waters receded, a green lacework, interspersed with the buds of white everlastings, covered the red sands; frogs were everywhere underfoot, goanna were stranded, the hunting was good.

When I first drove along the Stuart Highway north of Taylor Crossing to Warrabri, I heartily agreed with those who had said it was the most barren stretch of country they had encountered.[7] I couldn't cover the distance fast enough. Now I can drive barely a mile without seeing something worthy of comment. In what was once open spinifex plains broken only by the odd acacia stand, I now see highly differentiated foraging grounds, rich in small fruits and goanna; in burnt-out plains, I now see prime hunting-ground and I wonder, 'Whose fire burnt through here?' Local people always know who has lit a fire because only persons in the correct relationship to a particular tract of land may do so. In the wide, dry creek beds, I now find the wild potato runners, I recognize the potential water sources, the places where frogs may be hidden deep in the cool, damp sand. I scan the horizon for smoke; I see a red tinge in the rock and I look for ochres.

In the vast grandeur of the rolling sandhills I now recognize the body shape of certain ancestors, but in the finer details of clustering rocks, the overhanging wild figs and the patination on leaves, I have also learnt to see signs of 'intent towards man'.[8] At one point on the northward-bound track to Warrabri we would crane our necks and look for a particular tree – its name would be called by somebody in our party and soft singing would accompany the telling of the story associated with the dreaming which that tree represented. At other points we would drive quietly, so as not to disturb the dreamings who had passed through this area. Women knew every inch of the country and always impressed upon me that I must travel with others, that there must be somebody with me who knew the country. It was their country, their *yawulyu*: I was never afraid that we might lose our way, and indeed we never did!

My decision to focus on ritual was tentative before I entered the field but quickly confirmed by the women of all the language groups of Warrabri - Kaytej, Alyawarra, Warlpiri and Warumungu/Warl-manpa - all of whom acknowledged the importance of ritual to their sense of personal and social worth as women.

Through a study of Aboriginal women's ritual activity I hoped to answer questions which had nagged me since I began anthropology as an undergraduate in 1972. In some studies of Aboriginal religion I had read that women were deemed to be of less cultural importance than men, although their economic role and usefulness were acknowl-edged.[9] Other studies assigned to women a separate and secret ritual life.[10] How, I wondered, did Aboriginal women themselves perceive their role? Did they endorse a derogatory self-image or did they nurture a more sustaining one? Did they merely submit to male authority or did they have an authority base of their own? Were men the only guardians of the religious Law or did women too share that role? To some of my questions I found answers but more questions emerged as my work continued.

Having learnt something of women's ritual realm, having seen that their independence and autonomy of action were not illusory, I was forced to come to terms with the dynamics of women's culture and its interrelations with, not subsumption by, that of the men. In Central Australia where male and female worlds are substantially independent of one another in economic and ritual terms, men and women elaborate separate gender-specific power bases. The cultural ramifications of the separation of the sexes are so far-reaching that they preclude one from evaluating or comparing the contribution of each sex to their society within one domain. I chose to begin within woman's domains, to document her culture, for I felt that only by doing so could I begin to speak with any confidence of the nature of the society, or find it possible to tag male-female relations with labels such as male dominance, complementarity or sexual asymmetry.

I found my work proceeding on two fronts. Firstly, I set out to understand and to document women's self-perceptions. This was essentially an ethnographic problem in that one must be accepted as a person worthy of trust before attempting to participate and record.

Obviously I had preconceived ideas about the nature of the relationship between the sexes and although some of my ideas altered rapidly as fieldwork commenced, my own personal values and life-style were obviously continuing influences on my research. These developments clearly affected my acceptability to Aboriginal women and their responses to me were partly triggered (how much I shall never really know) by my attempts to adjust to certain attitudes and to accommodate people's perceptions. This complex of perceptions and adjustments affected the manner in which and the extent to which I was incorporated within women's culture.

I found this aspect of the documentation of women's ritual lives to be relatively straightforward; the major limitations were my stamina – unused to all-night dancing at the ceremonial ground and all-day hunting in the nearby sandhills; my lack of specialist skills in the fields of linguistics, ethnomusicology, sign language and choreography; and the limitations of my vehicle on trips into country. To provide a complete description of *yawulyu* and the country to which it relates would in fact require a team of specialists. In my first year in the field I decided it was more productive to participate and to be guided by women's interests and concerns.

In this way I sought to carve out a domain of study which was deemed important to women, not one arbitrarily imposed by me. Nonetheless, I was trained to observe, so I took down everything I saw and heard: my field notes became a miscellany of jokes, kinship terms, mail arrival and departure times, tragedies, domestic regimes, ritual vocabulary, site locations, and so on. I wrote myself questions and in my more confident moments sketched tentative analyses of the ritual lives of women at Warrabri. I re-read the work of the desert ethnographers Baldwin Spencer and Francis Gillen and Mervyn Meggitt and although the words were familiar, the images were not.[11] They saw women as denied access to the spiritual domain, as ritually impoverished, as pawns in male political power plays. Something was awry. So on the second front I sought to relate the image women projected of being 'boss for themselves' with evidence for male claims to control of women. This was essentially a conceptual problem for I needed a way in which I could analyse and compare male and female assessments of their own worth in a language which was free of pejorative overtones. I turned to theoretical frameworks within which feminist social scientists, both inside and outside Australia, have tackled 'the problem of women'.[12]

Of course ethnographic and conceptual levels do not exist as separate planes of understanding but are interwoven in both the fieldwork situation and the analysis of 'raw data'. Beyond achieving a coherent synthesis of these levels, I felt it necessary also to explore the possible dysjunction between, on the one hand, women's ritual representations of their role and status as women and, on the other, their role within Aboriginal society, the wider society of Northern Australia and their place within the anthropological models constructed to represent these levels of experience.

In learning of the way in which religious practice, life histories and community affairs are intertwined, of the way in which women perceive their place in various contexts, I was fortunate to have patient and perceptive teachers. In the field I found my closest friends to be my 'daughters', 'sisters', 'mothers', and 'grannies'. It was my matriline which took the responsibility for teaching me as a woman and in particular my 'sisters' who taught me the appropriate behaviour towards men. I was always safe when wandering with my 'sisters' because we shared major avoidance relationships. My 'sisters', 'mothers', 'cousins' and 'aunts' took me hunting, joked with me, scolded me, protected me. They worried on behalf of my children. If any of us were ill, they were anxious lest my parents would think they were bad 'sisters', 'mothers' and 'aunts'.

Later some of the women actually met my parents, first on a trip to Melbourne with a dancing group, and again when my parents visited Warrabri in 1977. Several of the women stayed in my home in Canberra while I was still in the field and on other occasions women have holidayed with me in Canberra and Adelaide. From these experiences I was known to have a family and a country which was declared to be too cold, full of 'money houses' and traps such as escalators: concerns of family and home were included in conversations about my well-being and position at Warrabri.

Older women laughed indulgently at my questions and reassured me with 'We'll show you by and by.' They were intrigued by the idea of someone wanting to learn from them because, they commented, 'White fellas always ask the men, but we know too.' I had gone into the field to learn but I found it was a two-way process in which the women sought an understanding of aspects of my personal history. At Warrabri the first question concerned my marital status. Where was my husband, I was asked. I explained I was divorced. How did I support myself, was the next question. On a pension from the government and a scholarship from the university which had sent me here to learn, I explained. (This was accepted readily because Canberra is known to be the source of all money.) 'In that case,' said Nakamarra, my older sister, 'you are just like us.' In the next eighteen months I came to understand the ramifications of this comment.

My economic and emotional independence of the world of men meant that I was 'safe' with women's secrets. Aboriginal women often worry that if they confide in a white woman she will repeat the information to her husband. Those who had worked as 'house girls' observed that on returning home in the evenings husbands often asked their wives, 'What did you do today, dear?' and were told.

I was classified as a 'widow' of independent means and because my children were past infancy, I was of the correct age and social standing to begin a course of ritual instruction. I was freed of the immediate and time-consuming task of child-rearing and therefore I could spend the necessary time at *yawulyu* and in the *jilimi*. My daughter was seen to be approaching marriageable age and my son to be nearing initiation and thus I could begin to ask questions about women's ritual responsibility. Above all I was seen as self-sufficient, and determined to learn to do things for myself. In Aboriginal society women of importance are capable, not dependent. In this context my driving and mechanical skills were duly admired, as was my sewing ability, although my reluctance to handle rifles was sometimes mentioned as a weakness.

My initial inability to track animals and my slow progress in learning to distinguish certain tracks caused some annoyance and puzzlement. I was obviously adult but quite useless. I tried to explain I had grown up in cities but this meant little as most of the women had not seen any town larger than Alice Springs. I did not know how to gut a goanna or distinguish a witchetty-bearing bush from any other acacia. To them it appeared that I did not even know how to make tea. I learnt the recipe - two handfuls of sugar, one of tea, add water to fill the billy can - but persisted in making my own inferior brew of weak black tea.

My first goanna was a disaster. The hunting dog had already stunned it. I picked it up, swung it against my erect crowbar as I had seen women do many times, and missed. The bloody body of the warm goanna wrapped itself around my leg and I flinched. The women were slightly more sympathetic about my desire to photograph the goanna hunt which moves very quickly at times. One woman kindly stuffed the goanna back into the hole so that I could photograph it being dragged out. For me the recognition of my competence in the bush came when one of my 'daughters' accepted without looking the fruit of a *Solanum* which I offered her. This round yellowish tomato-like fruit grew on a small spreading bush very similar to another *Solanum* which was poisonous. On that occasion, we were in an area where both poisonous and edible species grew.

In the first few months at Warrabri I was free to move about the Warlpiri women's camps. I was accepted as a pupil who could be given certain ritual and linguistic instruction. But I always felt a little uneasy: it was as if I had been accepted because I was a white woman and the Warlpiri had learnt not to argue with whites. I was a Nakamarra, a 'widow', a mother, but I was also a white woman. Maybe I was a little like the welfare people. Finally these women asked me if I would like to view an as yet 'unopened' dreaming, that is, a ceremony which had not yet been viewed publicly and was thus considered to be 'closed' or secret. I replied yes, if they wished. I already knew that one paid for such privileges in hairstrings, bush tucker, or other dreaming knowledge (and more recently in cash) but I was not prepared for the price – a trip to New Zealand! They explained the Education Department had paid for previous dreamings to be opened by financing trips to Canberra, Adelaide and Melbourne and that now they wished me to pay for a trip to New Zealand. I hesitated. I tried to explain I was not that rich. 'Canberra is,' they answered. We continued to work together but subtle changes and a new interest in this white woman, the Warlpiri Nakamarra, were apparent in the Kaytej camp. Perhaps she could be invited to attend Kaytej ceremonies.

During the early months of establishing myself at Warrabri, a 'niece' of my older Warlpiri 'sister', who lived in the Kaytej camp, had been shyly approaching me and had come hunting with me on several occasions. I had taken some women to Phillip Creek on a nostalgic trip to their former home and, at the request of Kaytej women, I had recorded some love songs. I asked Napurrula, who was to become my close friend and teacher, if she would help translate the tapes and she agreed.

After several weeks she quit her job as a house girl for a family on the settlement and began working more and more closely with me. Through her I was invited to attend Kaytej rituals at which I was watched very closely. After about a month the women decided I could be told something of their dreamings and still later they told me that in those months of watching and waiting, they had 'won' me from the Warlpiri. Indeed when we visited women in other parts of Central Australia, my Kaytej teachers would relate how they had won me, taught me and that now I knew the Law. Although they were excellent teachers, they overestimated my ability to understand and I feared I would disgrace them. I now realize though that they effectively shielded me from blundering too dramatically. Learning by mistakes is a dangerous process and not one employed by Aboriginal women. I learnt by imitation and from their direct instruction and encouragement.

I worked with Kaytej women consistently for the remaining fifteen months, but because of their ties to other groups, I also had access to Warumungu and Alyawarra women's rituals. I realize in retrospect that the women with whom I developed the closest emotional ties were all of my matriline or joint owners with me of certain dreamings. I was considered to belong to a particular family and all relationships were reckoned from there. Even when we visited afar it was kinship links which mattered.

I was friends with many younger women who would visit my place in the evening and sometimes sleep there with their young children who were the peer group of my children. But most of my close friends were older women in their fifties and sixties – women who were freed of child caring, who indulged their grandchildren but firmly handed them to mother when they cried. These were the ritual boss ladies who took me under their wing and carefully taught me, gradually at first and rapidly towards the end, to be a woman in their society. As well as these women who were my close teachers there were many other women with whom I chatted during the day, whom I took hunting and helped find lost children.

Obviously for the women there were practical advantages to having me work with them. I had a vehicle which was for women a privilege they rarely enjoyed at other times. I was literate and prepared to use the telephone and to seek assistance for those who wanted it. (This willingness confirmed me as 'welfare' in the eyes of some.) Several Europeans were upset by my activities in this sphere. I threatened their cherished right to control information and services as well as cash flow. I could answer the questions which parties of roving whites asked and thus relieve women of an irksome burden. In every community I know there is a 'front guy' who plays the role of informant to official enquiries and thus protects the older people from continual interruptions and the prying of visitors. The 'front guys' willingly surrendered their task to me while I was around.

I could also attend meetings and transmit information back to the women. Often white male officials consulted only with the Aboriginal men, and a select group at that, and relied upon the information spreading outwards. Sometimes it did, but not always. Women often requested that I sit in and listen at meetings. Men also asked me to attend and to relay information back to the women. Some visiting parties welcomed my presence – the Central Australian Aboriginal Legal Aid Service and the Central Land Council, for instance – others – such as the Department of Aboriginal Affairs and the Health Department – did not.

Several times I was impressed by the Aboriginal male's concern to balance the correct consultation procedures with respected female leaders against his own self image as a 'leader' in the eyes of white male advisers or politicians. Aboriginal men have since explained to me many times over that consultation must be with both men and women and that they cannot speak for their womenfolk. Aboriginal men do not want to appear subservient to their women but they know they must consult. Often this was difficult to explain to young male advisers who asked for an answer on the spot. I offered one solution. Men would either ask me to attend or they asked the white officer to get me to question the women. To me they would add, 'It is not my business to speak for women,' or, 'You tell him he must also ask women. We can't do it. He needs a woman to work with women.' I have since been impressed that it is not just any woman. 'For matters of gravity and importance, do not send us young girls,' both men and women have told me.[13]

Obviously I had unequal access to certain groups of women. I knew few women in the opposite matrimoiety. At times when I was asked to fetch someone or assist in a particular activity, the request was made in terms of kin obligations but I also learnt from whom I could ask favours. As time went on I was expected to know without being told. It was in this way that I learnt how much is negotiable, largely a matter of personalities and the tolerance of the other party. In reading descriptions of Aboriginal social organization, it is easy to gain the impression that everyone follows the rules. They don't, but I needed to understand the rules before I could begin to experiment. I frequently blundered unintentionally and was told to ask someone else for the information. Even my closest friend and most constant teacher would refer me to the person who could most correctly answer my question. Often it was not that she didn't know the answer, but rather that she did not have the right to answer. Once I had been given the information, I was able to discuss it with her and she would then correct or comment upon the information. On one occasion she sought out the other informant and scolded her for instructing me so poorly: 'Tell her properly; she's learning the Law.'

I realize also that I was taken to a selected range of sites and hunting areas. Each group at Warrabri had favourite and permissible hunting areas and did not want others to know when they had been there. Observing these restrictions may have limited my access but it was also advantageous in my relationship with the Kaytej women. Once they tested me out by taking me to a site which belonged to certain Nakamarra and Napurrula Kaytej women. I was told not to tell others of its existence, that we had visited it, or of the resources we had exploited there. I complied. When asked later by a Warlpiri woman where I had been, I said, 'Ask Nungarrayi, it is her country.' I was made to recount this story to several groups as if to confirm the lesson I'd learnt and to demonstrate to others my increasing competence.

Women were always careful to differentiate for me what was for my eyes only and what was general knowledge. Other information I was given could be passed on to women like myself in Canberra but not to Aboriginal women who stood outside the ritual land-holding and managing group. Canberra women were not considered to be susceptible to the ills which could befall an Aboriginal woman viewing these things. I marked with a large cross the tape or page which the women designated for my eyes only. They could then see that I would know at a glance which material was 'open' and which was 'closed'.

Women's knowledge is jealously guarded and women are therefore reluctant to deposit their secret sacred material at places like the Institute of Aboriginal Studies, which has no separate storage place for women. All the restricted material is housed in an area designed to safeguard men's secrets. When I showed one Aboriginal woman friend around the library she was upset by this lack of recognition of women's secrets but considered it consistent with other practices in 'my culture'. 'That's your law', she observed and with a shrug of her shoulders communicated the horror, despair and cynicism with which desert people regard 'white fella law'.

I had thought that living in a house would separate me from women with whom I worked but instead I found it had considerable advantages. Many Aboriginal people already lived in houses; my neighbours were Aboriginal. I was within hearing distance of the Kaytej camp and on a major route from one set of camps to another. My yard became a thoroughfare. The house gave me somewhere safe to store tapes which was important, for the women were always particular that I kept them out of sight. The house also gave me a place where I could sit quietly with one or two women and work on tapes. This was critical for they could give me there, in private, information which could not be passed on to me in the camp or even in the women's ritual area. The women were very considerate of my need to learn in a short time what they had acquired over a lifetime, and would make extra comments on tape which I would be able to hear on the play-back and discuss with my helper.

The house also provided me with facilities such as a shower which the women used and shelter which I could share during the wet season with homeless families. I could and did sleep in the camp but the settlement life-style offers little privacy and my exit in the evening was a polite way of affording us both space. Although I had many visitors, both night and day, the house was, importantly, a place to be alone with my children. It was perhaps the reason why, during our stay, we did not contract any major illness – a misfortune which plagues most fieldworkers and one which would have spelt doom for my project.

In particular, my home became a women's refuge where wives could sleep safe from drunken husbands. I was impressed by the respect men showed for this. They would often wake me in the night and demand to know where was their wife or to ask for food, but invariably they were apologetic in the morning. Other whites considered me foolish for buying into such matters and told me that any violence which rebounded on my head was my own fault. Aboriginal men, however, were generally very protective of me and grateful that violence with their wives had been averted the night before. The women who sought refuge in my house recognized my vulnerability and left early in the morning so as not to embarrass me in daylight hours. The older women armed me with fighting sticks and instructed me in their use. They also advised me on which women should be given refuge and which left to brawl in public and defend themselves.

The major drawback with the refuge was that I knew I was leaving and that there would be no other place for some of the women to stay once I left. Several of the teachers and nursing sisters offered protection but their role on the settlement was different from mine. They did not have the time to sit and learn. In the belief that women hate to be alone, women would be rostered to keep me 'company' in the evenings. It was assumed that as long as my light burned I was in need of company which they freely gave. This made the writing of notes very difficult. At times I went to bed, feigned sleep, and then began writing when everyone else was asleep. One child observed this habit of mine and from then on it was known that Nakamarra never slept: she wrote in her blue book all night.

Over the nights when my house was used as a refuge I became very close to a number of women and indirectly to their marriages. Alcohol was invariably the immediate cause of the feared violence but the women also recognized the deeper causes. They talked about their lives as women on settlements and their past in the bush, and they asked me about European marriages and male-female relationships. I cherish the memory of these conversations, which often extended late into the night and entailed frankness, humour, inquisitiveness and devastating insights from my female companions.

It was in these sessions that women felt comfortable in explaining to me their impressions of the lot of white women. On balance it was not something they sought to emulate. The desire of what they took to be 'women's liberationists' in my culture to break down sex-role stereotyping to achieve social equality with men was viewed as yet another cross which white women had to bear. They often sympathized with the lot of a white wife and mother; 'Poor thing shut inside all day, like a prisoner'.

For themselves, they sought to have their distinctively female contribution to their society recognized and accorded the value it had had in the past when it was critical to group survival. The role they wished to see recognized was not one of dependence or subjugation as wives and mothers but a role of independence, responsibility, dignity and authority wherein they were enhanced as women, as members of their society, as daughters of the dreaming. They did not wish to see their solidarity as women further undermined.

After a year of working with these Kaytej women, I was told the reason I was trusted with women's secrets was that I didn't talk to men. Unlike other white women I did not deem it necessary to check out their story with a male for confirmation or correction. I trusted their judgment and only conferred with men when told to do so by the women, which they often did. I was a go-between who could be asked to attend men's meetings and to report back to the women. The men welcomed this because it simplified many transactions for them, but as time passed it became more difficult for me to play this role. I was expected to conform increasingly to the correct rules of behaviour and thus I had to avoid 'sons-in-law'. This effectively cut me off from one-eighth of the adult male population.

Whenever I reported back to the women from a men's meeting, they always discussed whether the decisions were correct or not. A man's decision was not accepted without comment and on one memorable occasion, after I had attended a council meeting and reported back, the women went fuming to the council and insisted on speaking. This subsequent challenge to male authority I would not have thought possible. The women argued that the men had overstepped the mark in attempting to apply restrictions to the women. Having stated their case and dismissed the objections, they went on to accuse men of breaches of the Law ranging from the non-maintenance of dreaming sites to misrepresenting to me women's role in the maintenance of country. At the end, they left the meeting in triumph.

To the Kaytej I had been on trial while I was working with the Warlpiri. To whom did I talk? Did I ask men questions? I was dedicated to learning a woman's point of view and before entering the field had deliberately avoided seeing any films which concerned men's rituals. I continued this practice with respect to men's affairs once in the field. I feared that if I knew what the men were doing while the women were elsewhere, my understanding of women's perceptions would be skewed. I would always be in danger of unintentionally disclosing something. Even familiar English words I had learnt, such as 'bullroarer', had to be repressed. I learnt to use only the female indigenous name for such items.

It was much later that several older men approached me, rather hesitantly, and told me that they too had some ritual business which I might see if I wished. They quickly added that they knew the women were teaching me properly but I might like to know that they were also important in the upholding of the Law. Women weren't the only ones with Law, they told me, thereby standing the concept of male dominance on its head.

It is interesting that the men assumed that the women would not have either discussed any men's business with me or told me that men had no business (as men tell white male researchers of women's activities). In a sense they were right, because the women had not told me much about men's business. To begin with, it was outside the scope of the interest I displayed in women's rituals and they did not consider it essential to my understanding of women's rituals. I did not feel they were frightened to discuss men's business. They left that to the men in the same way that discussion of the dreamings of other women was left to the correct spokesperson for those dreamings. Furthermore, their own ritual activity kept them busy most of the day. There was little time to feel excluded from male rituals. As one woman sympathized with me one day when I was tired after an all-night ritual with one group and a full day of hunting with another group, 'If Canberra wants you to learn all this, they should send you a helper.'

Here was a confident group of women secure in the value of their own knowledge and worth, whose self-perceptions began within their own ritual and social worlds and extended to the wider society. In the attitudes of men and women, it was obvious that the body of knowledge and beliefs about the ancestral travels was shared jointly as a sacred trust, but it was also obvious that men and women had distinct and separate responsibilities for the ritual maintenance of this heritage.

The task of learning to be a woman and a Nakamarra was not an onerous one nor was the life filled with drudgery. It was full of the support and humour of women who were dedicated to teaching me 'straight'. As time passed, I was expected to bear more and more of the responsibility for my actions within the value-system of the women. During the first round of initiations I attended with my Warlpiri women friends, we once blundered into the ritual area when the men were not ready for us. There was a fine to be paid and, although the women were upset at the transgression, I was explicitly excluded from the censure. It was a different matter a year later when I was expected to know where and how I should dance, when I should speak and when I should retreat. If I transgressed I was called mad or deaf. I should know. I had been shown. I was no longer an outsider. My decisions as to who would travel with me or suggestions as to where we would go became more and more subject to audit by the women, who would tell me that as a 'daughter', 'sister', 'aunt', I should do a certain thing.

I had relearnt much of what it meant to be a woman. I was not defined in terms of my mothering roles alone, although these were important. I was a mother, an adult female, and within limits I could leave the children in someone else's care. Certainly I was constrained by those religious beliefs of women which excluded them from certain activities, but then I knew things which men did not know. I had learnt that a woman is called an adult not merely because of her years: she must also grow in wisdom, status and knowledge as she matures. To be old is to be respected but not necessarily deferred to. Old women with no interest in the Law have no special ritual status in the community. As women leave behind their mothering roles they move into more prestigious women's activities and play an increasingly important role in community decision-making.

All the while I was learning to be an adult woman I was also learning how to relate to men. I established few easy relationships with men of my own age. Boys to the age of about ten would talk openly with me but from that age to about forty, I had few male contacts. It was older men who stood in the relationships of 'father' or 'father-in-law', 'mother's brother', 'husband', 'maternal granny' (my mother's mother's brother), or 'older brother', who most frequently talked to me, offered information and assistance. After a year I realized I hardly knew any of my 'daughters' husbands' ('sons-in-law'). If they wished to communicate with me they sent messages through their wives. I knew all my 'husbands' and 'maternal grandfathers' with whom I could joke endlessly in language and signs. My 'older brothers' and 'maternal uncles' would advise and help me but I knew few men younger than myself. In fact there was tension and embarrassment if I was in close confinement with such men. My 'fathers' and 'father-in-law' treated me kindly and gently. In describing the relationship between 'father-in-law' and 'daughter-in-law' one old man said, 'He should love you like a daughter'. That was one of the few times I ever heard 'love' used as the basis of a relationship.

Such tact had been exercised in getting me out of the way of my 'sons-in-law' that when confronted with one in the local magistrate's court one day, I failed to recognize the man by his physical appearance. I did of course know his name and when it was called, I flinched. In an attempt to recognize this man I had stared directly at him but he had averted his gaze from mine. I had always been led to avoid these men by circumnavigation of any area where they might sit or camp or were known to be working. If by accident I approached one along a path, one of my 'sisters' would gently move me to another path where there was more 'room'.

My 'husbands' however were continually spoken about in front of me. They were the subject of ribald joking and serious discussion about their merits as husbands. In a very short time I learnt with whom I might joke, with whom I might have affairs, whose name I should not speak aloud and from whom I should seek favours. In all this I was learning to be a Nakamarra. As I began to understand the kinship system so I learnt how to name people. In this way I learnt a wide range of behaviour which conditioned my response as a woman to men. I also learned how to reprimand men who behaved improperly.

One thing I noted happened frequently: while men – white and Aboriginal – were around my house, the number of women visitors declined, even if it was a man they knew and liked. When men stayed overnight, as did field officers of the Central Australian Aboriginal Legal Aid Service or Central Land Council, I was warned not to speak with them about women's business and to put my notes and tapes in a safe place. As a widow-pensioner I was deemed independent and any liaison I might have with a man was regarded as temporary, and of no threat to the safety of the women's secrets I knew.

Once, an ethnomusicologist who was working with men related to Warrabri men, visited with his wife and stayed in my house. I was warned very seriously that I must not tell him anything of women's business nor should I ask about men's business. This advice concerned how I should behave, not what I could know. Women and men do know much of each other's ritual business but it is not for public discussion or acknowledgement. During initiation time I was often alerted to women's precise knowledge of male rituals but it was not for open discussion. The information was transmitted in signs or in the songs, dances and designs of rituals at which I was present. Women did not speak of these matters in public and although I was permitted to attend, I was warned not to ask questions.

Men exercised great tact in that I was never made to feel that I was excluded because I was a woman. Mostly one is not in the position of having the existence of men's business flouted under one's nose. It is obvious that men are at business either by their absence from camps or the distant sound of their singing, but it is not crass. Men's exclusion from women's ceremonies is not crass either. Men avoid all paths which lead by or to the camps of women and not infrequently travel circuitous routes to avoid passing near or stumbling upon women at business. The women, like the men, may keep men tactfully informed, for example, by wearing their ritual designs after the ceremony, the exact nature of which must remain unknown to the men.

The ritual violence, which in the ethnographic literature is given as a major factor in the subordinate position of women, was not what I had been led to expect. It was not blind terror which kept our heads bowed at initiation, it was respect for the Law which restricted both men and women. Respect for the Law also kept men away from women's camps and ritual business. Both men and women spoke of the sanctions in the same way: they told me it made them 'too sorry' to look. The Law is backed by sanctions, the most dramatic of which men are always said to control. Persons who transgress male rules are punished violently by men, for it is their ritual which has been violated. Similarly women punish the persons who violate their domain. Women's rights to impose sanctions have been severely undermined on settlements, as they can no longer visit the sites from which they derive the power to do such things as to send men up in a 'puff of smoke'. Aboriginal men of course are relieved that women no longer have some of these powers and attempt to brush aside and joke about those that women have retained. However, women may still inflict a lingering illness and death on a man. On settlements men have the opportunity to gang up on women. This was not possible in the past where the family group was smaller. I believe women are responding to an enhanced male solidarity by increasingly living in the *jilimi*, which provides a focus of female support and solidarity.

I was acutely aware that my presence affected the behaviour of both women and men at certain times. During one fight several said they were pleased I was present because it prevented bloodshed, while another wished I wasn't there because blood had to be shed to finish the argument. Blood was not shed at all and the conflict was resolved at the fight which I witnessed. Fights did however create a dilemma for me. Should I interfere or remain an observer? When my home was used as a refuge I was obviously interfering, but it was not resented by men or women. It was a welcome alternative. Fights were most frequently scheduled for weekends when fewer whites were present on the settlement and I took my cue from the women as to whether I should attend and how I should respond. At times I found this very difficult and I still have trouble relating cheerfully to one man who, in my view, bashed his wife cruelly for an adulterous liaison when he had a long record of affairs.

Almost in the last month of my stay in 1978 I realized I could have asked many more questions of men and on subsequent visits I have. But I consider it was critical that in the initial fieldwork period I was clearly identifiable and identified as a mature widow with children and an interest in women's Law. I joked only with my 'husbands' and 'grandfathers', I reared my children with care but allowed them independence. When I did leave I told the all-male council the date of my departure and explained what would happen to the notes and stories I had written. They asked what had they done wrong that I should leave. Why were they being punished? Could they write to Canberra and ask for me to stay? If not could Canberra send a replacement? Would I leave one of my kids and take one of theirs? (a request from a 'husband'). I promised to return. I have on many occasions but it is not the same. I learn new things, I am told the news from the perspective of several months' absence. It concerns the major births, deaths, marriages and affairs. They ask after my children, my parents and do I have a husband yet?

With the benefit of hindsight informed by fieldwork in other Aboriginal communities in Northern Australia; the opportunity of returning many times over to the field to work alongside Aboriginal women in the *realpolitik* of land claims, law reform and sacred site registration; the experience of reading my work back to Warrabri women for critical comment; of being able, over a period of six or so years, to consolidate and extend friendships both when revisiting Warrabri and being visited in my home in Canberra, I have to admit that the main limitation on my access to women's worlds during that initial fieldwork of 1976-8 was the speed with which I was able to learn to be female in desert society. There were so many aspects of life I had to reconsider, so many strands of the once neatly woven social fabric which needed to be unravelled and rewoven.

For me, and I suspect for other fieldworkers, a major problem was that while in the field, I was locked into the immediacy of the situation. I hated going to sleep in case I missed something vital. I had only eighteen months to learn. Looking back I also realize how fortunate I was to choose ritual as the subject of my project for, in work I have undertaken with Aboriginal women in other parts of the Northern Territory, I have noted that when asked questions concerning their lives, aspirations and fears, women almost always prefer to explain within a ritual context.

The nature of my project helped to determine how I was classified and the kind of access I was allowed to information. If one consistently asks about ritual matters, answers will be slanted to accommodate the question. I asked about women's rituals and learnt much. Certainly the transformation was apparent to my close Kaytej friends, one of whom said to me shortly before I left in 1978, 'Nakamarra, when you came here you were young, now you are Nakamarra, my *pimirdi* (father's sister), an old woman.'

NOTES

1.   Under this Act Aborigines may bring claims to unalienated Crown Land or land in which all interests other than those held by the Crown are held by or on behalf of Aborigines. Certain reserve lands, described in Schedules 1, 2 and 3, were also made Aboriginal land. Title to successfully claimed land is held by a land trust established for that purpose. See map p. 49.

2.   Bowen 1964:4. Bohannon undertook extensive fieldwork with the Tiv of northern Nigeria, and later, under the *nom de plume* Elinore Bowen, wrote *Return to Laughter*, about the plight of an inexperienced fieldworker in an alien culture.

3.   See Golde 1970; Mead 1977. In *Women in the Field*, Golde edited a collection of writings by women anthropologists in which they speak about the way their gender and presence may have altered, negatively or positively, the 'flux of life under observation'. Margaret Mead, in *Letters from the Field 1925-1975*, (1977), chose a different framework within which to explore the mystical experience of fieldwork. In letters spanning 50 years, she offers glimpses of the changing nature of anthropology and of her role as anthropologist.

4.   For an explanation of this reference to the sub-section system, see Appendix 2. Professor Kenneth Hale of M.I.T., Cambridge, Mass., U.S.A., has wide experience with Australian languages and has written extensively on Warlpiri.

5.   See Appendix 2 for a detailed description of the kinship, sub-section system and land-based relations described in this section.

6.   See Appendix 2 for further details concerning *kirda* and *kurdungurlu* and the system of land tenure of Warlpiri and Aranda.

7.   Gillen (1968:171) in his camp jottings of his 1901-2 journey through Central Australia notes that the area north of Taylor Crossing where Warrabri is now situated was one of the most barren stretches of country that he and Baldwin Spencer encountered in their trek north. See below fn1:11.

8.   Stanner 1979:115.

9.   Warner 1937; Stanner 1979:118. W. Lloyd Warner's influential *A Black Civilization* was based on fieldwork in north-east Arnhem Land between 1926 and 1929.

10.   Kaberry 1939; Berndt 1950, 1965; Ellis 1970. The work of these women is further discussed in Chapter V. Phyllis Kaberry, author of *Aboriginal Woman, Sacred and Profane*, worked in the Kimberleys of Western Australia in the mid-1930s; Catherine Berndt in South Australia, Western Australia and the Northern Territory since the mid-1940s; Catherine Ellis, an ethnomusicologist, in South Australia since the early 1960s.

11.   Spencer & Gillen 1899, 1904, 1927; Meggitt 1962. Baldwin Spencer, Professor of Biology in the University of Melbourne, and Francis Gillen, Special Magistrate and Sub-protector of the Aborigines, Alice Springs, published *The Native Tribes of Central Australia* in 1899, based on their fieldwork in the Northern Territory. This and their later writings, based on subsequent fieldwork, provides an ethnographic base line for Aranda society. Mervyn Meggitt, an anthropologist who undertook fieldwork at Hooker Creek (Lajumanu) in the 1950s, wrote *Desert People*, which remains today the standard ethnographic reference to Warlpiri society.

12.   This body of literature is further discussed in Chapter V. In particular see White 1970, 1975; Mitchell 1974; Rosaldo & Lamphere 1974; Reiter 1975; Hamilton 1975, 1978a & b; Leacock 1978.

13.   See Bell & Ditton 1980:21.

Chapter II
CHANGE AND CONTINUITY

Returning to Canberra from the field in February 1978 was in many ways more traumatic than going into the field: white faces, new smells, the pace of life, speech styles, all seemed strange and for a while I wandered around in a daze. But I now had that cherished anthropological tool of trade. I had my own field data. The pressure was on me to 'write up', to organize and to make anthropological sense of the ethnographic details of women's ritual life, to translate the individual experiences into a portrait of a society. I tried following the advice the King gave to the White Rabbit, 'Begin at the beginning and go on until you come to the end; then stop.' But where was the beginning? I needed to back-track to make sense of women's perceptions of their role and status. In mid 1977 I had begun recording life-history material and, fragmentary though it was at the time, I began to see the need to develop a framework within which the women of Warrabri might live historically, within which I could marry the oral traditions with the written record, within which the changes wrought by a shift from a hunter-gatherer mode of subsistence to a sedentary life-style could be explored.

Before entering the field I had read all the historical material I could locate, but most of the sources concerned brave white Australians venturing in Central Australia where they faced hardship, financial ruin and deprivation. From the Aboriginal point of view, the past century of white intrusion into the land of their ancestors was one of dispossession, violence and disruption.[1] The written history was a celebration of the arrogance and chauvinism of late nineteenth and twentieth century society. Irreplaceable ritual objects were stolen; water-holes were despoiled; the ecological domain of indigenous flora and fauna was rapidly transformed by intensive grazing; punitive parties massacred groups indiscriminately while rescue

41

'pacification' parties brought people in from the desert.[2] Even the authors who took care to credit Aborigines with feelings and insights into their changing situation wrote little of women: their presence can be inferred only from statistics.

However the women with whom I worked did not consider themselves to have been invisible: they had strong feelings about the past. All the women I know at Warrabri who are over sixty can recount stories of the 1928 massacres; women over fifty tell of sexual abuse by a missionary at Phillip Creek and of enforced movement of people from Yuendumu to Hooker Creek, while women over forty recall the forced removal of part-Aboriginal children from their families to institutions. Women in their thirties struggle to rear children in a community tormented by disease, alcoholism and poverty. Women in their twenties query the value of their Western education in view of chronic unemployment on settlements, while girls of twelve and thirteen become mothers, deserted wives and recipients of social security. Warrabri, women agree, is a sad, sick place.

They look back to an era when their contribution to the society was respected, when their status was backed by authority derived from their relationship to country. 'When we lived in the bush,' women say, 'we were not frightened of men, our marriages were safe, there was no sickness, there were no jealous fights, no alcohol, no money and we did not starve. Our children were healthy, our daughters married their promised husbands, our sons spent years in the bush for business and we were able to enjoy the bounty of our country and to celebrate the continuity and strength of our religious beliefs in rituals which were powerful and renowned for their intricacies.' Much of this may be nostalgia, but in the light of the events of the past century outlined in this section much is shown to be based on experience.

Unlike Diane Barwick, who analysed changes in the lives of Aboriginal women in the nineteenth century, I had no written sources from which to trace the changes in the lives of desert women. In 'And the lubras are ladies now', she was able to draw upon the records of the Board for the Protection of Aborigines and upon Parliamentary Papers, to document the nature of the shift in gender values of residents of Aboriginal stations in Victoria between 1860 and 1866.[3] I searched in all the likely places but have not been able to unearth any long-lost pastoralist diaries, missionary journals or campfire jottings of local identities which might deal with the families of Warrabri residents. This is not to say that some may not be uncovered at some future date. In Hilda Tuxworth's[4] romantic pioneer history of Tennant Creek, she draws upon the diary of the 'white missus' of Banka Banka Station, but these documents are not available for researchers. I found little else.

Then, in the work of Eleanor Leacock, I saw a way of balancing women's reminiscences of the past with the written history. In presenting her analysis and overview of what she takes to be qualitative changes in women's role and status amongst hunter-gatherers, Leacock relied heavily upon *Jesuit Relations*. On the basis of evidence drawn from this seventeenth-century record of the Montagnais-Naskapi of the Labrador Peninsula, Canada, Leacock argued that male-female relations had been essentially egalitarian and that it was an ethnocentric projection of the hierarchical social structure of our society which led to the failure to recognize the autonomous and public role of women in hunter-gatherer society.[5] Elaborating the ideas of Frederick Engels in *The Origin of the Family, Private Property and the State*, Leacock explored the ramifications of the transformations of family structures and relations. As if answering my questions, she wrote:[6]

> To understand the effects of colonialism requires more direct input than fieldwork typically allows from women and men who are reviewing their own cultural heritage, both pre- and post-colonial, as they weigh alternatives for personal and political action.

I pondered my field notes and began to reread the early historical sources. I realized that in the journals of Charles Chewings and Francis Gillen there was evidence that women's claims to be owners for country, to have a decisive role in marriage arrangements, to be independent producers, were not mere nostalgia.[7] Both men were keen observers, had substantial knowledge of Aranda culture and, unlike other observers, they recorded details of action which included women. On my first reading I had not realized the significance of their data because their analyses were dismissive of women.

It was another eight months before I could discuss my intuitions with the women of Warrabri. In August 1978, in the course of the Alyawarra and Kaitijta (Kaytej) land claim, I returned to Warrabri and was able to press older women for more life-history material, to explore their memories of their first contacts with white men and to record their accounts of their role on cattle stations. I had a framework in the making but it was embryonic. I knew that to make sense of my data I had to confront the dynamic interweaving of sexual politics and social change.

It was not until a field trip to the Warlpiri sacred site of Pawurrinji, in the sand-hill desert country west of Warrabri (the site celebrated in the first *yawulyu* I had witnessed), that I felt confident. Once in the country where the pacification and punitive parties had swept through fifty years before, the women were a mine of stories of the nature of the impact of the changes wrought by the colonization of desert lands.

One senior Napanangka told of her first sighting of a white man but because she was under a speech taboo, following the death of a Jupurrula, a close husband, she turned to a younger Napurrula, a sister-in-law, who was sufficiently distantly related to the deceased to be able to speak. Another old Napurrula, who was a close sister of the deceased, and therefore under a speech taboo, confirmed in signs the account of the younger sister. Story-telling is a group activity: the presence and assistance of an audience ensures that there will always be a number of persons to bear witness to the content of the story and to quell any accusations that the story-teller may have erred or touched upon matters which were improper:

We [Napanangka and Napurrula] were only young girls, about that big [eleven or twelve]. It was the killing time [late 1920s]. We were in Miyikampi country, playing in the water with Nampijinpa's mother [a Nungarrayi now deceased]. We saw a white man coming. 'What is this?', we asked ourselves. 'Looks like a ghost.' We were frightened. He was leading a camel. We didn't know that camel. My grandfather [Jungarrayi, Napurrula's mother's father], old *pampa* [blind one] was handcuffed and tied to the tail of that camel. He was 'showing' the white man the country. They were going to 'muster up' all the *yapa* [Aboriginal people]. We ran away. We dragged leaves behind us to cover our tracks. We hid in a rabbit hole. We started 'killing ourselves' [i.e. hitting themselves as in a mourning practice] and defecated. We ran away to Jukurtayi-marnjimarnji, near Pawurrinji. We climbed that sand-hill, too high for that white man to climb. When they finished with that Jungar-rayi he came back. He told us about tobacco. Everyone was hungry for tobacco.

These women fled to the north and eventually found sanctuary on a cattle station where the white manager was sympathetic and was integrated into the Aboriginal life style. He married a Kaytej woman now resident at Warrabri and their children have married back into Kaytej families. Other women fled to the south where they set up camp to the west of the ration depot at Barrow Creek. Nungarrayi, who must have been under five at the time, told me of an incident of the late 1920s-early 1930s:

We would go out in the mornings with my grandmothers and aunties, getting bush tucker, all the time. We only went to the ration place for tobacco. We like that white fella rope tobacco. Then one morning, we were out hunting, still near the camp. We heard shots. We ran back. We could smell smoke. I felt sick. It was too late. The white fella had burnt the camp and shot our dogs. We camped closer to the ration place after that. No more naked ones: we were wearing clothes now.

As young girls, these women had moved confidently in their own country, under the guidance of older women, but through traumatic circumstances, they were thrown into closer and closer contact with white frontier society. In this setting of sustained contact with whites, qualitatively different male-female relations developed. The changes were subtle and in no two areas were the experiences identical. But overall, in speaking of the transition from bush to settlement life, women emphasize that it was the arrival of the 'white missus' which created the role of domestic labourer for Aboriginal women; the missionary presence which created shame; the institutionalization of settlement life which created households wherein women were dependants.

The idea that men have certain roles and that women occupy a particular place is today as clear-cut as it was in the past. Women's work is still women's work: men's work is still men's work. However, the context within which this work is undertaken, the way in which the work is evaluated and the nature of the work have altered radically. While women's separateness was underwritten by a critically important economic and ritual role, while it was possible to draw directly on the land, women's authority and autonomy were secure. Although today women continue to assert their rights within their society and to celebrate these in their rituals, their position *vis-à-vis* men has been considerably weakened. For the context within which male-female negotiations now occur is an arena where male control is the norm and the roles made available to women are restrictive and predicated on an image of woman as sex object, wife and mother. Where once there was independence there now is relative dependence.

In Aboriginal Australia before white settlement, women worked constantly and that contribution made them indispensable to their menfolk. Rations relieved women of the burden of food-getting but made them primarily someone's wife and mother. Today women have no security as independent producers but are dependent on social security payments which entail relationships over which they have no control. Women have become members of a household, one with a nominal male head and notional breadwinner; she is a dependant. In the past women lived with men in small mobile bands where female solidarity was possible. Today women live on settlements where male solidarity is given new support and additional opportunities to be realized. Men now monopolize the work which men and women previously shared.

While women are recognized as the 'feeders and breeders', men are groomed as politicians by the white male administrators and liaison officers. Aboriginal women have been cut out of much of the political life of larger settlements and left in their camps to produce babies and small artefacts. Such is the wont of women, runs European reasoning. Further, because it is inappropriate for Aboriginal men and women to sit together in large mixed gatherings, most consultations with settlement communities take place between Aboriginal and white males.[8] By the time it was proposed that councils should be established on settlements, the die was cast. Men had become the political spokespersons and women the 'followers'.

To facilitate this discussion of change and continuity in women's worlds I have isolated three critical dimensions of Central Australian Aboriginal women's worlds: the past, the present and the *jukurrpa*. We find the events of the past century provide a context for the ritual action of today and a perspective on the world in which the rituals are staged. But the way in which Aborigines have made sense of the past century is not in terms of an event-person oriented chronology. They have asserted continuity and found it in the dogma of the immutability and the omnipresence of the Dreamtime Law. Through the flexibility of the system of checks and balances by which this dogma is maintained, Aborigines have been able to assert a degree of control over their rapidly changing lives; the past has been encapsulated in the present, the present permeates the past.

On the one hand the *jukurrpa* maps out the themes of ritual, dictates ceremonial and social structure and governs the behavioural interactions of living persons; on the other hand we have only the here and now (in this case Warrabri in the late 1970s) to provide the raw materials for the rituals in which the Law is made known and thus transmitted to others. Men and women and the groups resident at Warrabri have been differently affected and their various responses are evident in the organization of settlement life at Warrabri. Thus, in this chapter, from within the three dimensions of time as outlined above, I am probing the nature of the changes in the lives of desert women, but I am also looking to continuities with the past. What are the forces which have shaped the contemporary scene? How have women fared in a century of rapid change? How are we to relate their own reflections about their past with the meagre and biased sources? Are these women 'bosses' or 'prisoners'? How may women be reclaimed from the male-oriented and male-dominated record and given their historical due?

In my interpretive analyses of events of the past century, I am not writing a history of the peoples now resident at Warrabri, nor of the progress of white Australian settlement in Central Australia. Rather, I am exploring the context within which the shift was effected from a hunter-gatherer mode of subsistence to a sedentary life style; from small mobile kin-based groups to large population-intensive government settlements; from independence to dependence; from autonomy to control. I am seeking answers to my questions concerning the nature of the changes in woman's worlds, and hence in her role and status.

As far as we can know, prior to a white Australian presence in Central Australia, Aborigines of these desert regions (such as the Kaytej, Alyawarra, Warlpiri and Warumungu) lived for most of the year in small kin-based groups which moved across vast tracts of land in accordance with the seasons, the availability of water and food and with ceremonial obligations. The population density was low and large gatherings could only be sustained in times of plenty. Access to the country of one's forebears provided substance for the Dreamtime experience and an identity based on the continuity of life and values which were constantly reaffirmed in ritual and in use of the land. Economic exploitation of the land to support material needs, and its spiritual maintenance were not separate aspects of people's relations to country, but rather each validated and underwrote the other. The land was a living resource from which people drew sustenance – both physical and spiritual. The nexus between the two was shattered with the alienation of land by mining and pastoralists' interests. Women were particularly affected as they drew directly on the land for the survival of their families.

Kaytej country extends from around Barrow Creek and the Stirling Swamp area to north of the Devil's Marbles and west to the Hanson River.[9] Warrabri Kaytej hold dreamings for these areas but focus on the northern area around the Devil's Marbles and to the west. It is in this area, in the wolfram mines of Wauchope and pastoral properties at Stirling and Greenwood, that these women first came into contact with whites.

Alyawarra country centres on the Sandover River to the south, but extends as far north as the Davenport Ranges.[10] Northern Alyawarra have married Warumungu and, like the Kaytej and Alyawarra, share a complex of relationships based on their ritual maintenance of land. Alyawarra women experienced white Australian society on the cattle stations at Elkedra, Ammaroo, Utopia, Kurundi, Epenarra, Frew River and in the wolfram mines of Hatches Creek. Thus they share with Kaytej many experiences of white Australian intrusion into their country. Indeed, the Alyawarra and Kaytej have much in common: they are members of the Arandic language family; they share a similar system of land tenure, initiation and bestowal practices.

The Aranda of Central Australia are one of the best known of Australian Aboriginal groups.[11] Like the Warumungu, they were directly in the path of development from the south to the north: ideal subjects for Baldwin Spencer's investigations, T. G. H. Strehlow's religious men and Geza Roheim's *Children of the Desert*.[12] Yet, as Mervyn Meggitt complains, we know little of many aspects of their lives in spite of the long period of contact and the number of observers.[13] This is particularly true of the northern Kaytej and Alyawarra now resident at Warrabri, but for different reasons. They were not in the path of the telegraph lines as were the Kaytej of Barrow Creek, nor were they subject to pastoralists' usurpation of their lands in the nineteenth century as were the Alyawarra in the Frew River area.

A Twentieth Century Landscape

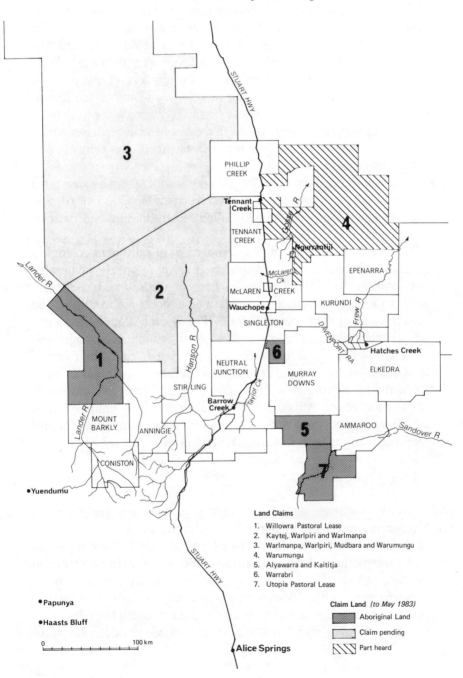

Land Claims

1. Willowra Pastoral Lease
2. Kaytej, Warlpiri and Warlmanpa
3. Warlmanpa, Warlpiri, Mudbara and Warumungu
4. Warumungu
5. Alyawarra and Kaititja
6. Warrabri
7. Utopia Pastoral Lease

Claim Land *(to May 1983)*

Aboriginal Land

Claim pending

Part heard

Of the four language groups resident at Warrabri, the lives of Warlpiri are the best documented, but the focus is more on the western Warlpiri of Yuendumu and Hooker Creek.[14] The Warlpiri of Warrabri are mainly from the Lander River area, people who fled the massacres in the 1920s to either Tennant Creek or Wave Hill and who were later drawn into the mission at Phillip Creek and thence to Warrabri. Their contact has been within the context of pastoralism, mining, towns, missions and reserves – the dead hand of institutionalization has fallen more heavily upon the Warrabri Warlpiri than on the Kaytej and Alyawarra. In the Lander and Hanson River areas, Kaytej and Warlpiri have intermarried and there are jointly maintained countries in that area.

The Warumungu have the longest and possibly the most disrupted history of all as their country around Tennant Creek was settled in the 1890s and their land quickly alienated by mining and pastoral interests.[15]

Each of the 'countries' outlined above lies in a different ecological zone. The Kaytej and Alyawarra, who enjoy relatively favourable environments for Central Australia, have smallish named 'countries', a tight family structure and rituals which stress the exclusive and closed nature of their spiritual world. The Warlpiri and Warumungu, on the other hand, have less well-watered country, few ranges and more sand-hills. Their 'countries' are ill-defined, sprawling tracts of land, cross-cut by dreaming tracks; their family structures and rituals stress the inclusive and incorporative nature of their relationship to the spiritual realm. Although differences exist in land tenure systems, social organization and rituals, these groups are united in their common belief in the power of the Law laid down in the *jukurrpa*.

FRAGMENTS FROM THE FRONTIER

Women are rarely mentioned in the literature as owners of country in their own right or as decision-making individuals; they appear as wives and mothers, their relationship to the *jukurrpa* always mediated through another. Yet I believe women enjoyed direct access to the *jukurrpa* from which flowed rights and responsibilities in land, a power base as independent economic producers and a high degree of control over their own lives in marriage, residence, economic production, reproduction and sexuality. In the light of women's insist-ence that they were and still are full members of their society, let us look again at written records and oral traditions. The portrait of women's lives which emerges reveals a persistent tradition of women's rights and responsibilities in land and of autonomy in decision-making.

Women trace their relationship to the ancestral heroes and thus to the land, in a number of ways. Through mother, father, place of birth, conception and residence flow qualitatively different rights and responsibilities. In the comprehensive nature of the web of relation-ships linking land and people these rights and responsibilities are united with those of the men. To understand this extremely flexible system, it is necessary to look to the politics of kinship and to the way in which relationships are based on land. Like the Warlpiri men of Meggitt's study, women also define country (and relationships) in a way best suited to their purpose.[16] This is possible because the land tenure system is one of interlocking, overlapping groups recruited according to diverse criteria.

Evidence for this fluidity and for the nature of the checks and bal-ances is, I believe, apparent in the survival of knowledge in areas where massacres occurred and entire patrilines were killed. Giving evidence in the Willowra land claim, one witness recalled the 1928 massacres: 'I saw my father, grandfather, all his brothers killed', he said.[17] This must have amounted to the near extinction of the patriline but the knowledge survived because there were others closely related in both the father's and the mother's line who could rekindle and rebuild the knowledge. The land survived and so did people who could care for it. One of the old men of the desert, a Japaljarri, once told me that although there had been a fire and the sacred trees had been burnt, the new ones were coming up just like the new *kirda* for that country.

Chewings,[18] who engaged an Aboriginal woman as a guide (on his return trip from Victoria River, 1909), lends weight to the notion that women not only know country but also have rights in land. Obviously her own people considered this woman competent and felt it appropri-ate for her to act as a guide.

In Spencer and Gillen there are various comments which indicate that very old women know of *churinga* (sacred objects), that female *churinga* exist, that women own *churinga*, that *churinga* are brought to women's camps, that the female ancestors travelled in all female mobs.[19] Gillen notes that women are the direct descendants of ancestral beings such as the 'seed' totem.[20] Chewings also recognized the power of older women, but nonetheless he and these later observers insisted on referring to old women as the no longer useful or desirable members of their society.

In his comments on myths of origin, Gillen states that men refer to the wandering bands of female ancestors by a term which means 'belonging to men'.[21] This may be so, but Kaytej women today do not refer to female ancestors in this way and insist they never did. Instead, as we shall see, the women cast the wandering bands of men in the Dreamtime as the uninitiated and in need of care.

As women move through the country in search of food they sing of the travels of the ancestors who gave the land form, shape and meaning; they cull, prepare and share food according to the Law which those ancestors made known in the Dreamtime; they explain to their children the significance of the land and its bounty; they impress upon children the integration of person, place and the Dreamtime heritage as one living complex whole. This role of mother, gatherer and provider is one in which women proudly state their responsibility to nourish their society. Certainly much of women's time is caught up with child care and food gathering, but this needs to be seen as a pleasurable activity rather than as the eking out of a living in constant drudgery.

With their children and female relatives, women hunted in the country of their ancestors. Their bounty included a wide range of foods from roots, seeds and berries, to honey ants, lizards, goannas, snakes, rats, frogs, birds, crabs, mussels, fish and larger game such as echidna, cat and perentie. Women also exploited their country for ochre, resin, spinifex, wax, bark and timber. Hunting parties achieved other ends, the most important being an affirmation of women's relationship to the land - a relationship which embraced rights and responsibilities.

Some of my children's happiest memories are of days spent hunting with their close 'family': their *jamirdi* (mother's father's sister) Napurrula and their *kapirdi* (older sister) Nungarrayi. But hunting is no haphazard activity, nor do women go hunting solely for food. Time away from the settlement, time with close kin, time in one's country are all as important as the exploitation of local resources. My Kaytej

My daughter, Genevieve and her 'cousins', under the watchful eye of her *jamirdi*, her 'mother's father's sister', sort through mussels collected from the waterhole at the old Phillip Creek Mission. See Map p. 49.

My son, Morgan, assisted by his 'brothers' unloads the tyre from the roof of the Toyota.

friends preferred to hunt around Devil's Marbles, near Taylor Crossing or in the country east of the Highway near Warrabri. This was their country; the virtues of it would be extolled and the significance of particular signs explained as we walked through.

On one trip to Taylor Crossing we went ostensibly to hunt for the 'fat goanna' which several visitors to Warrabri had reported being caught and sighted in the area recently. With crowbars for digging sticks, billy cans for coolamons, matches for firesticks, a blanket to sit on (no need to prepare a cleared area and make a 'cloth' of crumbled ant-hill), we were the modern well-equipped hunting party. However as soon as we were in the country, the influence of settlement life melted.

Pairs of women fanned out in different directions, their calls echoing back and forth across the creek where, with Napurrula, I wandered in search of the bush tobacco which grew in such areas. We dug for frogs buried deep in damp sand in the bank of the dry creek, pulled up the crunchy little bush onions, found a shady spot, lit a fire and waited for the others to return. In the quiet of the afternoon we watched the shimmering haze over the hills beyond the creek and the women began reminiscing about when they walked through this country as girls, when they had first seen white men; when they had drawn rations at Barrow Creek, Singleton Bore and Wauchope: 'We went to the safe places,' Nakamarra said. 'That old man at Singleton Bore used to chase us. We were walking always walking, not like today, too much sit down in one place.' Finally the other women drifted back, we ate our fill and shared the remaining food: I was given the tail of a goanna (a sweet white meat), and my favourite part of the animal. At sundown, we loaded into the vehicle and returned to Warrabri.

Much food is consumed as it is culled; much eaten is in 'half-way' camps before returning home. Women distribute the food they collect but they also distribute the food men collect. I have seen men bring home and distribute a bush turkey (bustard) in the evening and then in the morning the women undertake a secondary distribution, through which they may emphasize ties of marriage, ritual relations and friendship.

While most anthropologists allow that in pre-contact days women's contribution to the diet was considerable,[22] up to eighty per cent in desert regions, this datum is nonetheless frequently belittled. The male catch, the meat, is said to be of a higher cultural value because it is through the distribution of meat that men establish and maintain political alliances. This evaluation of the relative contribution of the sexes needs rethinking in the light of my data from Warrabri women.

Firstly, Warrabri is the wrong country for large game: kangaroo are rarely caught. Men therefore have little meat to distribute. Further, at Warrabri - as on most settlements - it is the women who do the shopping, which includes meat, and it is theirs to distribute. I do not think this is such a break with the past as it may at first appear. Women, today, as in the past, catch small game, which in addition to grubs, goanna, eggs and so forth, constitutes the major regular protein intake. Women distribute the food they have gathered (like the store-bought meat) according to kinship obligations and to parties with whom women wish to establish and maintain relationships.

Secondly, in addition to woman's control over her important contribution to the survival of the group, we need also to reconsider diet from an Aboriginal point of view. Meggitt,[23] for instance, records that men, who at certain periods of ritual may eat only meat, complain of their hunger and desire for a balanced diet which includes vegetables. This points to the fact that the men did not assess women's contribution to the diet in terms of calorific and protein intake alone.

While women's access to food and their right to distribute it mark a degree of independence for women and a dependence of men on the produce of women, the community's reliance on women's contribution has another facet. Because women are the economic mainstay, they must camp near sites where they have access to food resources. In this way women determine camp location and movements and, by claiming that there is no more food to be found, apply limits to the time men may spend in ritual.[24] This is only one of women's several influential activities in a complex web of checks and balances, but it does serve to underscore the point that women were in charge of important decisions concerning not only their lives but also those of the men and thus the whole group.

The patterns of hunting I observed would differ from those of the past, when women lived in small bands. Obviously men and women would have spent some time moving from place to place together; nonetheless, the way in which women gather, consume their catch, explain the country to their children and celebrate the bounty of country, is not new, nor is the idea that what women find is women's to bestow. Women will bring back food for a husband but their primary concern in hunting is to feed themselves and those with whom they are camped.

The major difference today is that women no longer have the daily opportunity to consume their share before they return to camp. Once they have purchased food in the store they are prey to all askers. Women have thus lost the right to distribute food amongst a finite number of close women relatives with whom they have chosen to spend the day, and must instead make decisions concerning requests for food from their settlement co-residents. Control of food was possible in the past because women were separate while food gathering and in control of their produce, at least until they returned to camp.

I wondered whether men resented the way in which women ate their fill before returning to camp to distribute the few remaining morsels. I also wondered whether men tried to force women to share the entire day's catch with them. For women living in the *jilimi* this is not a problem; they return to the company of other women after a hunting trip. Some women, however, may return to a married camp. I have heard men say tentatively, 'Anything for me?' and accept what was given. I have also heard men joking that if they really wanted to eat the food they would have to accompany the women. One said to me, 'That's what happens when you stay in camp.'

Women were responsible for the care of children to the age of about five when, if not already displaced by a younger sibling, they were weaned. Thus it was at the mother's knee that children learnt first of the importance of country and the Law and it was women who mapped out for children the knowable world of kinship, land and dreaming. Fathers regard their children very affectionately and indeed play with and handle children often, but a crying child is the responsibility of its mother. The role of 'growing up' children extends for women to their adult sons and daughters: at initiation women continue to assert their nurturance role and to base these claims on their rights in land.

The sharing with other women of activities such as child care and food collection and preparation provided the basis for later happy conversations and, I would suggest, a basis for female solidarity. Sally Slocum, Nancy Tanner and Adrienne Zihlman,[25] in their reappraisals of the role of woman the gatherer, argue for the social importance of women's activities in the evolution of our species. Certainly men's

One of the methods of transporting witchetty grubs, an extremely nutritious item in traditional diet. Sometimes witchetty grubs are tucked into the hairstring belt of the successful hunter and proudly displayed when she returns to camp.

Nungarrayi and Napurrula butcher meat while Little Nampijinpa with a tomahawk assists by clearing the ground on which the leafy 'tablecloth' is laid.

hunting parties in the desert are usually small and involve a minimum of communication and shared action, whereas women's hunting parties are the context within which children first learn about country. Through shared experiences such as hunting, but also in other domains, women develop strong ties with other women such as co-wives which are often more enduring than the tie to an older promised husband. The idea of men exploiting the potential jealousies of co-wives is, in my experience, a male myth. The relationship between co-wives often precedes and post-dates that of the marriage: many are sisters (actual or classificatory).[26] Men assiduously avoid fights between women because they are the affairs of women, but also, in my experience, because in these fights women enumerate the short-comings of the spouses and lovers in a way that men prefer not to hear.

Gillen[27] reports how the young men eagerly cleaned their clothes for the young ladies of Barrow Creek to admire. Certainly these women were already married to promised husbands considerably older than they were, but this did not stop romances between young men and women nor, women say, has it ever done so. Chewings recounts one incident in which women, while employed to mind sheep (another clue to their independence), were engaging in affairs with young lads.[28]

Women displayed a fair degree of independence in pursuing the men they desired, as Chewings reported, but they also were able to retain the men in their own country. Women were not grabbed and dragged off to another country: rather, men stayed in the country of the woman in order to be near her. Chewings[29] tells of a young man in his 1909 party who stayed with his love, in her country, and did not attempt to carry her off to his country, and of another incident of a man inducing a woman to elope, but remaining in the woman's country.

One incident glossed by Chewings[30] as wife-stealing appears on closer examination to be that of a woman exercising control over her own sexuality without damaging the marriage contract. While on a visit to the Winnecke mining-centre, the wife of a Kaytej man eloped with a local. Her husband unsuccessfully pursued the couple. He was 'crest-fallen'. Several months later the couple arrived in Alice Springs, where the woman stayed and was reunited with her husband, 'as though nothing had happened'.

In a more complex case reported by Chewings,[31] a man who eloped with a young woman was punished, but the woman was not. The culprit was then deemed to have been too severely punished and the punisher was forced to relinquish his wife. Chewings cites this example as evidence of women's low status. But the woman, who went unpunished, only stayed with the new husband until he was well and then left him for his unfaithfulness. As today, there appears to have been a fair degree of give and take between wives and husbands, which Chewings analysed from the perspective of the Victorian era. He thus imposed upon Aboriginal women a notion of womanhood from a different social order.

In the past, as today, men socialized with men and women with women. In the evenings the men and women came together to share both the news and the produce of the day's activities. In this ebb and flow of daily life the independence of the sexes was apparent. Women brought with them the knowledge of their importance and a sense of their own worth, a dignity based on their contribution to the society. There was no need for women to mark further their independence in a retreat to or a display of sexual solidarity, as they tend to do today, for in living they realized their independence.

I have outlined rights and responsibilities which indicate that women were autonomous decision-makers. They may determine where a family group will camp; they may curtail male ceremonies; they may run away and form liaisons with young men; they may marry and remain in their own country; leave men who are unfaithful; and maltreat those who accuse them. They control their own sexuality: it is theirs to bestow as they please and to a large measure they also control their own fecundity.

Does this sketch of women's domain bespeak a persistent tradition of female autonomy? It is difficult to say, but if land is the power base which I understand it to be, then women, through the maintenance of responsibilities and exercise of these rights, have long enjoyed autonomy. That women such as the Kaytej, who have lived continuously on their own land, show a higher degree of autonomy in decision-making than those, like the Warlpiri, who have been displaced, appears to support my argument.

Women's status and the relation between the sexes must be evaluated in view of the different experiences of these people in the past century as well as in view of the differences between Aranda (Kaytej and Alyawarra), Warlpiri and Warumungu. For others, each group has its own stereotypes, which, as we shall see, reflect events of the past century. Kaytej have become known to whites as 'treacherous bastards' and, according to Meggitt,[32] are regarded by Warlpiri as 'a sullen, suspicious and hostile people'. Warlpiri, on the other hand, are deemed by the Kaytej to be 'hungry buggers; hungry for land, for young men, for sex'.

Let us look at the impact of each wave of intruders into desert lands – especially on those of people now resident at Warrabri. The first recorded physical presence is that of the early explorers,[33] who are generally assumed to have had little impact on the lives of the people through whose country they fleetingly passed. However, in the changes in the Aboriginal response recorded over several decades, it is apparent that Aborigines very quickly became aware of white Australian treachery, and of their lack of regard for Aboriginal treasures and customs; it is also clear that this information travelled well ahead of the actual frontier of settlement.

On 26 June 1860, in the first recorded clash between Aborigines and white Australians in the Central region, the explorer John McDouall Stuart was attacked by upwards of thirty warriors:

> . . . [S]uddenly up started three powerful, tall fellows, fully armed, having a number of boomerangs, waddies and spears, . . . their distance from us being about 200 yards. It being so near to dark and the scrub we were then in being very disadvantageous for us, I wished to pass them without taking any notice; but such was not their intention . . . and performing some sort of dance; they were now joined by a number more, which in a few minutes increased to upwards of thirty: every bush seemed to produce a man . . . I told the men to get their guns ready . . . they paid no regard to all the signs of friendship I kept constantly making.[34]

Stuart attempted to leave but as soon as he turned a boomerang was thrown. By this time the Aborigines were only forty yards away. After a second volley of boomerangs, one of which hit the ear of a horse, Stuart gave the order to fire. However in view of the determination the Aborigines showed, his party of four, he felt, was too vulnerable to stand and fight. Stuart decided to camp further on.

Hilda Tuxworth[35] suggests that one of Stuart's men teased a small Aboriginal child: 'His cries for help brought tribesmen and a short struggle followed. No lives were lost – Stuart named the stream "Attack Creek".' In a less whimsical vein, historian Mervyn Hartwig[36] reports that the reason for the hostile reception lay in the fact that the two parties were competing for the limited supply of water available in the district. Where water was a scarce resource, for there to have been thirty or more adult males in one area (if Stuart's statistics are to be believed) indicates that the Warumungu had decided to make a show of strength. Stuart also comments that he had the impression he was not the first white man they had seen.

Aborigines who claim to be the descendants of those Warumungu people today tell of the attack with a degree of pride. They mention as the possible purpose of the attack the protection of women, the scarce water resources, and fear of the intruders. Given the novelty of whites and their gross infringements of Aboriginal law, I think it is reasonable to assume that news of Stuart's explorations, and the behaviour of other whites, had reached the Warumungu. Whatever the motivation, the result of the attack was that Aborigines in the area gained a reputation for treachery, and whites armed themselves for protection against the 'savages'.

Of the several early explorers who passed through Kaytej and Alyawarra country, Stuart reports frequent meetings with local people in the 1860s, but Ross, exploring the overland telegraph route in 1869, reported no encounters.[37] Certainly the contacts with Stuart were not marked by mutual understanding and, as Hartwig suggests, probably the first information that Alyawarra had about whites was news from western Queensland Aborigines of white pastoral alienation of land in the Hubert River district in the 1860s.[38] This, I suggest, could have preceded the exploration of the telegraph line route and possibly even Stuart via Aboriginal travellers and messengers.

From Stuart's observations[39] we gain insights into the location and size of groups in the 1860s. He saw evidence of occupation in the Davenport Ranges and a *wurli* (bush shelter) on the Hanson River. The Kaytej were obviously cautious because they followed him but did not venture close as he travelled through their country in the Taylor Creek area. In the Bonney Well district he came across a party of fourteen Aborigines at breakfast and let his horses drink from the water left behind when the group ran away in fear. He camped at Bonney Well, depleting the water-hole at the rate of 15 cm a day.[40] This was a favourite campsite according to Kaytej today and we frequently 'camped out' in this area.

In 1878 surveyor C. Winnecke also depleted an important water source when he allowed his horses to drink at a soak on the Sandover River on which sixty Alyawarra were said to depend.[41] One wonders how many other instances of whites' despoiling and depleting Aboriginal resources have gone unnoticed and unrecorded. Certainly the impact on women's lives would have been dramatic: their carefully managed resources were destroyed by persons with whom they could not communicate and to whom the Law did not apply; their ability to care for country and their dependents was immediately jeopardized; no longer was knowledge of country sufficient for survival.

To me Warburton's entry in his journal of 26 June 1873 is a stark reminder of the impact of 'transient' visitors. When 48 km north of Waterloo Wells he wrote of finding two sacred decorated boards, measuring 15 ins x 6 ins, which were hidden in a hole in the top of a hill and of taking them.[42] A violation of a sacred site such as this would have been widely reported amongst desert people but the whites understood neither the ramifications of their actions nor the enormity of the theft. This was not an isolated incident. Dr E. C. Stirling (Director of the South Australian Museum) and C. Winnecke's party stole Aboriginal possessions from Haasts Bluff.[43] Spencer and Gillen 'paid' for the items they removed (pipes, tobacco, tomahawks and knives for irreplaceable ritual items).[44] But the casual note struck by explorers, scientists and travellers who actually recorded at least some of the treasures makes one wonder how many were stolen, bought or lost but not recorded. Gillen's[45] comment that in 1902 the Hanson River blacks who came into Barrow Creek were impoverished, is not surprising when one considers the actions of the punitive parties which rode through their country in the 1870s and the activities of early explorers.

Intensive white Australian colonization of the desert began in earnest with the construction of the overland telegraph line from Alice Springs to Tennant Creek in the 1870s. The influx of male workers directly affected the Kaytej and Warumungu through whose country the line was built and less directly the Warlpiri and Alyawarra, whose country lay to the west and east of the line. The telegraph stations established at Barrow Creek and Tennant Creek in the early 1870s, plus Wycliffe Well and Kelly's Well, sunk in 1875, provided a focus for Aboriginal experience of whites.

The telegraph station also became the scene of the first recorded racial violence in the lives of Kaytej. Whereas the confrontation at Attack Creek in 1861 had been warrior versus intruder, a traditional show of strength, a ritualized display, the Aboriginal attack on Barrow Creek in 1874 indicated that in the intervening years Aborigines had realized that the newcomers were not easily repulsed by such means. Barrow Creek was attacked by young men who took advantage of the terrain, blocked an exit by which several telegraph workers attempted to escape and kept up surveillance on the station for several days. Dissatisfaction with the distribution of rations was, Gillen suggests,[46] a possible motive for the attack, in which two whites, Stapleton and Frank, and an unknown number of Aborigines were killed. But a deeper cause may have been that after two years of telegraph stations Aborigines had decided whites were not transients: they took both land and women; they threatened the very fabric of Aboriginal life.[47]

In the punitive parties which followed the Barrow Creek attack, Aborigines soon learnt that overt resistance would be met with violent retaliation. Unfettered by instructions and spurred on by the righteous indignation of the press which called for swift, severe and prompt retribution, officially sponsored punitive parties rode through the country within a 85-km radius of Barrow Creek – through the Taylor and Hanson Rivers and Central Mt Stuart region – killing as they went.[48] Officially, eleven were killed, but a higher death toll is likely. One result of the attack was that the Kaytej became the villains of the Centre, their reputation for treachery kept alive by the sight of the roadside graves of Stapleton and Frank.

In Hartwig's view,[49] the Barrow Creek incident ended the period of conciliation and heralded the beginning of the era of pacification. During the next decade, when cattle and Aborigines were increasingly competing for water resources and land, whites knew they could insist on putting down the 'murderous' Aborigines while Aborigines learnt the futility of open confrontation. The bleached bones north of Barrow Creek, at Skull Creek, the violation of sacred sites, the loss of relatives who took with them to their graves knowledge of the country, the grief and fear which kept people out of certain tracts of land, were constant reminders to the Kaytej of the meaning of white presence in Central Australia.

Violence was not confined to Kaytej country; it was endemic. Arthur Ashwin,[50] writing of the 1870s in Warumungu country, gives a gruesome account of his contacts with the 'natives' just north of Powell Creek:

> I let six staghounds go, and away they went towards the rising morn. Then we heard a stampede like a mob of cattle breaking through the scrub; then a native yelling for about five minutes; then all was quiet.
>
> About ten minutes later the staghounds came back to camp and were tied up again. They were covered with blood. Milner said, 'Aye, mon, Arthur! they have done good work; I think the fear of God will be with the natives to-night.'
>
> In the morning I went out to where I heard the yelling . . . About 400 yards from the camp there was a native lying dead with his throat torn out. The staghounds must have bitten others of the natives, for there was blood on their tracks for two or three hundred yards further afield. There must have been quite 200 natives, judging by their tracks a quarter of a mile wide, and all making for Ashburton Range, about one mile distant.

Earlier, in 1870, Ashwin had been a member of the party of Ralph Milner of Killalpaninna near Kopperamana mission (South Australia), which attempted to cross with stock from South Australia to Port Darwin in order to claim the £1,000 prize offered by the South Australian Government. John Milner, Ralph's brother, was clubbed to death by Aborigines at Attack Creek just south of where the incident Ashwin describes here occurred.

While explorers, construction teams and the manning of telegraph stations brought violence to the frontier, what brought Kaytej and Alyawarra into sustained contact with whites was the alienation of vast tracts of land in the 1870s' pastoral boom in Central Australia. Spurred on by high cattle prices in the 1870s, by Winnecke's finding of an overland route from Queensland to Alice Springs in 1877 – a route which by following the Sandover River cut right through Alyawarra country – and by heavy capital investment, a new wave of whites took up residence. Cattle runs in the Frew, Elkedra, Murray Downs and Barrow Creek regions were established.

With the drought of 1899 and falling cattle prices, runs were abandoned or fell into the hands of large companies, some of which did not stock their properties. In that decade the northern Kaytej and the Alyawarra learnt at first hand the meaning of the presence of white pastoralists. As people were torn from country and pauperized with rations, the nexus between land as economic resource and land as spiritual asset was shattered.

The pastoral frontier remained male-dominated. Hartwig[51] gives the ratio of one white women to ten white men in the last quarter of the century. Some of the liaisons between white pastoralists and Aboriginal women were enduring and the children of the union raised as heirs to the property; others were more brutal and short-lived. But whatever the nature of the relationship, it was through this contact that Aboriginal women became visible in the accounts of life on the frontier.

The presence of eight Aboriginal women at the Frew River station was mentioned by the *Adelaide Observer* (11 July 1891) as one possible reason for the attack of June 1891 by Alyawarra and Wakaja. Further attacks occurred and by 1896 the ill-fated station was abandoned. Eylmann,[52] who had spent more than a year in the Centre between 1896-98 and had visited the Frew, wrote:

> The station dwellers are said to have always treated the Aborigines with the greatest severity and mercilessly shot down every cattle thief they could get hold of. When I was there I found two human skulls in one piece, one which was pierced by a bullet, and I heard from a really reliable youth about twenty years old that the whites had once brought in a large number of lubras – among them his mother and two sisters – and let them go only after several weeks. When the insolence of the stockmen had gone much too far, the warriors of all hordes in that country attacked the station for several days; but their intention, to burn down the buildings and murder their oppressors, was thwarted by the watch and ferocity of a large number of kangaroo and blood hounds which were kept inside the pallisades. (Translation by Hartwig, personal communication.)

For the Aborigines the toll of such attacks and counter-attacks was great. One report of 1898 states that there were '45 bucks and 460 gins' in the Frew River area.[53] We have no statistics with which to compare this for the decade earlier but the implications of the sex imbalance, even if overstated, are horrendous.

By the 1890s Hartwig[54] suggests that the treatment of Aborigines was becoming less harsh, probably because the pacification drives had been increasingly successful. By 1894 he reports that, with the exception of the Frew, sizeable Aboriginal camps were attached to all cattle stations and telegraph stations. By the turn of the century there were ration depots at each of telegraph stations where Aborigines were employed to cut wood, mind herds and to act as trackers.[55] In Tennant Creek in 1890, ten aged Aborigines were receiving rations; a year later there were still only ten, but the Aboriginal population of the area had grown to a hundred.[56]

The underlying rationale of ration distribution – that the fit should work and the aged and infirm be supported – was at odds with Aboriginal values. 'They [the fit] hang about whining and in constant hunger,' wrote J. T. Beckett, Chief Protector of Aborigines, Darwin.[57] By way of contrast he noted that the Alyawarra remained in the bush and were far more dignified. They, one might add, had won a temporary respite; the Warumungu had not been so fortunate.

The Frew River area was again occupied in 1918 when pastoralists returned to northern Aranda country. The holdings of the Chalmers family in the 1920s alienated much Alyawarra country and gold mines were worked in the Kurundi area. According to Beckett,[58] when Messrs Hanlon and Wickham reoccupied the Frew and put horses and cattle on the run, the natives met them with friendliness: 'A perfect understanding was arrived at by which both sides undertook to respect each other's rights'. In return for services he paid them generously in rations. Thus nearly half a century before anthropological research was carried out in the area, a process of mutual accommodation was evident.

Experience of whites was not consistent through northern Aranda country. After the first violent contacts with whites, the Kaytej of the Barrow Creek area stayed near to the telegraph station and today their camps remain at the nearby Neutral Junction station. Beckett[59] noted that the 'Kaitichi' (Kaytej) had settled around Barrow Creek telegraph station, were drawing government rations and 'deriving little good from the same'. He reports that their many waterholes were then filled in with sand drifts and that they had come to rely on government wells. The northern Kaytej avoided this early contact and were not settled until the second era of pastoral development in the 1930s.

There was some pastoral development in Warlpiri country during the 1880s, but it was the second wave of pastoral expansion in the 1920s which brought violence to Warlpiri and Kaytej that is still remembered by many Aborigines today. In particular the Coniston massacres are a well-documented, though certainly not isolated, example of latter-day frontier violence which has become a touch-stone for many Aborigines.

Established in 1917, by 1924 Coniston was in the grips of a severe drought which forced Aborigines and cattle into competition for the same limited water resources. An elderly prospector, Frederick Brooks, was killed by Aborigines on 7 August 1928. Official reports of the subsequent punitive parties launched by whites acknowledged that thirty-one Aborigines were killed, but Aboriginal oral tradition and my own genealogies suggest a much higher number.[60]

So once again Kaytej country was the scene of tragedy, the dimensions of which were quite different for invader and invaded. One member of the punitive party, Morton,[61] stated:

We then went about thirty-six miles along to a soak on the Hanson River and found a large camp of natives there, approximately forty altogether. There were about nine adult male natives. We rounded this mob up. There were only myself and Constable Murray there then ... the natives were all armed with native weapons ... Two blackfellows yabbered to the lubras to run away quick because they were going to kill us ... We each fired several shots at the blacks with a result eight were killed.

The party had ridden east from the Lander towards Tennant Creek and then followed the Hanson River to Atheympulungku, a favourite watering place in the dry. Kaytej men and women, when they speak of these experiences, always mention that those massacred were engaged in ceremonies. To attack in such circumstances is an act of treachery. Jupurrula,[62] whose father died on the Hanson, recounted his story:

And poor old my old fella, they bin make big business. And old fella go round and they didn't know the trouble there. They ran in, they grab them there, make it prisoner ... they ran into Murray them. Grab 'em them. Two of them bin shot in the Hanson ... [after] showing them all [rockholes and water] along the country you know. They bin have chain in the neck, all the way along ... When they bin find 'em all the people then, last one alright. 'Right you two done it now, you two can be shot, Bang.'

Not all guides were shot as we saw in the story of Napanangka (see p. 44). Some guides travelled with local missionaries who rounded people up for their own safety. Nungarrayi, a senior Kaytej woman, recalling the impact on her as a child, told how the missionary party followed close on the heels of the punitive parties.[63]

My father showed the white men Wakulpu bush, Kulartakurlangu, Wapurnungku [west of Wauchope]. He took the white man around. I can't say his name, it's *kumunjayi* [taboo]. He was a policeman ... and a missionary. The missionary followed my father. I was staying at one place, Greenwood. The missionaries were still following my father. I was worrying for my father. I was really worried because we had heard that the white people were killing a lot of people. He was going with the missionary whose name was Mr White and my father would light fires so they could see that he was alive. I would be waiting there and then I look up and know that my father was there.

The name of Murray, the police constable who led the punitive parties, remains forever *kumunjayi*. In forum, such as a land claim hearing, women allude to the massacres as Nungarrayi did in speaking of her father, but will not provide details. Because the experience was shared by so many now resident at Warrabri, there is no need for explicit statements, and further, to speak of such events is too traumatic.

Many were killed, some escaped, some retreated into the sand-hill country, others sought refuge on stations and at ration depots known to be safe. Older Kaytej women who were children at the time remember the first white men they saw and how their anxiety was overcome. Nungarrayi[64] recalled:

We saw him and we said 'What's this?', and then we got scared. We said, 'This is something different. This might be a monster; a devil.' Then he showed us a lolly and we got right down and a lot of us ran off scared to get away, and he put down a lolly for us. We could see him from the scrub where we were hiding, and we said, 'That white one is something! He's gone off. Might be a ghost or something; he's gone off,' but we were really hungry so we snuck up and we grabbed that lolly and we raced off with it, and we saw a biscuit. We just put it on the edge of our mouths to taste – and it was good too! Like *kunpu* [a sweet sap from the trees]. We had no clothes; we were running around all naked. This white man started making wells and he went around to Warnku and to Martungkunya and made wells [near Wauchope].

All the bush people first were very frightened and they all got together and they ran off naked, but then the biscuits and the lollies quietened people, calmed them. My father was working. It was my grandmothers [both on her father's side and her mother's side] who saw these people and who were there with me.

Pastoral expansion in the 1920s and 1930s alienated the best waters, while personal and ritualized grief kept people out of the areas associated with violence.[65] In this way Aborigines came more and more to depend upon rations. This involved a complex 'coming in' process which may well have begun with curiosity but which all too quickly became dependence.

Not surprisingly, there are many different perspectives on 'the killing time'. Difficult access to water and a desire to keep their land free of intruders certainly were major factors underlying the attack on whites. Aboriginal survivors of the massacres suggest that Brooks' failure to return an Aboriginal woman with whom he was camped at Yurrkuru (Brooks' Soak), Coniston, was the reason why he and not someone else was the victim of their anger. The need to protect women from the clutches of white men who did not understand the nature of the terms on which Aboriginal women were able to be with them is frequently discussed today as a reason for the violence and for running away from the advancing settlement. Women are more ambivalent in their discussion of such matters than are men. Women suggest that they could go freely to such white men and that they enjoyed both the relationship and the goods they thus procured. They insist it was only with their consent that they entered into such relationships. Aboriginal men on the other hand argue that white men stole their women. There is a degree of pride in each explanation. There is also a tension in these accounts, for while women may have enjoyed the novelty of white men, the long-run effects were devastating.

Gold rushes to the Tanami in 1910, the Granites in 1932, and Tennant Creek in the 1930s, along with the establishment of wolfram mines at Hatches Creek, Wauchope and Barrow Creek, caused further despoiling of lands and created new centres of population. What distinguished the mining from the pastoral experience was that Aborigines were employed in considerable numbers. Usually Aborigines worked for rations with men and women toiling alongside one another on the windlass, in clearing and loading. In addition to the larger mines there were also the lone prospectors who took up life-long residence near their mines and entered into long-term relationships with Aboriginal women.

Probably the next most important formative experience of white culture for future Warrabri residents was World War II, or what they call the 'Army Time'. During these years when the Army employed them, Aboriginal men enjoyed equal wages, good rations and training in the fields of mechanics. Most of all, the experience widened their horizons: they learnt to drive, to tell the time, to calculate distances and to recognize cash money. Women, on the other hand, found a narrowing of opportunities. No longer did they work alongside their men. Employment was limited and their contacts with white men were in the context of a large, impersonal town.

In 1943 a ration depot was established in Tennant Creek for Darwin evacuees, thus swelling the population. Two hundred Aborigines were moved to Phillip Creek in 1944-5 and it was here that many future Warrabri residents first experienced the dead hand of institutionalization. Even so, many ex-Phillip Creek inmates retained some independence from the mission. Women, now in their fifties and over, remember that in their youth they would collect rations from the mission and move out some five to ten miles from the mission to favourite waterholes. They remained there until the rations ran out, when they returned to the missions to replenish their stocks. Thus in the 1940s it was possible to retain some autonomy and to live in small groups, but the demands of the white institutions to assimilate Aborigines placed enormous strains on parents and children alike.

Welfare personnel removed children from homes they deemed unsuitable and placed them in 'good' white homes. Part-Aboriginal children were forcibly removed from their parents and placed in institutions or with 'good' white families. There are adults alive today at Warrabri and elsewhere who speak of their lost siblings in Adelaide, Darwin and elsewhere.

Those parents whose children were of school age felt the punitive arm of the mission even more keenly. The dormitories at Phillip

Creek were not only segregated on the basis of sex and degree of Aboriginal ancestry but also by age. A hostage system operated whereby if parents and older siblings wanted to see their relatives, they had to remain within walking distance of the mission and visit during the day. Children were locked in at night. For their parents there was also a restriction on camping too close to the mission buildings. This regime was not accepted passively but those who attempted to escape were quickly taught the error of their ways. Today women speak of the mission with mixed feelings. On nostalgic trips we took to Phillip Creek in 1976 and again in 1977, they remembered with humour the escapades and affairs of their life at Phillip Creek.

My 'aunt' Napurrula[66] told me of how she eluded the missionaries at curfew one evening and ran away to join her parents in Tennant Creek where her father was working. She showed me the remains of the kitchen and indicated the location of a bin in which she had hidden. She then walked the 30-odd km through the night into Tennant Creek. She was probably aged only about eleven at the time, but her determination to be reunited with her parents was strong enough to overcome the fear all Aborigines – especially children – share of the dark.

Under the 1940s assimilationist policies, many Central Australian Aborigines were forcibly removed from town centres and their own country to new centralized settlements which often were situated in alien territory. Yuendumu, the one Warlpiri settlement actually in Warlpiri country, was established in 1946 with 120 people from Bullocky Soak and 150 people from the Granites ration depot. Hooker Creek settlement was proclaimed in 1947, but not occupied until 1952 when people were trucked to the settlement. They then walked back to Yuendumu. Two further forced resettlements and Aboriginal walk-backs occurred in 1958 and 1965.[67]

For those Aborigines who came into the towns after the War there was little work. Women were sometimes able to find domestic employment and the men casual work as stockmen. By the 1950s the best country in the Centre was despoiled by cattle. Wolfram prices had fallen and there was little employment in the mines. It is hardly surprising, given the loss of land and the savage repression of pacification drives, that people stayed near ration depots. However this presented a problem for the administration. They needed to find a place to resettle the Aborigines who congregated in towns.

After several abortive attempts to find water at Powell Creek, Attack Creek and Morphett Creek, Warrabri was chosen in 1954 to be the new home for the Warlpiri and Warumungu of the Tennant Creek area. Although the Warramunga (sic) reserve was proclaimed in 1934, it was not occupied for, once again, sufficient water could not be found. From the point of view of the Welfare Department, Warrabri would be an ideal site because it fulfilled all their conditions: there was sufficient water, the possibility of agricultural development, and the 'local tribes' were all friendly to each other.[68] Furthermore, it was far enough away from Tennant Creek to protect Aborigines from the 'contaminating effects' of town life. To the Welfare Department this area of 440 square km was a perfect choice.

The name 'Warrabri' – a combination of the 'Warra' of Warramunga and the 'bri' of Walbri (Warlpiri) – was a further attempt to create unity. But the country remains known amongst desert Aborigines as *Alekarenge* (Ali-curang), after a site associated with the mythological travels of the ancestral dog. For the Aboriginal residents, Warrabri is the antithesis of all that Welfare expected. The words of the Warrabri school song:

> There's a place in the Centre
> And we call it Warrabri
> Where we all live together as one,

hold a promise which has not been fulfilled.

Living 'together as one' at Warrabri was a European ideal of the late 1950s and 1960s. The Government presented Warrabri as a model for cultural assimilation and social progress: it provided the opportunity for what Welfare saw as the 'socially backward' native to be trained while protected from the harmful effects of the towns. In such an environment correct social values could be gently inculcated; an acceptance of a European life-style would be facilitated.

According to the 1961 *Welfare Report*, Warrabri's hope lay in the newly trained and literate under-thirties. It was they who would prosper as Warrabri became economically viable and self-sufficient. This goal of Welfare has not been achieved. Warrabri is an unhappy, divided community where in 1976-7 some 60-70 whites delivered services to and administered the affairs of the approximately 750 Aborigines who were effectively marooned and stranded at Warrabri. Although Aborigines are extremely emotional about country, burst into song and dance and go into trance states when they sight their country, I have never seen such reactions when people return to visit or move to Warrabri. Enforced co-residence at Warrabri engenders tensions and conflicts which find no easy outlet. Alcohol and violence constantly disrupt family life. Outstations such as those which have relieved the pressure on other settlements are not an option for most Warrabri residents because the settlement is hemmed in by cattle stations. How then have the people fared at Warrabri?

THE PRESENT: WARRABRI
'Tell me where you camp and I'll tell you your business.'

Within one day of arrival at Warrabri I had heard rumours of improper (but not unlawful) black-white affairs, suspected corruption, of white cliques, of hostility between the traditional owners of the country, the Kaytej, and the 'interlopers', the Warlpiri. In a community of 800-odd I had expected that it would be possible to become acquainted with most of the residents. Armed with Meggitt's *Desert People*, I looked for disputes which bore on kinship obligations and social structure and which threw into relief the values of the community. Very quickly I learnt that there was no unified, cohesive Aboriginal community at Warrabri; public debates were nonetheless instructive.

Early in my fieldwork I listened to an eloquent exchange outside the co-operative store: the disputants debated whether or not the strip of land outside the store was an appropriate place to stage their fight. The Warlpiri women argued that as a neutral piece of ground, where all the residents of Warrabri felt free to gather and listen, this was an ideal place to argue. The Kaytej women responded that *yapa* (Aboriginal) business belonged in the camps away from the gaze of white fellas. Encapsulated in this dispute are structural principles and Aboriginal perceptions which underpin the Warrabri life style. The Aboriginal community at Warrabri may not be homogeneous, but in order to cope with the pressure of settlement life people are developing ways of thinking about their changed situation.

It is no longer possible simply to move away from trouble, nor is it possible to ignore the white presence. At Warrabri solutions to the problems created by population density and a sedentary lifestyle can

73

be seen clearly in the spatial organization of camps. Once again country is a major factor in the choice of a camp site on a settlement. But the impact of the changes of the past century are also evident in the orientation of camps and the division and links within the population. It is helpful to think of the Warrabri situation as one which entails an east-west division of the Aboriginal population (a division based on affiliation to country) and a centre-periphery distribution of power and resources amongst the Aborigines and whites of Warrabri (a distribution which owes much to the lessons of the past century).

These two spatial models exist on the ground, as well as in the minds of Warrabri residents. The first reflects the orientation of the Aranda (the Kaytej-Alyawarra) to their country in the east, in contradistinction to the Warlpiri and Warumungu, who look to their country in the west. This division is not an artefact of settlement life, for these people really do hold country to the east and west of the settlement. However, on a settlement, the east-west distinction is rather more dramatically drawn in terms of numbers, permanency and location of camps, and attitudes and values than would have been possible in the past.

The second model, that of the centre-periphery, reflects the distribution of certain introduced resources. Those who live in the centre (that is, in the European-dominated settlement core) control information coming into and moving out of the settlement, the kind of material goods that circulate, and the fortunes of those particular families who have emerged as supporters of white interests. On the periphery, in the camps, are those who have either rejected white values and thus remain materially impoverished, or those who are excluded from the centre because of their aberrant behaviour. The Kaytej and Alyawarra, who live on the periphery of the settlement, do so, not because they have just come in from the bush (as we have seen the Kaytej have a long and bitter history of contact with whites), but because they have made a deliberate choice to remain as much as possible outside the sphere of influence of the centre.

The Warlpiri are territorially aggressive and dislike their subservient position at Warrabri. The Kaytej, on the other hand, are numerically weak and prefer to avoid open conflict. An uneasy resolution has been for the Warlpiri to seek socio-economic status in terms of employment and control of such bodies as the local council, while the

Warrabri: A Schematic view (1977)

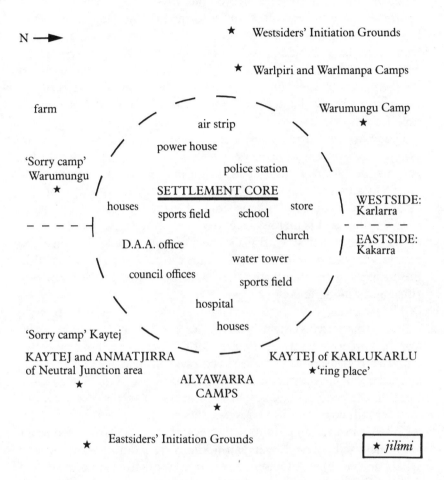

N ➤

★ Westsiders' Initiation Grounds

★ Warlpiri and Warlmanpa Camps

farm

air strip

Warumungu Camp
★

power house

'Sorry camp'
Warumungu
★

police station

SETTLEMENT CORE

houses   store   WESTSIDE:
Karlarra

sports field   school

church   EASTSIDE:
Kakarra

D.A.A. office

water tower

council offices

sports field

hospital

'Sorry camp' Kaytej

houses

KAYTEJ and ANMATJIRRA
of Neutral Junction area
★

ALYAWARRA
CAMPS
★

KAYTEJ of KARLUKARLU
★'ring place'

★ Eastsiders' Initiation Grounds

★ *jilimi*

Kaytej and Alyawarra remain secure in terms of their rights in the country.

Warrabri Aborigines, it appears, have at times deliberately rejected and at other times incorporated aspects of the white culture to produce distinctive settlement lifestyles. While owing much to linguistic, kinship and ritual affiliations, they recognise that the population density and institutionalized structure of settlements have introduced new indicators of status. In the settlement, eastsiders and westsiders have responded differently to the conflict between the demands of a settlement and Aboriginal social structure. Differences in the role and status of women are one facet of this complex process. The women's world continues to be underwritten and informed by the Dreamtime Law, but it is also a world into which new ideas, resources, people and behaviours have exploded with such rapidity and intensity that the very fabric of social life is under threat. Women continue to assert the continuity of their role as nurturers in their daily lives and rituals which stress renewal and the all-encompassing nature of the Dreamtime Law.

If one asks a Warrabri resident, 'Where do you camp?' the most common response is *kakarra* or *karlarra* (east or west). Colonization has torn people from their country but the most basic identification is still in terms of country. The Warlpiri camp at Warrabri, or 'the village' as it is known locally, is situated to the west of the settlement core facilities and is thereby oriented towards the traditional country of the Lander River Warlpiri. The Warlpiri people are thus the people who camp to the west; they are the *karlarra* people. Within the camp there are finer distinctions to be made which reflect kinship, ritual and economic factors.

The Warlpiri have further elaborated their distinctive life-style through their involvement with the cash economy. Until recently Warlpiri predominantly held all the jobs at Warrabri, spoke on council, were registered to vote, received pensions and starred in fights, consumption of alcohol and court appearances. The Warumungu camp in the sandhill country to the north-east of the Warlpiri, but they are still considered to be westsiders.

The Alyawarra camp (lying some several hundred yards from water and toilet facilities and over half a kilometre from the hospital and school and store) is as far as possible from the settlement core. These are *kakarra* people. Their camps have moved frequently to avoid trouble generated by the settlement and to preserve their separateness from the westsiders. Many Warlpiri have no idea of the composition or location of eastside camps, whereas most eastsiders know the westside camps which are clearly visible from the store. The Kaytej camp is located to the east, with one camp to the northside for people who hold country around Devil's Marbles, and one to the south for the Barrow Creek Kaytej camp. Location of camp is towards one's country, but its distance from the settlement centre also reflects the aspirations of the residents. At Yuendumu and Papunya the camp patterns are similar. The Pintupi camp of Yuendumu is oriented to their southern country but lies at a greater distance from the settlement core than the Warlpiri camp. It is the Pintupi who, like the Alyawarra and Kaytej, quickly take advantage of good seasons to move out of the settlement in trips and in camps into their country.

For the Alyawarra and Kaytej, there are disadvantages to camping some way from the core facilities. Women must carry water and rations over long distances, but remoteness protects them from westsiders' accusations of jealousy and illicit affairs. Their geographic position also symbolizes their distinctive identity, which is further strengthened by the close-knit family life of the eastside camps. Within the eastside camps women exercise a degree of control and autonomy which is lacking on the westside, where families sprawl out over large areas. Amongst eastsiders most disputes are settled within the camps and between the families involved: police rarely intrude. For the westsiders police patrols are a fact of daily life.

In the previous section, I outlined the context within which the various groups now resident at Warribri have found their way there. How then do Aborigines speak of their past experiences of whites? One legacy of the Phillip Creek experience is fearful attitudes towards school and fearful expectations of schools as white institutions. Parents and children still attempt to evade the fights and alien discipline of schools by retreating to the bush or to camps some distance away. Although there are teachers who desperately want the school to work, the constraints of the bureaucracy and the philosophical underpinning of western education render the school an alienating environment.

Another unfortunate legacy of the Phillip Creek days is the Aboriginal women's tolerance and acceptance of sexual abuse. Young nubile girls fared rather badly at Phillip Creek. Bereft of the protection of mothers and aunts, the dormitory girls were exploited by one missionary who was eventually ambushed by concerned mothers, brought to trial in a European court and sentenced.[69] Middle-aged women at Warrabri have told me of their experiences with this man and then gone on to discuss without rancour other examples of liaisons with road gangers and itinerant workers of Tennant Creek and Warrabri.

Sexual abuse, children held as hostages, and restrictive legislation are all important aspects of colonization that remain fresh in the minds and experience of Warrabri Warlpiri. Patterned responses developed at the mission are nourished by expectations that white behaviour towards Aborigines is predictable. The situation is one where they are always the losers. There is no such thing as a free lunch, even from missionaries, and Aborigines have learnt that welfare is also an expensive gift. For these Warlpiri in particular, whose country and families have been rent asunder by the colonization of the Northern Territory, by massacre and by welfare, a new identity has emerged based on 'traditional' Aboriginal criteria. They are now the 'eastern Warlpiri', marked off from the other Warlpiri communities by a softer speech and variations of the Law. This is not merely an ethnocentric view but one shared by other Warlpiri and neighbouring groups. In the 1950s Meggitt found four communities of Warlpiri – Lander Ngalia, Yalpiri, Wanegia, Walmalla.[70] The Warlpiri at Warrabri belong to the northern and Lander River divisions, but their experiences of the last fifty years are forcing them into a new 'community', the Warrabri Warlpiri.

Warribri Warlpiri, unlike other Warlpiri communities, have become virtually the monogamous Warlpiri. Of 128 marriages for which I have data, 120 were monogamous. Men may have more than one spouse in a lifetime, just as may women, but the pattern is one of serial monogamy.[71] This shift to a marriage pattern which approximates more closely to the white ideal might appear to release women from an unrelished bondage: in fact it has placed women at a disadvantage. No longer can they appeal for protection to relatives who arranged their marriages, but neither can they turn for assistance to white law-keepers, who tend to dismiss marital violence as domestic strife in which they are reluctant or refuse to interfere.

The Warlpiri view the Kaytej and Alyawarra with suspicion, regarding them as foolishly ignorant of many white ways. The Kaytej view the Warlpiri as the instigators of most fights, the consumers of alcohol, and as those lacking a strong Law. Although the Kaytej have been unjustly treated as pastoral employees, the experience appears to have been less destructive of family life and group cohesiveness than the Warlpiri's mission experience at Phillip Creek. The Kaytej and Alyawarra have been able to preserve an autonomy not manifest in the life style and history of the Warlpiri. Although Kaytej and Alyawarra first drifted into the settlement as long ago as 1958, they have retained a high degree of mobility and still spend much time on neighbouring cattle stations, visiting, working and attending to ceremonial business.

Although the loss of the best country has meant dependence on white foods for most Alyawarra families, changes in Alyawarra communities have been qualitatively different from the Warlpiri case. Hunting remains an integral part of the lives of most eastsiders. This is understandable as they are in their own country and at liberty to make use of its bounty and indeed they do. Further, because the eastsiders are less committed to school attendance than the westsiders are, children accompany their female kin on hunting trips during the week. They thus learn of country and of the competence of older women. The country of the eastsiders is richer than that of the desert Warlpiri and the dispossession of lands has been qualitatively different. Kaytej and Alyawarra women take full advantage of their rights in Warrabri country and fulfil their responsibility to teach children their heritage.

Alcohol is less of a problem for eastsiders than it is for westsiders, where initiation business may be disrupted by drunks. Access to alcohol for station people is and has been limited and any extended drinking was done in town during the stand-down period. Cattle station people had little cash in hand so drinking sprees could not be sustained. Further, their life style on stations offered some purpose.[72]

Initiation rituals are performed by both sides but the eastsiders are more private about their business. This is both a continuation of traditional values and a response to white intrusion. School holidays are a convenient time to hold ceremonies and the favourite days for staging rituals associated with initiation are Boxing Day and Christmas Day. Whites, as Aborigines correctly observe, are usually in no fit condition to pry into their business on these sacred days of the Christian calendar.

Most Warrabri eastsiders come from nearby cattle stations where several large families form or formed the core of the station community. Law and order is maintained by these groups and the voice of women is heard loudly and clearly in the decision-making process. Whites rarely interfere in the affairs of the Aboriginal camp on a cattle station and therefore the concept of a male-dominated council has little or no currency.

Before the arrival of the Aboriginal Benefit Trust Fund Toyotas in the mid 1970s, travel was on foot, horseback or by generosity of the manager. This caused dependence of a kind in that no protest against non-payment of wages and poor work conditions could be sustained. On the other hand, the station people enjoyed a rather more stable relationship with the manager. On most of these stations the management is of many years' and sometimes several generations' standing: a working relationship has developed between Aboriginal employees and managers which allows work to proceed but ritual business to continue away from the view of the management.

The Christmas stand-down period from December to March provides a convenient time for people to retreat to the bush to perform initiation and land-maintenance ceremonies. Settlement Warlpiri could theoretically do this, but Warrabri is not their country and their dependence on white food is far greater than that of the cattle-station people, who rarely see a wide range of goods amongst the rations they receive. Even during the working year, people could live away from the station in small family groups. Independence, pride and autonomy of action were thus retained.

Station life is also less disruptive of the rhythm of family life. Because one need not fear that the absence of a spouse indicates infidelity, less time is spent in jealous fights. Further, people are not constantly fending off the demands of marginal relatives for food and other goods. The pace of life is generally slower and some privacy is possible.

Marriages conform more closely to the rule of polygyny. Younger women still go to older men as promised wives but because these arrangements are within the ceremonial alliances of initiation, there are sanctions applied to cruel or irresponsible husbands which Warlpiri women cannot expect to see enforced. The complex web of rights and responsibilities in which a promised marriage is enmeshed provides protection and support for young wives. Eastside women expect and indeed receive such assistance from those bound by the alliances established during initiation (see p. 270-71). Westside women's marriages are not so conscribed and they consequently cannot expect support. On the eastside, joint arrangements are made by co-wives in the organization of the domestic economy and fights are rare. These women may therefore spend more time enjoying the company of their spouse in relaxed conditions.

Eastsiders are not as involved in the cash economy at Warrabri:

fewer are employed. They tend to be under-represented on the village council and as voters on the Northern Territory electoral roll. They keep very much to their own camps and spend a minimum of time in public areas such as store and school.

Above all, Warrabri is Kaytej country, and Kaytej men and women do not have to impress upon the outsider their importance. Kaytej women are the prolific dreamers of Warrabri. It is they who are in constant contact with the country of their parents and who daily find evidence of their rich heritage. Their relationship to land is being constantly reaffirmed through the use and the obvious fertility of their country. This is of economic, religious and psychological importance. In the life-history material I have collected from these women, a striking theme is the amount of time quite young women have spent in small family groups camping in and walking through their own country. As women tell these stories they proudly name the water holes, ridges and foods of the area. For westsiders, this sort of memory belongs back in the 1940s before the days of institutionalization.

If we focus on the *jilimi* - the area where women's authority is given its clearest expression - we see that the differences in the structure and organization of west- and eastside *jilimi* yet again reflect different historical and cultural factors. At Warrabri in 1976-8, the Warlpiri women had two large *jilimi* which divided along the lines of age, interest, and commitment to 'centre politics' and its rewards. The older women maintained the larger and more permanent camp which initiated or hosted most Warlpiri women's rituals and much of the 'sorry' (mourning) business. The women sat in the shelter of their bough shade to paint up but rarely danced in the area of the *jilimi*. Any performances were held closer to the centre of the settlement in the school grounds. Their control over their performances was thus limited but they had the advantage of displaying to others and to whites their ability and skill in staging certain women's rituals. Much activity did take place in camp, but the performances involving mass painting-up and the use of ritual paraphernalia were nearly always in a public arena which became taboo to men for the duration of the ritual. This obviously was not as secure as remaining in the women's *jilimi* where men may not enter at all.

Alyawarra and Kaytej women on the other hand remained within their special ritual area near to the *jilimi* and only brought the business to the school area when specifically invited to do so by whites. The

Alyawarra maintained an ever-shifting complex of *jilimi* which moved to accommodate large groups of visiting people from other cattle stations, 'sorry' camps, personality conflicts and changes in the weather. During my stay at Warrabri I saw this complex transformed three times. However, there was agreement about which women constituted the core of the *jilimi* and usually some of these women could be found in the *jilimi*. The area in which these women actually danced was attached to, but a little removed from, the *jilimi*. Ritual objects were stored in a lock-up shed in which several women slept during cold or wet weather.

The Kaytej women had one large independent *jilimi* and several smaller ones which accommodated the Barrow Creek and Neutral Junction people who visited and occasionally stayed at Warrabri. During 1977, following the death of one of its residents, the Kaytej *jilimi* split, after years of permanent location, and finally moved completely. When I left Warrabri in February 1978, the women were just beginning to return to the area to live, but by September 1978, a further death had resulted in the establishment of a 'sorry' camp some distance to the south.

When this camp first split, women moved out of the immediate vicinity but remained close enough to the *jilimi* site to meet during the day in the shade of some nearby salt trees. Misfortunes such as death are keenly felt by women, but both Warrabri Kaytej and Papunya Warlpiri have told me that they only temporarily vacate the actual ritual area after a death and that they ultimately form another camp close enough to the old one to be able to continue to use the ritual area. However the deaths have isolated one family in a 'sorry' camp on the south side of Warrabri. For them to participate in ritual is difficult, while socializing during the day in the Kaytej *jilimi* is almost impossible, as the camps are just too far apart.

The Kaytej *jilimi* living area was situated to the east of the settlement and to the north of the other Aranda eastside camps. Thus it is oriented to the country in which the residents have interests and responsibilities. The internal organization of the Kaytej *jilimi* and ritual area was indicative of the serious and devout attitude of these women to their country. Within a large cleared area, the women had built two long constructions which ran north-south and faced each other across a cleared space. On the east side were the long, low sleeping quarters which could be adapted to afford protection against rain or to take advantage of winter sun. The building was, like most other desert *jilimi*, a long, snake-like building which expanded and contracted to accommodate visitors and other temporary residents. Within the sleeping quarters, the space was further divided into individual areas which held the swags of one or two closely related women and their children. In the Alyawarra *jilimi* and sometimes in the Kaytej, these swags were separated by a low wall and each individual area always had an individual fire. (Warlpiri women do not have such markers of privacy within their *jilimi*.)

During the extraordinary rains of February 1977, the Kaytej *jilimi* was one of the few dry places. Women would sit inside the dry sleeping quarters of the *jilimi* and explain with a sense of pride and achievement the virtues of the *jilimi* which they themselves had built. Their skills were based on a lengthy tradition of craftswomen. Across the open space where cooking and general socializing occurred was the long, but not so low, daytime shade of the *jilimi* complex. This opened to the east and thus provided deep shade in the hot afternoon but took advantage of the early sun on the crisp desert mornings. Women spent their days peacefully chatting, caring for children, cooking, mending and sewing in this shade. My experience of *jilimi* life contrasts with Meggitt's observations[73]: 'The old women also constitute cliques, generally centred on the widows' camps which are hot-beds of gossip'.

Economically the *jilimi* women still enjoy a measure of independence and rely on their own income. Today this is in the form of pensions – primarily old-age pensions and some supporting mother's benefits. Pensioners are considered to be important within the Aboriginal community as they are the persons who receive a reliable income. In the Aboriginal view caring for the aged is an appropriate policy of the Department of Social Security. Other pensions are less reliable and subject to variation. It is not unusual to find families attached to a *jilimi* in order to share the benefits of the pensions which the elderly and widowed receive.

Anthropologist Annette Hamilton[74] has argued that people's perception that social security payments such as child endowment are 'women's wages' has placed women at a disadvantage *vis-à-vis* the men who receive other benefits in their role of household head. She argues that in accordance with the independence of the sexes each perceive the money received as theirs to spend. Women whose only allowance is child endowment are in greater difficulties in this respect than are women who receive widow's pensions.

Nevertheless, at Warrabri and elsewhere many *jilimi* are in fact relatively independent in terms of pension income, which the older women may supplement by calling upon debts owed by such persons as sons-in-law. Thus while the basis of independence has changed, women may still remain substantially independent in economic terms. They do not however exercise the same degree of control over their produce as was possible in the past and they are responsible for a wider group of persons.

In the past, in small family camps, there would have been maybe two or three women to form a *jilimi*, but on settlements the residents of the *jilimi* may number upwards of twenty. Thus the possibility of women forming larger and potentially more powerful *jilimi* has increased. That women have chosen and, in ever increasing numbers, are choosing to live in the *jilimi* instead of entering second or third marriages is, I think, indicative of women's perceptions of and responses to their changed lives in the 1970s. The physical separation of the sexes which the *jilimi* represents is a mode of expressing continuity of a key facet of the relations between the sexes. The *jilimi*, like the east-west division of the Warrabri population, is an elaboration of a traditional form. In the past the separation allowed each to demonstrate independence without compromising the essentially complementary nature of male and female activities in the maintenance of their society. Today the separation of the sexes and women's independence are no longer mutually reinforcing values. There is an increasingly felt need, on the part of women, to assert their sexual solidarity.

Where one camps immediately indicates important allegiances but also important aspirations. As one woman who moved between an eastside camp and a house in the centre explained to me, 'We have two different sets of rules at Warrabri. While we are in the settlement, we do it *papulanji* [white] way. In the camps we do it *yapa* [Aboriginal] way, but some people think they are white.' This adjustment, this cultural hopscotch, applies to speech, dress and family life-styles. An interesting comparison can be drawn with Yuendumu where camp values permeate the settlement area. For instance, after a death the hospital is swept to make way for use when mourning is completed.

Unlike the east-west division, which is an elaboration of a traditional form greatly magnified, the centre-periphery is an artefact of settlement life. White intrusion constitutes such a violation and invasion of the Aboriginal life-style that to speak of white rules and Aboriginal rules eases the strain a little.

One painful example of the compromise is changes in the practice of not calling dead names for a certain period after a death: this is the *kumunjayi* system.[75] In many small ways offence can be given. For many people who knew a man now deceased who was named 'Peter', that word is taboo. Every packet of Peter Stuyvesant cigarettes which is sold in the store gives offence. In other areas of settlement life, it is more blatant. Schools want individual names for their charges: hospitals want unique names on their record cards. Name changes are annoying and clog the computers and government departments. One way of accommodating the demands for rapid registration of names at birth is to give rare and hopefully unique names to children and then not worry about it for some time. This does, however, result in some strange names. To speak a dead name aloud is to cause grief to all relatives of the deceased. Children on occasions may be excused as not knowing any better, and be asked to supply names, but I have seen fights arise from this compromising practice.

One solution for teaching assistants and health workers who are constantly being addressed by white supervisors is to allow names to be called in the settlement area and preserve the *kumunjayi* system in the camps. It is as if one crosses a line where the intrusion of whites is no longer the prime consideration. This 'solution', although it allows some social intercourse in the settlement area, still violates the custom and is emotionally disturbing for many people. Eastsiders appear to hold closer to using their own naming system than do westsiders, who have been 'registered' for longer. In fact, some eastsider mothers have told me they do not know the name of their child. In answer to my question, 'What should I call this one?', women might say, 'I call it Nampijinpa (that is a skin name). They didn't tell me its name.'

Naming is but one example of the way in which rules are bent to accommodate the whites of Warrabri. An examination of the institutions and facilities of the centre reveals that although key whites control opinion and resources, the Aborigines are manipulating and integrating the power structures within their own systems of obligations and rights.

Within the centre, politics are qualitatively different from those on the periphery. It is white goods, services and control of opinion which are at stake. The major institutions developed supposedly to deliver services only to Aborigines – but which are also used by whites to build power bases (for personal and ideological gains) – are mutually interdependent at one level, but independent at others. Let me explain.

Institutions such as the school, hospital, store, police and Department of Aboriginal Affairs have secured the loyalty of particular families at Warrabri – many of these relationships continued from Phillip Creek days when certain persons had certain jobs. Each of these institutions operates as a separate unit and vies with the others for control of opinions and resources. For example, during the operational days of the farm and while it was under a white manager, the Aboriginal employees enjoyed privileged access to housing, vehicles, and cool storage for meat and vegetables. They also had a literate spokesman should they ever run foul of the law and need assistance with bureaucracies. In return they offered support for the employer should any prying individual ever suggest that the farm was not run efficiently or in accordance with the wishes of the people. When the confrontation came between store and farm over marketing policy, it was the store with its more entrenched interests which was victorious.

The 'mutual admiration societies' of Warrabri flourish where a white 'boss' has spent many years in the community. For example, after seven years' residence, it has been necessary for Aborigines to come to terms with the continued presence and power of the store manager. Further, it is practically impossible to ask most whites to leave after a long time at Warrabri because they can ask Aborigines to repay all outstanding debts – a very effective way of ensuring that opposition to whites' continued presence will fade.

Aboriginal employees have attempted to come to terms with the compromised position in which they find themselves by incorporating the white 'boss' within the social system at the level of subsection affiliation and hopefully thereby imparting notions of correct behaviour. Most whites are delighted to be thus honoured and interpret the 'skin' to be a mark of acceptance. (Some whites stay forever outside the system and never receive a 'skin'. Their residence at Warrabri is limited.) The other strategy is to designate the control or orientation of an institution of the centre as west or east or as a male or female domain. This creates a more ordered social environment in potentially chaotic areas of daily interaction.

The school is a fairly harmless example of attempted incorporation as very little real power flows from affiliation with the school. In 1977 the head teacher was designated Jampijinpa and his teachers often received the subsection (skin) Jangala or Nangala (see Appendix 2). Within the local social organization the teachers thus became his children, which, in Aboriginal terms, explained their subordination to his authority and the respect teachers customarily show for the Principal. One old Warlpiri man, the then power behind the school board, was also a Jangala. As is possible with the subsection system, he deemed himself to be 'father' to the head teacher, who then had to respect him and his decisions.

An amusing aspect of teachers' skin classifications is that frequently they have been given a skin in another community, but then do not behave *vis-à-vis* other teachers at Warrabri in the appropriate manner. Before conferring 'skins', some of the Aboriginal teaching assistants prefer to wait until they see which way the affections of new teachers lie. Any romance between teachers is regarded as improper unless it conforms to the Aboriginal system. Indeed, the fragility of white romances is often attributed to their improper classifications. 'We knew it wouldn't last', women say. 'He's the wrong skin for her.'

The school is perceived as a female domain as far as social interaction is concerned. It is an extension of women's role in socializing children but westsiders have more invested in the school than eastsiders. The hospital is perceived as a female domain and the allocation of skins to white workers conforms to the principles of matrilineal descent. It is, I believe, an extension of the matrilineal focus of certain traditional health-curing activities (see p. 152).

At the level of inter-connectedness, the complexity of black-white relationships is bewildering, but underlying it are deliberate strategies pursued by both blacks and whites. Linking the divisions are sexual, kinship, ritual and financial ties. Not only is the kinship network of Aboriginal people of importance, but the extended white families on settlements must also be noted. At one time the store manager was married to the nursing sister in charge of the hospital at Warrabri. The other nursing sister there was married to the police sergeant; the police constable's wife worked in the school. The bookkeeper of the store was the sister-in-law of the manager, while the mother of the nursing sister worked in the co-operative store. Police, store and hospital were thus closely linked. Any attempt to change store policy, to bring charges against the police or to suggest community involvement in the hospital could be thwarted by a closing of the ranks. Although the school is not involved in the ongoing policies of the other institutions, the policeman's wife did work as the head teacher's secretary and common political allegiances were a further uniting force.

Prior to 1976, regular meetings of the 'heads of departments' at Warrabri - that is, school, housing, co-operative store, Council, Department of Aboriginal Affairs and the farm - were able to provide a united front in the face of any external threat. During 1976, when the Community Adviser prepared a report on the corruption and irregularities on the settlement, his report, without his permisson, was circulated amongst the 'heads' and discussed at an emergency meeting. The Adviser finally left and the Department of Aboriginal Affairs spent the next year smoothing over the troubled waters.

Aboriginal kinship and ritual links underwrite and bolster these white family alliances. The Aboriginal managing director of the store is also the police tracker. The Warrabri Council president is married to the head health worker in the hospital. The wife of the police tracker is a sister of the woman who works in the co-operative store. These women are all full nieces of one of the most important ritual leaders on the Warlpiri side. It is he who is the uniting power behind the co-operative store and the Council and it is he who is consulted by the white store manager. These ties are exclusive to the westside. Eastsiders sometimes announce, with a degree of pride, that such 'business' has nothing to do with them. At other times they complain bitterly of their exclusion from the major networks.

If one tried hard and always faced the east, it would be almost possible to collect sufficient data to write an ethnography of the 'traditional' life of the Alyawarra and Kaytej at Warrabri. In the most easterly camps, situated about half a kilometre from ablution blocks and over a kilometre from school and store, no English is spoken. These are people who rarely venture into the settlement area. Police visit infrequently. Concerns of kinship and ritual obligations are paramount.

However, the very choice to live at the extreme edge of the settlement, and not to participate, leaves these people materially impoverished, a position they view with ambivalence. Until 1977 they had little say in the running of Warrabri, but as a result of a Department

of Aboriginal Affairs' directive, the Council has been made more rep-
resentative of local groups than it was previously. Elections were held
which re-structured the Council, but these could not erase years of
corrupt practices and the Council expectations about the nature of
centre politics.

The people on the periphery do not control the flow of goods or
opinion. Several enterprising whites working for the housing and
farm associations recognized that their organizations could find a
possible support group for a new empire which they might conceiv-
ably build. They sought to establish alliances with the eastsiders. For
many reasons, one of which is the Alyawarra's lack of interest in
achieving socio-economic status, the farm is now defunct. The scale
of the project was too vast and was not integrated into their life style.
When attempts to render the operation of the farm compatible with
their life style and aspirations failed, this group disbanded.

East-west, centre-periphery are, as I have already stated, cross-
cutting models of spatial relations which articulate power relationships between and amongst blacks and whites. The investment of
westsiders in centre politics is of long-standing. The experience of
institutionalized living and dispossession of their lands has created an
environment wherein Warlpiri now seek status in a blend of socio-
economic and ritual terms. In an attempt to render their existence less
schizophrenic, they have incorporated whites and their goods, to a
degree, within Warlpiri social structure. Where clashes are unavoid-
able the rules have been bent.

On the other hand, eastsiders have less investment in centre politics
and seek status in ritual, rather than socio-economic, terms. Settlement tensions have impinged less on Kaytej and Alyawarra as they
are still in contact with their country. In the shift from a semi-
nomadic to sedentary life style, they have managed to preserve some
autonomy of action and mobility and hence are less dependent on
white institutions and goods. Although they recognize the existence
of two different political arenas, and the advantages of a degree of
identification with white values, they see their Kaytej and Alyawarra
identity as precious and threatened by interaction with whites and
even with Warlpiri.

THE *JUKURRPA*

In the two preceding sections, I have not attempted to strip back the layers of 'contaminating contact' to reveal the pristine social forms of desert society, nor have I sought to extract from the contemporary scene what is traditional and what is a product of contact. Such procedures would assume that we can hold constant outside forces and focus on an internal, static field of actors and beliefs; rather, I have posited a dynamic model which takes account of sexual politics and social change. Such a model best accommodates the complex notion of dreaming as an era, as a force in the lives of the living, as a moral code and as ancestral spirits of the land which provides the framework for the world view of Aboriginal women.

At one level the *jukurrpa* is an era shrouded in the mists of time, from which people claim to be descended without actually tracing the links. Information concerning past generations is difficult to locate on a chronological scale because there is a taboo on the calling of names of the dead. This is often given as an explanation for the shallowness of genealogies, patrilines, matrilines, and so on. Such an explanation is tautological. It is more pertinent to recognize that the remembering of a unique name and exact dates adds little to Aboriginal understanding and perceptions of the past. What is stressed when identifying a person, alive or dead, is their relationship to others, their dreaming affiliations and their ritual associations. In this way it is possible to locate every person as a unique individual: no two persons share exactly the same social, ritual and kin field. Siblings are perhaps the closest. To say that 'our grandparents were siblings' is sufficient to bind two people as sharing the same country, rights and responsibilities.

The shallowness of genealogical memory is not a form of cultural amnesia but rather a way of focusing on the basis of all relationships – that is, the *jukurrpa* and the land. By not naming deceased relatives, people are able to stress a relationship directly to the land. It is not necessary to trace back through many generations to a founding ancestor to make the claim. By stating that a person is of a certain country, usually by reference to a grandparent who was of that area, the identity of a person is known.

Relations to country which underpin relationships between people are evident also in the way in which people refer to ritual objects. Frequently I heard women speak of certain ritual objects which represented a particular ancestor, site or track as 'mother', 'father', 'aunty'. Because it is from the land that one derives identity, relationships are stated and affirmed in terms of rights and responsibilities in the country of one's ancestors.

At another level the *jukurrpa* is only two generations behind the present generation; moving concurrently with the present; its heritage entrusted to the 'old people', to the deceased grandparents. It is this aspect of the *jukurrpa* which makes any attempt to establish an ethnographic base line a misguided endeavour. The *jukurrpa* is not a long dead and fixed point of reference. It is a living and accessible force in the lives of people today, just as it was in the past. Here then is the structural potential for change, the Aboriginal mode of incorporating change with their cosmos.

The dogma of dreaming states that all the world is known and can be classified within the taxonomy created by the ancestral heroes. All possible behaviour is covered by the moral code made known through the activities of the ancestral heroes. In the *jukurrpa* was established an all-encompassing Law which binds people, flora, fauna and natural phenomena into one enormous interfunctioning world. This Law and the order which the ancestral heroes established is immutable. The living persons who give form and substance to the Law live in ever-increasingly divergent life styles from those envisaged as correct by the *jukurrpa* of a century ago. For instance, people no longer live in small mobile bands but on large settlements; people no longer subsist from hunting and gathering but from rations and store-bought food; people are no longer independent producers but rely on social security and wage labour. These settlement-dwellers are the people who are acting out the *jukurrpa* and giving it form in rituals. Many new items can be accommodated: for example, crowbars as digging sticks and car springs as adzes. Other resources can be brought under control of the Law by classification within the subsection system; still others are utilized in a distinctively Aboriginal fashion: for example, cash money in ritual exchanges. Even residence in a new territory can eventually be legitimated once evidence is found of Dreamtime activity in the locality. Thus the Law is not challenged by certain changes; others, such as alcohol, are presenting problems.[76]

The ideology of dreaming is also an historical epistemology within which the sifting of mythical fancy from historical fact has little relevance. If we think of the *jukurrpa* as historical doctrine we may look anew at the meanings Aborigines attribute to the various forms of white intrusion into desert lands. In Aboriginal terms the events (described in white-oriented history) are construed differently from a person-event oriented chronology of the past century.

The twin notions of an ideologically fixed universe and a structural potential for change through actual behaviour are not irreconcilable; rather, they allow one to maintain a secure position known to be underpinned by the Law, while leaving one room to respond within particular constraints. Stanner puts it well when he says 'They attained stability but avoided inertia.'[77] It is possible to establish how life ought to be lived and to be relatively certain that in these values there is continuity with the past. It is somewhat more difficult to determine what is or was the actual behavioural content of the Law as applied and acted out in any given situation, unless one has actual documented observations.

The possible dysjunction between people's belief in the immutability of the dreamtime and the way it is upheld by living descendants was stated nicely for me by one woman. I was discussing with her what I took to be a breakdown in the marriage code amongst girls living in a town camp. Young girls were marrying younger and to men of their own choosing. 'Does this mean,' I asked, 'that the Law is breaking down?' 'No,' said the woman, 'people just get lazy. The Law is still there.' Of course in time the Law becomes, within limits, what people do, but there is the notion that it is there as the framework.[78]

The notion that there is a framework is apparent in the way in which women dream about the country in which they are living and hunting. While out in country for which a woman has rights or wishes to assert rights, she may have a dream or see something of significance she believes to be associated with the travels of her ancestors through this country. Dreaming activity on a particular tract of land is assumed and it is for living descendants to learn of and to transmit this knowledge. This is done in the context of ritual and visits to country, when direct teaching is possible, but it is also done by finding the evidence of dreaming activity and thus being able to reassert and reaffirm the knowledge of the activity in the area.

For instance, in the song repertoire of an Alyawarra woman at Warrabri there is an allusion to a boy of a Japangardi subsection. He is *kirda* for the country for which she as a Napanangaka (that is his father's sister) is also *kirda*. I had heard the song many times but on one occasion when I was translating songs with the woman, she explained that the Japangardi was her younger brother's son who had fallen from a windmill and died while still a child. She told of his place in the family and of how old his siblings were when he died. From this I was able to fix a date to the song. To her this was interesting but unimportant. She related how she dreamt of him on the day he died. When she returned to camp she knew of the death before she was told. This song is considered to be her song and when she dies it will be put aside as will all her property, name, swag, camp site and so forth. If her bush name is also the name of a site, that too will be put aside.

Many places have several names or are specified at different levels: according to features at a site: one name may apply to the entire area, another to a specific rock or tree. One of these names may be lost, but at least one will be retained.[79] Eventually another *kirda* or *kurdungurlu* in the country will dream of her singing the story of the Japangardi and the song will be re-found. On this occasion, name or relation will not be specified; the hero will simply be a Japangardi of that country, not a particular member of a family. A date will not be specified nor a particular place. Often it is a person who is to assume responsibility for the country who has the reactivating dream, but not always. The onus is on the finder to perform and teach the content of the dream, be it song, design or both, to other members of the land-maintaining group. Because other women have heard the song when it was originally sung by the first finder, they will be able to correct the singing when it is re-found.

I have seen Warrabri women do just this. On one occasion a particular phrase of a song was sung in conjunction with the second phrase of another closely related song. One older woman claimed she had heard the song some twenty-five years earlier but had remembered it. Of course it is impossible to know whether the two versions were actually the same. The important quality being stressed is the recurring nature of the song which is derived from the country and which is evidence of recurring activity in that area. At the cultural level one can assert that little has changed, but at the verbal level much may have changed. These changes do not in themselves alter the direction or intent of the ancestors - for that is bound by the Law - but because the Law is only made known through human agents, over generations, changes must occur.

Although each song, dance and design bears the stamp of its finder, the dogma of dreaming which entails this necessary and continuous process of re-invention ensures that no one person may claim to be an individually inspired creator; living persons may only assert and reaffirm the Law and act as the custodians of knowledge of the Dream-time experience. This process of reinvention is necessary because of the taboos on a person's property at death. It is continuous because the dreamings must be shown to have continuity and people to have access to the Dreamtime. Renewal depends on access to country. Over the generations a song which referred to a specific incident will become shrouded in oblique references, intelligible only to the con-temporaries of the person depicted in the song or design. However, once the reference is no longer to a particular person but to a subsec-tion, the song becomes part of a more general repertoire of ancestral activity in an area. Ultimately it will concern the ancestors them-selves.

BOSSES NOT PRISONERS

Warrabri women's interweaving of the past and present within the seamless web of the *jukurrpa* has created an illusion of stasis. For the anthropologist it is tempting to read directly from the present to the past and to declare that women are, and always have been, excluded and oppressed. Such a conclusion is oversimplistic and accounts for neither the sexual politics of desert society nor the inevitability of change. Women's role has changed and with it the relation between the sexes. While it has always been possible to accommodate gradual change and for the Law to remain untarnished, the dramatic changes of the last century have taxed the dogma of immutability. In their rap-idly crumbling world, women have clung tenaciously to certain key values and to institutions such as the separation of the sexes in the *jilimi*. In so doing women have found continued meaning for their self-image as independent and autonomous members of their society.

If we look back to the events of the last century and to the context within which women came to live at Warrabri, there are some stark comparisons and striking similarities. For women of all groups there were limited opportunities for employment. Women on cattle stations fared rather better than their missionized and urbanized sisters in this respect, for they engaged in stock work, shepherding and woodchopping while the others were expected to be mothers and wives. Women, I am arguing, enjoyed a complex set of rights which were validated by their direct access to the Dreamtime and the use to which they put the land.

The other side of the coin is the responsibilities which devolved upon women. The land was held as a sacred trust, to be kept alive, to be made to come up green and lush. As one woman said, 'We've

The Karlukarlu women camped near Warnku (See Map p. 112) at Easter 1977 in order to cut wood from which to fashion various carrier dishes and ritual items. Here Napurrula, Nampijinpa, the Nungarrayi sisters and Nakamarra discuss the *kurduru* which Nungarrayi, as *kurdungurlu* for the country, is making.

got to keep that corroboree going so as to make this country good and make the people happy.'

Kaytej women worked beside their menfolk in the mines and on the stations. From the northern Kaytej women I have heard their reminiscences about working the windlass, chopping wood, breaking horses, mustering and droving. None of these tasks was considered sex-specific but they were none the less pursued separately from men. The enshrined stereotype is of men as glamorous stockmen and women as domestics and sex objects. This is not borne out by life-history material I collected, nor by reports of men such as Chewings, who states that women were engaged in wide-ranging jobs (guides, camel-minding) early in the century. Women did engage in stock work and continued to work as responsible individuals in 'traditional men's work' until very recently. In the remoter areas Aboriginal women worked in jobs which were not considered suitable for white women. Camel-minding, for instance, was a dangerous task. Mustering was hard work. For Aboriginal women it was a continuation of the past independence that they could be thus employed. It was the presence of white women on cattle stations and the missionaries in the towns which curtailed many of these activities.

Opportunities to engage in productive labour were limited for women on settlements and missions. Men were classified as the household heads and they did what little work there was. The changes were subtle - for instance at the Phillip Creek mission (unlike Yuendumu and Hooker Creek), men carried out all the ration distributions. Women were thus immediately classified as dependent on men. Women did find work as domestics but when this was in the context of a mission, they were domestics who served. No longer were they the individual producers they had been in the past. Thus I am suggesting it as not only the opportunities available to Aboriginal women but also the white perception of woman's role which constrained Aboriginal women. Missionaries needed to create God-fearing women who knew shame. In addition white bosses needed women to perform a number of duties and to fulfil a number of roles. Cattle station managers wanted workers who were all-round helpers. Of course in frontier conditions the usual double standard applied to women, who were expected to work hard during the day and to please the master in the evenings. Women on missions did not escape sexual exploitation either and the Phillip Creek experience was a traumatic one for many

Nangala and Nampijinpa, *kirda* for the country of Karlukarlu (See Map p. 112)
return to camp with the rough-shaped log cut from the bean tree slung in a leather
carrying strap. This wood may be shaped into the *murdu* water carrier, *parraja*, food
and baby carrier, or ritual items.

women alive today. One woman told me that following the encounter with missionaries her family moved and did not return to Tennant Creek for a decade.

Women in the towns, near the telegraph stations and mines, were undoubtedly drawn into liaisons with white men. Women today claim that their grandmothers entered into these relationships because their sexuality and their feelings were theirs to bestow as they wished. Today also younger women insist that liaisons with younger men, white or black, are their affairs and do not necessarily threaten marriage contracts. Trouble occurred when the Aboriginal male, who always had to tolerate a degree of discreet sexual freedom in his wife, found his marriage contract challenged. Aboriginal men expected their women to return after a brief affair with another man. If this did not happen, then the men expected the proper exchange of goods and services which accompany long-lasting relationships to take place. This was rarely the case with white men, who knew nothing of the Law. White men had no sense of lasting obligation in the eyes of Aboriginal men.

Often white men-black women relationships are written of in terms of prostitution where the Aboriginal male is the pimp, but many older Aboriginal women disagree with this characterization. They say they went willingly to white men, that they enjoyed the love-making and the payments they received. Women exercised their own initiative, and secured goods, admiration and pleasure for themselves. Ultimately it was the Aboriginal men who were dissatisfied because they were not being recognized properly. They were being paid, but the nature of the marriage contract which binds Aboriginal men was not honoured by white men. The Aboriginal male reaction was to remove women from the gaze of white men. So, from a position of independence, women became vulnerable, in need of protection in a way previously impossible when marriages were based on alliances (backed by a web of kin rights and responsibilities) between families, not individuals, and affairs were a woman's own business. Thus while women are visible very early in the literature as strong, independent personalities, they were quickly removed and 'protected' by their menfolk who wished to retain a basis to their claims that they had the right to bestow women's services.

On many cattle stations the liaisons between white males and Aboriginal women were enduring relationships with children raised as the

With an old car spring Nampijinpa shapes a *mardu*, a traditional water carrier, from the log cut earlier in the day. Although the tool is of the twentieth century, the way in which Nampijinpa uses it is the same as she would have used the traditional stone adze.

heirs to the property, only to be deposed by the arrival of the white wife in the second decade of settlement. Women on missions and in the towns were engaged in shorter, more brutal liaisons with white men and often their children were removed by Welfare to institutions or raised by the Aboriginal mother and her Aboriginal husband.

Assessments of the lot of these children vary. Hilda Tuxworth described the women as 'adaptable to all station duties, including handling cattle'.[80] J. T. Beckett wrote that:

> The lot of the half-caste man is necessarily much easier than that of his sister . . . the half-caste girl who remains with the tribe anywhere in the vicinity of a civilized settlement has one inevitable destiny, and that the most degraded.[81]

In many analyses Aboriginal women are denied an active decision-making role in black-white liaisons because observers tend to believe that women are a kind of property or object. In Aboriginal society, wives were not sold: they were able to exercise a high degree of choice; they fought, they insulted, they remained in their country where their power base was strong. The marriage contract was one between families, it did not entail control over sexuality but it did entail certain rights concerning the children of the women. My data here are based on discussions with women over the age of sixty who remember the first time they saw a white man and speculate as to the nature of 'woman trouble' today and in the past.

Much is made of men's rights in and control over women in marriage, but in the reports of early observers there is supporting evidence of women's rights in and out of marriage to suggest two things. Firstly, women did not in the past and do not today confuse sexuality with the conditions of a marriage contract based on an alliance between families. Secondly, women display a good deal of independence and freedom within the bonds of marriage. Men, I suggest, are co-conspirators in these power plays. We need to re-examine much of the literature on prostitution and wife lending/trading in view of these tactics. As Meggit[82] writes, men are more 'concerned to maintain male superiority than to redress the wrongs done to women', and this, I argue, has allowed women a great deal of latitude in their affairs.

The male-dominated nature of the colonial frontier in the Northern Territory impinged on both eastsiders and westsiders, but in each situation women played different roles and enjoyed a different status.

Westsiders' formative experiences were within the context of institutions like the church, mission, and settlement, whereas eastsiders learnt of whites while living in small family camps on cattle stations or near mines. The context within which the Aranda women of Warrabri and the Warlpiri women have learnt of white society and been dispossessed of their land is different and accounts for some variation between the groups. We do, however, need to look into the relations now and in the past between women and land. There are marked differences between the westsiders and eastsiders which have no doubt been magnified by the events of the past century but which undoubtedly reflect the world-view of each group.

In the land-maintaining rituals of Warrabri women, there is evidence for the differential impact on eastside and westside women of the changes of the past century. Aranda rituals are closed, private, exclusive family affairs that make few concessions to the outsider. The Warlpiri, on the other hand, stage wide sprawling, all inclusive rituals designed to incorporate and to recruit people. In the Aranda system of land tenure people are mapped onto land with a tightness of organization and structure made possible by their relatively well-watered territory. However the Warlpiri system of land tenure is more diffuse; the land-maintaining group is a shifting and negotiable ensemble of persons held together by a widely flung web of relationships.

Within the context of cattle station life the Aranda have been able to accommodate their land-maintaining rituals. They have remained in family groups and near their own land or land to which they have ties that can be activated. The demands of the cattle industry have dovetailed with their desire both to be out in country and to organize their own work routines. Women have been able to maintain a tie to the land which includes use of the land and employment as independent workers. Most importantly, cattle station people have retained control over many affairs which the station managers did not want to know about.

Warlpiri, on the other hand, have experienced missions and ration depots where white control was extremely intrusive and the heavy hand of administrators ever present; where male-female liaisons were short and brutal. They have come into towns, been moved to settlements and attempted to live as large communities - rarely possible in the past - but in so doing, they have lost their access to and use of land. They have attempted to incorporate others in their rituals but have lost many secrets in the process.

For Kaytej and Alyawarra, their tight organization, coupled with the possibility of remaining in small family groups on cattle stations, has enabled the women to feel that their rituals are still of relevance to their land and that they are in control. They continue to feel this, although some rituals are no longer possible. Because of these factors, Kaytej women have maintained their position *vis-à-vis* men. They have worked beside them, remained on their own country, and hence have retained the power basis for certain claims they may make on men. Most importantly, they have continued to live in small family groups where they are consulted and able to express their demands to be heard and their right to be respected.

Warlpiri women, on the other hand, have not enjoyed this small supportive family atmosphere. They have lived in situations where the expectation is that women appear subservient in public. They have been cast as wives, as mothers, as ones who support a male but who are not consulted in the distribution of resources. They have not lost the privileges which flow from living on one's own country while men have gained some privileges from their new designation as 'household heads'.

All of these accommodations, however, occurred after the brutal and violent pacification period. This was felt particularly acutely by the Kaytej in the 1880s and by the Warlpiri in the 1920s. The Kaytej have therefore had several generations in which to assimilate and make sense of the changes. One response of the Kaytej has been to turn inwards and reject all white values as distasteful. In this way we can understand the apparent enigma of Warrabri where the Kaytej, with a long contact period with whites, famed for their treachery at Barrow Creek and feared from then on, massacred in reprisals and subject to two major pacification drives in Central Australia, have nonetheless retained a tight reign on their rituals and country.

Small family groups on cattle stations have been able to develop and exercise hunting and gathering skills in a more meaningful way than have the settlement people. The area around cattle stations does not become as devastated as it does around settlements. Also, the country was very often that for which the family had a special responsibility and, in terms of the pride and skills passed on to one's descendants, this has been very important. The heavy hand of the assimilationists did not fall upon the cattle stations with anything like the weight it did on settlements and missions. Polygyny persisted with all the checks and balances intact, initiation continued to be performed in the bush, as did birth – until very recently. In summary, women and men were manifestly engaged in a joint enterprise of maintaining their country and their families.

I have gone to some lengths to spell out the context of a century of contact for the residents of Warrabri for several reasons. There is a big difference between the vitality, range and theme of the Warlpiri and Kaytej, but there are also many similarities – mainly of a structural nature. I am suggesting that the differences between the small tight group organization of Kaytej and the more sprawling communities of Warlpiri has been further elaborated and magnified in the last hundred years. Kaytej women have become so private about their rituals (which have always been a closed affair) that observers such as Strehlow[83] believed that the rituals no longer existed. The contact period has been brutal and women have turned to and grasped different strands for support. Warlpiri women have sought to throw off the burden of constant food gathering by seeking security in the 'love marriage', Kaytej have sought to come to terms with their radically altered world by elaborating existing rituals which have continued meaning. This has been possible because people have remained on their land whence they may draw constant affirmation of their worth.

To pursue my argument that a shift in the meaning and consequence of women's separation from men in ritual and daily life has occurred, I have explored the changing face of desert society. The cross-cutting cleavages and ties of Warrabri, exemplified in the east-west division of the Aboriginal population and a centre-periphery division between the white-dominated service core of the settlement and the Aboriginal camps scattered around this periphery, provide the *milieu* within which women give the *jukurrpa* ritualized form.

The shift from a hunter-gatherer mode of subsistence to a sedentary life-style on government settlements, cattle stations, missions and towns has meant more than the loss of land for Aboriginal men and women. Today they no longer control the resource from which both physical and spiritual sustenance may be drawn. The use one makes of the land and the spiritual maintenance of that land in ritual are intertwined and underwritten by the Law.

In spite of assertions that the Law does not change and that everything is known within the Law, there have been changes. Some entail incorporation, others rejection. The Law had always been able to accommodate change but those of the last century have proved to be of such an intensity and quality that the very basis of Aboriginal exist-ence is threatened. In the face of this upheaval women have continued to assert their importance as nurturers of people, land and relation-ships, but they do so in a radically changed *milieu*.

In terms of the cash economy, women today are the members of households with a male breadwinner as head; they are subject to Aus-tralian law, their role usurped by health, education and law-enforcement agencies. In their camps they continue to play out the role of autonomous individuals but it is a losing battle. They no longer enjoy the relation to the land which allows them to assert and reaffirm their direct access to the *jukurrpa* and their heritage as daughters of the dreaming. Their continued assertion in ritual that the Law is rel-evant to their lives has allowed women to cope with many of the changes of the past century, but the nexus between land and people has been shattered. The land is now used by persons not bound by the *jukurrpa*. Nevertheless the loss of control over land has affected men differently from women and Kaytej differently from Warlpiri.

The sexual politics of desert society have become increasingly enmeshed in those of the wider society of Northern Australia in a way which impinges upon women's role and status. For Aboriginal women there is a continuity of self-identity but this is given expression in a radically changed world and fashioned with dramatically different tools. For the anthropologist there is the necessary task of sifting out from women's assertions a new evaluation of women's role.

Today and in the records of the past there is evidence to back women's assertions of independence and autonomy. In looking back to a bygone era, Aboriginal women are not indulging in fantasy; they are yet again demonstrating that there are a number of world views and that their view of their past explains their present-day predica-ment more satisfactorily than the statement that women are the prop-erty of men, or persons who enjoy few rights, and that this has always been so.

In the past male-female relations were flexible and subject to change; each party had room to manoeuvre; each had a power base. But in the living out of this set of relations today, the roles have become increasingly rigid, the give-and-take a fiction, the checks and

Back at Warrabri Nampijinpa and little Nampijinpa eat from the *mardu* made earlier that month. This sweet milk is made by mixing the seeds of *wakirlpirri* (*Acacia oriacea*) with water.

balances skewed. Aboriginal men have found a more accommodating niche in the emerging male-dominated colonial society of Northern Australia. It is their power base which has been deemed a negotiating forum, not women's. Men may continue to manipulate the system, for they are the politicians in the eyes of many white Australians. Women have limited access to this world of decision-making. To mark their status as 'boss for themselves', women are now turning to the *jilimi* as power base and retreat and to *yawulyu* as an expression of women's rights and responsibilities in land. However, in the process, they restrict their access to important institutions within the emerging political order and become not 'as prisoners' but nevertheless marginal to the main stream of settlement and Northern Territory life.

NOTES

1. See Baume 1933; Terry 1934; Hartwig 1965; Hagen & Rowell 1978, 1979; Peterson *et al.* 1978.

2. Stuart 1861:136; Hartwig 1965:391; Gillen 1968:147; Strehlow 1970:120, 1971:592-593.

3. Barwick 1970:31-8.

4. Tuxworth n.d.:50-54.

5. Leacock 1978:247-75.

6. *Ibid.*:273.

7. Chewings 1930, 1936; Gillen 1968. Charles Chewings first visited Australia in 1881 and in various capacities – camel trader, geologist, explorer, pastoralist – continued in close contact with Aborigines for many years. His interest in their traditions is evident in the records of his 1909 survey of a stock route from Central Mt Stuart to Victoria River (published in 1930), and his *Back in the Stone Age* (1936). Francis Gillen, in his diary of camp jottings of the 1901-2 fieldtrip with Baldwin Spencer, notes everything which comes before him, including women who behave and speak forcefully. See fn.1:11

8. Bell & Ditton 1980:5-8.

9. See Koch *et al.* 1981:1-3.

10. Yallop 1969; O'Connell 1977:120; Bell 1978; Hagen & Rowell 1978:1.

11. See Spencer & Gillen 1899, 1927; Roheim 1933; Pink 1936; Strehlow 1947, 1970, 1971; Yallop 1969, 1977; O'Connell 1977; Denham 1978.

12. See Spencer & Gillen 1899; Strehlow 1971; Roheim 1974. Spencer and Gillen (1899) worked with people who had 'come into' the newly established telegraph

stations. T. G. H. Strehlow (whose father, Pastor Strehlow, took over the management of Hermannsburg in 1894) undertook linguistic and anthropological research with Aranda speakers from the 1930s until his death in 1978. Geza Roheim worked in Central Australia in the late 1920s. He was much influenced by the ideas of Sigmund Freud (see p. 242).

13. Meggitt 1962:xii. See fn. 1:11.

14. See Meggitt 1962, 1972; Peterson 1969, 1970a; Munn 1973; Cawte 1974; Hale 1974.

15. See Spencer & Gillen 1904; Stanner 1934; Nash 1980; Hagen *et al.* 1982.

16. Meggitt 1962:67.

17. Transcript of Evidence 1980:179A.

18. Chewings 1930:334.

19. Spencer & Gillen 1899:134,312,338.

20. Gillen 1968:153.

21. Gillen 1968:140.

22. The various estimates of the relative contribution of the sexes to the diet were calculated after cattle had grazed on the land and rations had been introduced. This renders the reliability marginal. However, all sources indicate the critical importance of women to the physical survival of the group. See Hiatt 1970:2-3.

23. Meggitt 1962:307.

24. Hamilton 1978b:5.

25. Slocum 1975:46; Tanner & Zihlman 1976:585-608.

26. See Bell 1980a:253.

27. Gillen 1968:105.

28. Chewings 1936:85.

29. Chewings 1936:86.

30. Chewings 1936:80-81.

31. Chewings 1936:86-8.

32. Meggitt 1962:39.

33. For example see Gregory (1969) in 1856; Stuart (1861) in the 1860s; Gosse (1874); and Ross (Hartwig 1965:259).

34. Stuart 1861:133-4.

35. Tuxworth n.d.:1-2.

36. Hartwig 1965:244.

37. Hartwig 1965:241.

38. Hartwig 1965:241-2.

39. Stuart 1861:138; see also Meggitt 1962:17.

40. Stuart 1861:136.

41. Hartwig 1965:391.

42. Warburton (1875:181-2), quoted in Peterson *et al* (1978:Appendix 1).

43. Strehlow 1970:120.

44. Gillen 1968:129.

45. Gillen 1968:123.

46. Gillen (1968:107-9) provides a detailed record of the attack.

47. See Strehlow (1971:592-3) for an account of the incident by two elderly Aranda men.

48. Hartwig 1965:270ff, 419.

49. Hartwig 1965:278.

50. Ashwin 1927:14.

51. Hartwig 1965:345-6.

52. Eylmann 1908:462.

53. See Hartwig 1965:411.

54. Hartwig 1965:443.

55. Chewings 1936:68; Tuxworth n.d.:2.

56. Hartwig 1965:610.

57. Beckett 1914-15:26.

58. *Ibid.*:26-27.

59. *Ibid.*:27.

60. See also Meggitt 1962:24; Strehlow 1970:107.

61. Quoted in Koch *et al.* 1981:23.

62. *Ibid.*

63. Transcript of Evidence 1981:199-201. I have modified the transcript by omitting the questions of counsel from this text (see fn.3:1).

64. *Ibid.*

65. See Strehlow 1970:107; Bell 1979a:11.

66. See Bell in press.

67. See Peterson *et al.* 1978:14.

68. *South Pacific* 1959:75; see also *Welfare Report* 1961:4.

69. See Meggitt 1962:28.

70. *Ibid.*:48.

71. See Bell 1980a; see also Meggitt 1965:148.

72. See Bell 1978:36, 60-61.

73. Meggitt 1962:236.

74. Hamilton 1975:174-5; see also Bell & Ditton 1980:94-6.

75. See Nash 1980.

76. It is interesting to note that under the Liquor Act of 1979 in the Northern Territory Aborigines have been able to express, for the first time, opinions on licensing regulations and they have asked in the great majority of cases for their home areas to be declared 'dry' and restricted licences to be issued to close-by outlets for alcohol. It appears that one solution to the alcohol problem is to shut it out of the world in which people live their daily lives and confine it to the towns where the rules and law are different.

77. Stanner 1966:169.

78. See Bell 1980a:248.

79. Meggitt (1962:222) comments that the loss of place names from songs caused a re-organization of songs. In my experience the naming of the site is merely re-organized.

80. Tuxworth n.d.:47.

81. Beckett 1914-15:28.

82. Meggitt 1962:93.

83. Strehlow 1971:647.

Chapter III
THE SUSTAINING IDEALS:
LAND, LOVE AND WELL-BEING

THE KAYTEJ *JILIMI* AND 'RING PLACE'

Come then into the Kaytej *jilimi* of 1977, meet the residents and most frequent visitors, and explore their relationships with each other and with country. Locating Kaytej women at the centre of my analysis in this way involves no sleight of hand, for the Kaytej *jilimi*, the home of the ritually powerful and respected leaders, was the focus of activities in the main Kaytej camp for men and women alike. Rather than older women looking to younger women to support and care for them, younger women and men looked to the *jilimi* for support in a number of ways. From the *jilimi*, other Kaytej drew not only economic support but also a sense of purpose, strength and knowledge.

The women associated with the Kaytej *jilimi* were the moral watch-dogs of the entire camp, the repositories of wisdom, the conscious carriers of a proud heritage. Unhesitatingly these women would censure unseemly behaviour even in adult sons. I saw one mother shout and shame a son until he clambered down from a truck which was heading to another settlement where he planned to engage in a fight with his estranged wife. His mother had the right to interfere by virtue of both her authority as a land owner and her responsibilities as mother-in-law to the girl. The authority of Kaytej women was recognized by those who lived in or near the *jilimi* and thus came under its influence. The relative distance of *jilimi* from other camps is an indication of the nature of the dependence one on the other. Often a large family camp, where a husband, wife and their dependent children live, may have a small *jilimi* within the camp area, but in the Kaytej camp, the *jilimi* was surrounded by smaller family camps. The authority of the Kaytej *jilimi* was also apparent to outsiders who spoke with some awe of the 'Karlukarlu women'.

Karlukarlu is the name for the rock formation at Devil's Marbles near Wauchope and is also one of the names by which Aborigines refer to the surrounding country. Several of the major dreamings which are held and celebrated by these women focus on Karlukarlu country and on Wakulpu, a site which gives it name to country further to the west. Within the camp there are finer distinctions and group-ings, but the overall basis of membership is an association with the dreamings which pass through the country and sites of Karlukarlu and Wakulpu. Each of the women could offer a genealogical validation for her residence in the camp, but as these links could also be forged with other women who did not live in or near the *jilimi*, I looked further for an explanation of their co-residence in the Karlukarlu camp. It was only when I began collecting life-history material from these women that I was struck by the pattern of co-residence in the past. These women had all lived together for many years at the wolf-ram mines at Wauchope, Barrow Creek and Hatches Creek, and at Greenwood Station. Thus genealogy had been further reinforced by work and residence histories.

Nampijinpa, one of the core residents of the Kaytej *jilimi*, was a widow in her late fifties, mother of six, grandmother of sixteen, great grandmother of seven and one of two surviving siblings. Wiry, alert, a fine craftswoman, renowned for her facility in sign language, her precision in body painting, her spirited dancing, and knowledge of song, myth and country, I called her 'grandmother' but she was like no grandmother I had ever known. We were able to share jokes and engage in very open discussion on a range of matters which were taboo to other relatives.

Her father's country, Wakulpu, which lay to the west and south-west of Devil's Marbles, extended further west into the high and uncharted Warlpiri sandhill country of Ngunulurru which was her mother's country. To the south of Wakulpu lay Jarrajarra, another country in which her mother had rights: a country of substantial ranges and wide sandy flood-outs. Wurrulju to the south-west, a country of rocky outcrops, sandhills, dry river beds and soakages, was the country of the spouses of her children, that is her daughters- and sons-in-law. To the north lay Miyikampi, a Warlpiri country of clay pans and rolling sandhills and secret springs, which like Warlukurlangu to the south of Jarrajarra, was the country of her classificatory husbands.

As we can see from the map (p. 112), this multiplicity of interests in countries means that Nampijinpa's residential potential is exten-

The Ancestral Landscape: Nampijinpa's 'countries'

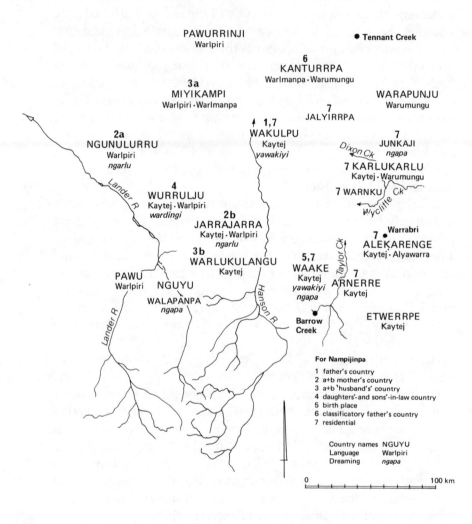

PAWURRINJI
Warlpiri

● Tennant Creek

6
KANTURRPA
Warlmanpa · Warumungu

3a
MIYIKAMPI
Warlpiri · Warlmanpa

WARAPUNJU
Warumungu

7
JALYIRRPA

2a
NGUNULURRU
Warlpiri
ngarlu

↑ **1,7**
WAKULPU
Kaytej
yawakiyi

Dixon Ck

7
JUNKAJI
ngapa

7 KARLUKARLU
Kaytej · Warumungu

4
WURRULJU
Kaytej · Warlpiri
wardingi

7 WARNKU *Ck*

Wycliffe

2b
JARRAJARRA
Kaytej · Warlpiri
ngarlu

3b
WARLUKULANGU
Kaytej

5,7
WAAKE
Kaytej
yawakiyi
ngapa

Taylor Ck

● Warrabri
7
ALEKARENGE
Kaytej · Alyawarra

7
ARNERRE
Kaytej

PAWU
Warlpiri

NGUYU

WALAPANPA
ngapa

Lander R

Hanson R

Barrow Creek ●

ETWERRPE
Kaytej

Lander R

For Nampijinpa

1 father's country
2 a+b mother's country
3 a+b 'husband's' country
4 daughters'-and sons'-in-law country
5 birth place
6 classificatory father's country
7 residential

Country names NGUYU
Language Warlpiri
Dreaming *ngapa*

0   100 km

sive. She could legitimately reside in any one of five or six areas. In this she is not unusual: we shall see that other women had similarly wide-ranging claims to different countries. That Nampijinpa has spent much of her life in the country of her father, in the country for which she is *kirda*, is due, in part, to very special events of the past fifty years. The demands of the *jukurrpa* and the constraints of colonization continue to shape the present. In the course of the hearing of a land claim (to the above countries), Nampijinpa[1] spoke of Wakulpu, the country for which she was *kirda*:

I grew up at Waake and Wakulpu. I was walking around there. I was living there. I was born at Waake. I was walking all around there and that's where I grew up. I became a mother there. I only came here [Warrabri] when I was big . . . Yanganpali [Wauchope], I was walking to all the places, soakages where I lived: Jajilper-nange, Wirlilunku, a swamp, Kurlalkinyje, Milpajirrame, Manta-karri, Wanjimarange, Wilyaninye, Jurujuparnta, Pajipajile. Wakulpu is the place right in the centre of a lot of soakages, in a way it holds the soakages.

My mother took me around first when she was still alive. We walked around . . . My father was in the same place around with us . . . My father, whose country was Waake, passed away at Bullocky Soak, Yamarku, on this side from Ti-Tree [i.e. to the north] . . . My father did not work. He was a bushman . . . We got rations there, my parents and myself. When that mine started [wolf-ram at Wauchope] a lot of people went there but we only went to get rations . . . We used to come where the wolfram was and get rations and then go back and eat them, back in our country. We stayed really at Wakulpu. We came east and we went to Barrow Creek for rations and especially for tobacco. Then we would go back and live, back to Wakulpu . . . We got rations at Wauchope. The old people used to get rations, our mothers and fathers used to get rations and tobacco. Then we would go back to the bush again . . . After I was married and had a child, I was living at Taylor Crossing. I was staying there as a married woman with children . . . And then I went to Wauchope, after that to Warnku . . . Now when I had big grown-up children. We came to this [Warrabri] when it was a new place . . . They were getting the children together for school. People were asking us to come here. Welfare . . . Welfare again .. We just came here but we really wanted to be at our place at Wakulpu.

In spite of rationing from centralized depots, Nampijinpa lived most of her life on or near her country and therefore sustained intimate contact with the country of her father and its main sites, Wakulpu, Waake, Warnku and Karlukarlu. On the other hand her Warlpiri mother's country of Ngunulurru was too distant from such contact. However, because her mother was able to forge a dreaming track link with the neighbouring country of Jarrajarra and because Nampijinpa participated in ceremonies, and lived in the area, she was able to consolidate her position as *kurdungurlu* for Jarrajarra.

When Nampijinpa dances for Wakulpu (or Akwerlpe as it is known in Kaytej), one of her favourite sequences is of food gathering west of Karlukarlu. The images and the humour of her dancing draw on her experience of the country and family. Her ritual range extends from her mother's country in the south and west and, by following rain dreaming out of Wakulpu into Warumungu country, goes as far north as Tennant Creek; it is underwritten by her unbroken contact with the country celebrated in the ceremonies.

Nampijinpa, a Kaytej speaker, married a Warlpiri man, just as her Kaytej father had married a Warlpiri woman. Her children have rights of *kirda* in their father's country but because they have been reared near their mother's country, they tend to emphasize their rights as *kurdungurlu* in Wakulpu. Nampijinpa expresses some pleasure that her children are learning of their Kaytej heritage and sometimes complains that Warlpiri forced her to speak their language.

In Central Australia there is no absolute relation between language and country: Akwerlpe is Kaytej country, but most often is given the Warlpiri rendering of Wakulpu; similarly the Kaytej country of Errwelje is known by the Warlpiri as Wurrulju. Jarrajarra is Kaytej and Warlpiri mixed. This, as we shall see, is one consequence of marriage and the reciprocal relations of *kirda* and *kurdungurlu*.

Nampijinpa's mother, born in the last decade of the nineteenth century, was, when I met her in 1976, frail but quick of mind. When we went camping out, Nampijinpa and I would carry the old lady and her swag to the camp of another 'daughter' so that she could be cared for in our absence. When we recounted our exploits on our return, she always listened attentively and added her sage comments. Her

114

dependence on her daughter restricted Nampijinpa's movements but no resentment was expressed. 'I do for her what she did for me', daughters often observe.

The old lady died while I was at Warrabri. As I have already noted part of mourning rituals involve women in speech taboos which are observed for varying periods of time according to their relationship to the deceased. During this time they communicate in a highly developed, complex sign language. Most of the women of the Kaytej *jilimi* were affected by the old lady's death, but due to her age and the general feeling that she had lived a full life and not died before her time, the taboos were lifted after a month, rather than two years, which is the case for younger persons.

When a death is imminent, families gather, for it is important that mourning rituals are observed and that the old people are buried on or near to their country. These are critical factors in feeling secure in one's country, and on approaching sites not visited for some time, travellers call out to the old people, to the grandparents, and explain the purpose of their visit. Land rights in certain areas have given people a security of tenure to the land, in which the old people may again be buried.

In giving evidence in a land claim, one Napurrula[2] explained:

This place [Warrabri] is somebody else's sacred site and they [her old people] are buried in someone else's sacred site tree over there. They want to go back to their own land and sacred site . . . because a lot of old people have passed away, and some of them young people never look back to that country and sacred site, even old people.

The site of which she spoke has now become Aboriginal land and, in mid-1982, one of 'the old people', her father's sister, was buried in the country. The spiritual essence of that old woman now imbues the country with new significance for her descendants. When they call out to the country, they speak also to her.

Nampijinpa had little or no experience of towns and was always reluctant to become involved with the institutions of white society. The memory of punitive parties which drove her family out of her mother's country in her childhood and the 'mustering' of people in the establishment of Warrabri were formative experiences. Like other *jilimi* residents her childhood was lived in the shadow of the 'killing time', the 1928 massacres, but such matters were discussed in hushed tones.

Napanangka, one of Nampijinpa's daughters, was a large, unhappy woman who worked as stockrider mustering and is now married to a man from Wurrulju, the country adjacent to Wakulpu. After her father-in-law, a Kaytej man, was killed in the massacres, his son was raised by his mother's second husband, a Warlpiri man of Pawurrinji. As we have seen, it was to the security of this country that many people fled.

Napanangka's children thus have the rights of *kirda* in both of the countries of their father (Wurrulju and Pawurrinji) and, as they live within striking distance of both, will be able to enjoy rights in both. From her father (that is Nampijinpa's husband), she has interests in dreamings further west in the Tanami Desert, but her residence in her mother's country and participation in its rituals emphasizes her ties to Wakulpu, for which she is *kurdungurlu*. Her husband's affiliation to Wurrulju intersects with hers because the mythological travels of the *wardingi* (witchetty) ancestor of Wurrulju meets with and crosses over that of *yawakiyi* (bush berry) of Wakulpu. In ceremonies for Wakulpu, husband and wife co-operate in the production of ritual items for use in ceremonies which men and women stage jointly (see p. 191ff).

Nampijinpa's other adult daughter was also a constant visitor to the *jilimi*, but her marital disputes alienated her from the camp and eventually she left Warrabri. The *jilimi* was no sanctuary for women who consistently behaved improperly but this is not to say that life within the *jilimi* is one of enforced celibacy. Women will often comment on how well another is looking and speculate, with a laugh, as to the cause.

The daughters of Nampijinpa's brothers, the Nangalas, were also constant visitors to the *jilimi* and participants in *yawulyu*. However these nieces were too young to assume the role of senior *kirda* in ritual. There were several older Nangala resident in the *jilimi*. One of these women, a senior *kirda* for Wakulpu, died in 1978. She had no surviving children, no sisters and her brothers had no daughters. Thus there was no-one in her immediate family to whom she could transmit her rights in Wakulpu, but through her participation in *yawulyu* she assisted in the instruction of classificatory daughters and nieces, and thereby assured continuity of knowledge.

The Kaytej Jilimi of 1977: A Fragment of a Genealogy

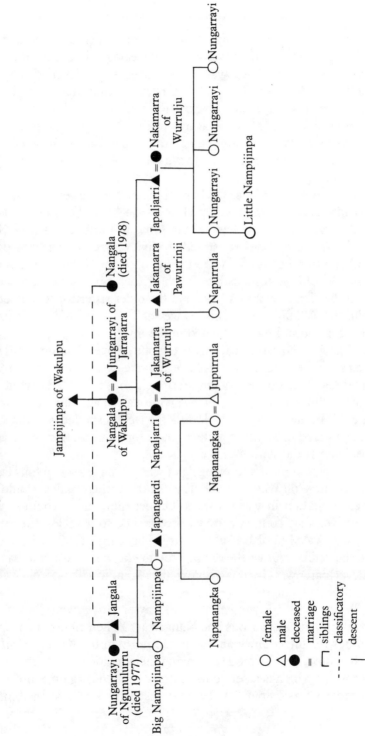

One middle-aged Nangala was always spoken of as belonging to Wakulpu, but I could never elicit a genealogical base for this claim. Rather it appeared she was incorporated at the level of subsection affiliation. Although her face had been horribly disfigured by yaws and speech was difficult, she participated in *yawulyu* and it was, I suspect, one of her few pleasures in life. Her handicapped son was a responsibility which limited her involvement and as he would never be initiated, he remained always the responsibility of the *jilimi* women.

Nampijinpa's older sister, born at the turn of the century, lived with her husband in a small camp close to the *jilimi*. During the day the sisters often retreated beyond the *jilimi* to the bough shelter where all the secret material was stored, to work on the ritual gear associated with Wakulpu country. When they danced for Wakulpu the younger sister would be responsible for the ritual paraphernalia associated with the site known as Waake and the older sister for that associated with the Wakulpu site. This, as we shall see, is also the relationship between the siblings celebrated in the myth.

The older Nampijinpa, or 'the big one', as we sometimes called her – an accurate name in terms of age and size –, had lived for many years at Greenwood Station in a long-term relationship with the white manager. Although she moved between the station and favourite camping sites on Bonney Creek – including the well despoiled by Stuart – she remembered fondly that 'killers' (meat for consumption) were always available at the station.

The Nampijinpa and Nangala of whom I have spoken thus far, call the country of Wakulpu and Karlukarlu 'father'. They would state their affiliation in various ways. On occasions they would say, 'I'm *kirda* for that country', or, with reference to a major site such as Waake, Wakulpu or Karlukarlu, say 'That's my place', or by addition of the suffix *arenye* (belonging to) to the country name say 'I'm Akwerlparenye. (In this context the Arandic cognate of Wakulpu would be favoured.)

When I asked women in the Kaytej *jilimi* who looked after Wakulpu, the answer was 'the Nungarrayi'. Their rights and responsibilities for the country and their centrality in the Kaytej *jilimi* were undisputed, yet the mode of tracing their relationship to the country is not that which is asserted to be the norm. Once again a multiplicity of factors was important. In most discussions of responsibility for

118

country, women would state that the *kurdungurlu* for Wakulpu should be the daughters of the Nampijinpa and Nangala. If this were always so, then the Napanangka and Napaljarri would take on the responsibility. Nungarrayi are the children of Japaljarri and are thus members of the same patrimoiety as the daughters of the *kirda* for Wakulpu. At the level of patrimoiety, Nungarrayi women certainly have a role in ceremonies. As it was explained to me – with a sweep of the hand – at the very first *yawulyu* I observed (see p. 20), one side of the society (that is, one patrimoiety) is *kirda*, and the other is *kurdungurlu*. However the Karlukarlu Nungarrayi had a more precise link than this notion of 'sides': they were carrying on their father's roles as *kurdungurlu*. The senior Nungarrayi[3] explained it in the following way:

> [My father was] *kurdungurlu* for Waake and Wakulpu. It was his ... Look after Waake and Wakulpu ... He looked after the two places, Waake and Wakulpu, and then I lost him; he passed away. Now it is me looking after my own country, Jarrajarra, and also Waake and Wakulpu. As my father could not go onto Waake country, so from when I was a young girl I kept on doing the *yawulyu*, looking after the country ... my sisters. They are looking after that country too ... and those daughters of my father and Nakamarra [his second wife].

Like Nampijinpa, Nungarrayi was reared in the shadow of the killing time and also like Nampijinpa she speaks obliquely of the events. Nungarrayi's father couldn't live at Waake because it was within the range of the pacification drives and ritualized grief kept people out of the area, but this information is only available to those with local knowledge. The memory of burnt camps, shot dogs, the wailing of mourners at dawn and dusk, her anguish for a father to whom she was extremely close, are only spoken of in private or, as we saw in the previous chapter, by highlightng the less tragic encounters with whites. However in her account of her coming to Warrabri related below, the legacy of fear of white authority is apparent.

Nungarrayi's father was by all accounts an impressive man and his three daughters are said to be in his image. The eldest in particular is one of the prolific dreamers of Warrabri, an intensely spiritual person often lost in thought, wise in the ways of the Law and country but also blessed with a wicked sense of humour. I called her 'daughter' although she was in her late fifties and she offered me the thoughtful care a mother may expect. Her skills extended to those of the ngangkayi (traditional healer) and her younger sister was an accomplished healer. When I was ill or concerned for my children (whom she called brother and sister) Nungarrayi would intervene.

Her knowledge of country, like that of Nampijinpa's, was based on intimate and sustained contact. But when we listen to her story we see that it was the country of her father's mother in which she spent most of her time.[4]

[I was born at] Yanganpali ... Wauchope [and grew up there]. When I was a little girl, about that high [indicating four feet] my father took me around there, to Wakulpu, Pajipajile, Wilyaninye, Kurlakinyje, Ngarnapirlapirla, Wurjulungulangu ... My father used to take us around looking for food. If there was no food we would go onto another place. The meat we used to get was mainly possum and sugar bag. My sister was living with us ... At Warnku, the place where all the Warumungu, Warlpiri, Alyawarra people meet up, at Yanganpali, they meet up there ... for ceremony ... We stayed at Warnku which was like a permanent settlement, a sort of a village. Alyawarra people came there, and Kaytej people and Warumungu ... To that same Warnku, to the one place ... Anmatjirri and Warlpiri people came. They came from all different countries to this one Warnku. My father was working at Greenwood Station.

[That was where we saw that first white fellow.] He had a buggy and a horse [see p. 68] ... I stayed with my grandmothers [father's mother and mother's mother] while my father was showing the missionary the Wakulpu country ... After Greenwood we went to Warnku. There were a lot of us living there for a long time and Singleton, Umburulungku, that's the Aboriginal name for where the old station was ... and at that wolfram mine too. My father worked there – he was working there with the equipment. I was now grown up. I was living along there. My father was still working at the wolfram place, and then he moved to work at Wauchope. My father was still working and then he passed away.

My big children were born while I was still living at Wauchope ... We lived there – Nakamarra [i.e. her 'mothers'], Nangala [her husband's sisters and *kirda* for Warnku] and Nungarrayi [i.e. her sisters] ... We came to live at Warrabri. A white man got us here

120

for school. We were a bit frightened. My two sisters, they didn't really want to come, they were frightened, but the white man caught them in the evening at night when it got dark. They wanted to stay there forever . . . They brought us with a car . . .

But we still visit Wakulpu and we want to go there . . . because it is a good place, and plenty fruits, bush tucker . . . We still go out camping towards that country: we go camping for a number of days in the direction of that country . . . We usually go out on weekends. There is water there, a swamp and soakages but we really need a bore to live there. In the olden days we lived at Wilyaninye, where there is a spring and lived off the spring water. When all the soakages dried up that was where we lived, at Wilyaninye, because of the permanent spring water.

Nungarrayi is now generally to be found at Warrabri, in her husband's camp or, during their many estrangements, in the *jilimi*. Her sons of her first marriage have grown up and married. By her second marriage, to a man many years her junior, she has a daughter. This child is in a favoured position to learn of Wakulpu country and, given her continued residence near the country and membership of the correct subsection – that is, Nampijinpa – she may become, in future years, a knowledgeable *kirda* for Wakulpu.

Nungarrayi, as a young girl, was promised to the old Jangala who was father for Nampijinpa of the Kaytej *jilimi* and thus her children could offer further support for their claim to be *kirda* of Wakulpu by emphasizing their relationship to a classificatory father (that is, their mother's promised husband).

On important ceremonial occasions, the three Nungarrayi sisters would gather to celebrate the dreaming activity of Jarrajarra, the country for which their father was *kirda*, and for Wakulpu the country for which he was *kurdungurlu*. Their closeness as sisters is reinforced not only by their residence at Warrabri but also by their marital history. Both went as promised brides to the same old man. Their bond as sisters pre- and post-dated the marriage.

Their father's second wife, now a middle-aged Nakamarra, is about the same age as the oldest of the Nungarrayi. This Nakamarra holds country to the south of Wakulpu and was another core member of the Kaytej *jilimi*. She has participated in Wakulpu *yawulyu* and through long residence in the country, knowledge, marriage ties and membership of the same patrimoiety as Nampijinpa, could play the role of *kirda*. I called her 'sister' and together we would plot and scheme the future of the various eligible Japaljarri (our potential spouses).

Other casual visitors to the Kaytej *jilimi* included several Napal-jarri, who, as classificatory sisters of Nungarrayi's father, could have been *kurdungurlu* for Wakulpu, but they knew little of the country. Nonetheless, the Karlukarlu women made every effort to recruit and teach those who stood in a potentially correct relation and these Napaljarri were no exception.

The other most constant visitor and, for much of 1976 and 1977, a full-time resident, was a Napurrula, Nungarrayi's father's sister's child. Intellectually Napurrula and Nungarrayi were well-matched; each had wide-ranging knowledge of country, multiple affiliations and ceremonial expertise. Napurrula was *kurdungurlu* for Jarrajarra and in *yawulyu* assisted Nungarrayi. They worked side by side in the preparation and execution of *yawulyu*. Napurrula would ensure that Nungarrayi did not err in her following of the travels.

Napurrula was my 'aunty', her father was the 'brother' of the first Nakamarra who befriended me and had introduced me to *yawulyu*. Through this side of her family she had rights in Pawurrinji but through her mother, the sister of Nungarrayi's father, she had knowl-edge of Wakulpu. Napurrula traced her rights from her mother's mother. She called the country '*jaja*' (Warlpiri for mother's mother) and her rights in the country were reinforced by her conception dreaming at her *jaja*'s place, Ngapajinpi.

Napurrula's mother's first husband was killed in his own country of Wurrulju and if she wished she could have claimed rights in that country also. The bond between grandmother and grandchild was close. In recounting her story, Napurrula[5] told me: 'I never left my grandmother alone. I used to be there always. I loved her very much. I always followed her, never my Mum'.

Napurrula was a little younger than Nungarrayi and Nampijinpa, but because she had borne no children of her own, her period of ritual instruction had not been interrupted by the demands of child care. She had fostered her brother's daughter's children and seen her deceased sister's son through initiation. In her twenties and early thirties, when most women were subject to the demands of child-rearing, she was learning and participating in *yawulyu*. When in the late 1940s her parents came in from the desert wastes of Pawurrinji to the ration depot known as the Six Mile (just east of Tennant Creek) run by the Aboriginal Inland Mission, Napurrula was swept up by institutional life of school and separation from parents. For others this was deadening but for her it was an opportunity to learn more. She watched and participated in Warumungu *yawulyu*, and from other women at Phillip Creek learnt of country as far north as Lake Woods.

As a young woman she had spent time in Alice Springs and Darwin, which also widened her understandings. Napurrula would locate her answers to my questions within this wide-ranging experience and offer insights which often prompted further comment from other Kaytej women.

In early 1977, the Karlukarlu *jilimi* was home also to several Napangardi who were *kirda* for Miyikampi and Kanturrpa but, following the death of a 'son', these women moved to the other side of Warrabri and although they continued to visit the Karlukarlu women, they did not participate in the maintenance of ritual items for some period. Similarly when the older Nampijinpa moved to Tennant Creek, her role in locally held ceremonies was necessarily limited. Over four years I have seen other women being groomed by Nungarrayi, Napurrula and the younger Nampijinpa to fill her place.

Place names, dreaming affiliations and the relationship of particular individuals to land may be discussed within the *jilimi*, but when women wish to engage in *yawulyu* or serious discussion concerning *yawulyu* places, they retire to the 'ring place'. Situated to the north of the *jilimi* and conceptually in the bush are the ritual store-house, bough shade and 'ring place' of the Kaytej women. In common with the location of 'ring places' in other communities, the Kaytej women's area is located so that it is inaccessible from the road and not visible from the other Aboriginal camps or from the settlement core.

The area has two main divisions. One is a large clearing facing west where women may sit to paint, display their boards, dance and occasionally sleep; it is known in Aboriginal English as the 'ring place' or 'business ground'. (Men use the same term for their ground.) The second area, which backs onto the 'ring place', has a store-house opening out into a bough shade facing east; it is in this space that all grave matters are discussed. It also provides another area in which women may paint, sit and work on their ritual objects, or simply chat and rest, but the atmosphere is far more serious.

In the past, women's 'ring places' (like those of the men) were the areas where offenders were brought to trial and disputes resolved by ritual means. Although many of these functions have now been usurped by school, hospital, church and police, the 'ring place' is still considered to be a peaceful place where it is therapeutic to sleep during times of illness, social unrest or personal sorrow. Important meetings involving women may also be held in this area. When a woman lawyer came to discuss with Kaytej women their concern about land rights and the village council, it was the 'ring place' which was chosen as a fitting area for such an important meeting.[6]

The 'ring place' is an area where women's authority is writ large. Men travel circuitous routes to avoid even sighting the area. And women, if disturbed there by children during ritual activity, will carry through disciplinary threats which at other times are not enforced. This of course is only possible when women are living on or near their land and their actions are backed by sanction.

From where the women sit in the bough shelter area they are able to keep all the activity of the *jilimi* and environs under surveillance; on approaching the area one waits to be signalled through. There, on most afternoons, Nungarrayi, Napurrula and Nampijinpa would sit in the shade of the shelter, to repair their boards and hairstring, to grind their ochres, to clean their headbands and feathers. As these items were handed down from a shelf at the back of the shelter, the women would speak the names of the dreamings and country for each set of items and address each by the appropriate kin term. Gone was the ribald joking of the *jilimi*; instead women spoke of the need to care for their treasures, to protect them from damage and 'to hold them' always.

Introduced items, such as store-bought cleaners, wool, fat and cash, are easily incorporated within the Kaytej ritual repertoire. For example, once wool 'hairstring' has been used in a ceremony and stored alongside other items in the 'ring place', it has the status of hairstring. Although the latter is valued, women are aware that access to store-bought objects opens up new possibilities: no longer need they rely on initiation exchanges for hairstring. Similarly, store-bought tomahawks allow women to cut their own raw materials for ritual boards and store-bought fat means that women's ritual activity need no longer be constrained by the availability of goanna and emu fat. Cash has also been incorporated in ritual exchanges and thus in

124

a sense brought under the control of the Law.

I remember one peaceful afternoon when some of the women were 'making' hairstring from eight-ply wool by greasing and reddening it with ochre, while others were bleaching the feathers and headbands which were stained with red ochre from the last time they were used. Nampijinpa had been cleaning feathers with a traditional white paste, made by mixing water with the grounds of a rock found near Devil's Marbles, and was admiring them in the sunlight. Nungarryi held the headbands she had been cleaning next to the feathers, and declared, 'I use White King. It gets them whiter.'

Ceremonial concerns dominated the conversation of the 'ring place'. The women spoke of their responsibility to care for and protect the contents of the store-house and of the loss of precious items in a fire some years ago. Today, they said they wanted brick museums like those which are built for the men. They related stories of past *yawulyu* and spoke of their plans for future ritual activity. They complained about their limited access to vehicles and the trouble they had notifying other women of ceremonies. Men were reluctant to assist or intervene both because it was not their job, and because some ceremonies, such as *yilpinji*, are feared by men.

However, women are not always thwarted. On one memorable occasion an Aboriginal male councillor woke the white mechanic at 5.00 a.m. and insisted he repair the truck because the women needed it. 'Of course they fixed it,' the woman explained to me, 'it is my duty and right to travel with this business. He might get sick if he doesn't help.' She was a woman from a cattle station and accustomed to being heeded in such matters.

At the back of the 'ring place' women sit to paint. First they grease their bodies and with broad strokes of the index finger, map out the basic contours of the design in red or black. Then, with small painting sticks, the white enclosure lines are applied. If the *yawulyu* was for Wakulpu, a *kurdungurlu*, often an actual daughter, would first paint Nampijinpa (that is, the senior *kirda*), then more junior persons, then finally another senior *kirda* and the *kurdungurlu*, such as Nungarrayi. Painting is a group activity which allows those with little expertise to acquire the knowledge necessary to apply designs and the like.

While women are preparing the ritual items and painting they sing gently and harmoniously of the Dreamtime experience which validates their use of the objects. During this activity the range of songs, rhythms, harmonies and symbolic meanings is far more extensive and complex than during the open and public singing which follows on the 'ring place' to the west of the store-house. It is a private time, when children and outsiders are not welcome; and songs known as 'dear ones' (that is old and cherished) are sung; it is also when verbal instruction occurs and ritual roles are sorted out. It was during this time that I was offered ritual instruction. It concerned the structural level of interrelation of sites, persons and dreamings – the masterplan of mythological activity in an area. Finer-grain analyses of song texts, designs and gestures were offered to me only after performances and after I had a general idea of ancestral activity in Kaytej country.

On days when a *yawulyu* was to be performed, the women would gather early in the afternoon and prepare their ritual paraphernalia. When the painting was complete, most of the women would move to the dancing place and sit facing west. There they would begin to sing the songs which call all peoples together. Women's rituals, like those of the men, are a time when distant people come together to exchange and assert their common bonds of responsibility to country. A fire is kept burning throughout the rituals and as a symbol of ritual continuity the same pile of ash is re-raked and relit for each new ritual.

The *yawulyu* performance is short and alludes to the preparation, rather than explicitly spelling out the matters which have beeen discussed and the songs that have been sung at the dancing ground. After the *kurdungurlu* introduce the country with several songs, the senior *kirda* appear holding the boards on high, and dance forward following the tracks of the dreaming until they arrive at the fire. (In Warlpiri rituals the *kurdungurlu* first collect the *kirda* and are said to 'wake them up' for the dancing.) They thus re-enact the way in which the ancestors demonstrated their roles to each other.

The seated *kirda* and *kurdungurlu* sing of the site at which the dreaming rests or visits; other *kurdungurlu* plant the boards and dance flanking the *kirda*. The place of the dreaming is thus marked out. The boards are then admired and called by the name of the country for which they stand. The participants also address them affectionately, with the appropriate kinship terms such as mother, father, aunty. In this way both the ritual relationship to country and the deep emotional personal tie to country are given expression. Once planted, the object becomes the focus of the performance as the dreaming travels are re-enacted. Both *kirda* and *kurdungurlu* dance

Napurrula draws the symbol for water hole at the base of the ritual *kurduru* which represents the travels of rain in Wakulpu country. She calls the *kurduru* 'jaja', (mother's mother).

and both *kirda* and *kurdungurlu* sing, but unlike some Warlpiri women, the dancers do not sing for themselves.

To follow the dancing, one needs to be able to read the symbols it encodes. From the position of the dancers, the role they assume and the body designs they wear, an observer can determine whether they are *kirda* or *kurdungurlu*. In the patterns of the dancing feet, the women's gestures as they dance, the orientation of the boards, an observer may learn something of country but details are not available to those unschooled in the dreaming. An observer would know the various roles different people were playing, the direction of the dreaming and, from the gestures, the broad category to which the song belonged. But the words of the songs and the symbols in the designs reveal little to the outsider unless instruction is offered.

Once the dancing is finished the women sing the dreaming into the ground and expect visitors to leave. They then smooth over all traces of where the boards have been, throw dirt to nullify any remaining power and rub the painted boards onto their bodies to reabsorb the power. This transference of power is extremely dangerous and in certain contexts, not discussed here, constitutes the most sacred moments of women's resolution of conflict *yawulyu*. Once stripped, the boards are carefully replaced in the storehouse. Women may either return to the *jilimi* or prepare to sleep the night at the ground. The paint on their bodies is allowed to wear off and is often the only sign that women have been engaged in ritual.

Such performances took place on average once a week during my stay at Warrabri, but the performances tended to cluster, either because during certain times of social unrest there is a moratorium on ritual action, or because of a tendency to concentrate ritual action at certain times of the year. Even during my quiet times though, women would be busy in the ritual storehouse area.

YAWULYU AND LAND

Yawulyu ceremonies of Kaytej and indeed of other women in Central Australia evoke the three major themes of land, love and health within the context of women's *jukurrpa* heritage. These interlocking themes are embedded in the central symbols of fat and colour and the attendant emotional, physical and psychological states.

Warrabri Kaytej celebrate these themes within the context of Wakulpu and neighbouring countries. From the red of Karlukarlu rises the power of life force and blood.[7] Through massage with fat, prepared during a performance of a *yawulyu* for the country around Karlukarlu, the power can be activated by women. Against this redness is juxtaposed the whiteness of rain and lightning as it flashes dangerously overhead at Devil's Marbles and as it forms the designs of Ngapajinpi – both person and place. This whiteness is disturbed

Alyawarra women dance holding up the boards for their country. The designs on their bodies and the boards tell of the travels of the ancestral dingoes. Here *kirda* and *kurdungurlu* give ritual form to the statement that women 'grow up' and 'hold up' the country.

and challenged by the brilliance of the colours of the Rainbow Men, who pursue women in the area which is the focus of many of the love rituals.[8]

With *yawakiyi* (bush berry) is associated all that is black in the natural world. He is confronted by bush fire, crosses over and travels with *wardingi* (witchetty), is accompanied by his faithful bird companions, the *yirpadirlpadirlpa* (little black birds) and is dependent for life on *ngapa* (water).

The travels of *yawakiyi* portray mourning, the devotion of his bird friends, and correct ritual relations between *kurdungurlu* and *kirda*. He goes into the ground at Wakulpu to re-emerge further on, but this point of his travels is not the responsibility of the Kaytej. 'Stop here,' women say. 'Don't run into someone else's country.'

In both rain and bush berry dreamings, fat is the medium through which the power of the dreaming is transformed and transmitted by the women who are *kirda* and *kurdungurlu* for the ceremonies and the country. Fat is the central symbol of women's ritual in that it links the major themes of love, health and land.[9] While the Dreamtime heroes pioneered the country, they rubbed themselves with fat and admired the beauty and redness of their bodies. To glow with health is to be as one who is covered with fat. A lover cannot help but be attracted by the glowing good health of the body which reflects contentment and the strength of one who has access to country of one's dreaming. As bullock fat is now readily available, it is possible to grease and paint more bodies more often than in the past when one relied on emu, goanna or witchetty fat. Fat is seen as imparting strength and requires special ritual attention in all women's health maintaining and curing rituals. Fat is also seen as a sign that one is loved, lovable and in tune with country.

The term *yawulyu* is known and used by women to refer to their own ceremonies throughout Central Australia.[10] However in different places it encompasses different themes. For Warrabri Kaytej it is a general gloss for all their land-based rituals, but at the level of the song, design, gesture and object, there is further specification. If a *yawulyu* is being celebrated to restore harmony, then the designs, songs and gestures will be those associated with the maintenance of social harmony and restoration of good health. If the focus of the *yawulyu* is emotional management, then powerful *yilpinji* designs, songs and gesture will be used. Uniting all *yawulyu* ceremonies is the celebration of country based on the rights and responsibilities of the participants.

It is in the context of *yawulyu* activity at the ring place that women speak of the dreamings which underwrite their use of objects and country. Nampijinpa, Napurrula and Nungarrayi co-operated in the telling of the dreaming stories, in calling the sites on the tracks and in enumerating those responsible for the country.[11]

For Wakulpu, Yaakiy [*yawakiyi*], both bush-plum dreaming. Yaakiy comes from Waake and went to visit his brother at Wakulpu, the other one comes from Yanganpali [Wauchope]. He stopped at the soakages along the way . . . at Warnku, he was just sitting in the shade . . . there is a creek there . . . Then he got up and went straight through to Wakulpu . . . The one from Waake, he stopped at Jajilpernange, Wulpuje. His brother at Wakulpu told him to go straight back.

There was one yaakiy who was sitting by himself at Wakulpu; he was sitting there by himself. His name was Amberanger. He was the oldest brother. That is his secret name. That is the dreaming's own name.

This other yaakiy came and was asking this one: 'Nambinyindu?' which means 'What name are you?' 'I am food. I am vegetable food', I think. 'What about you?' He refused to answer; he made a sign which means: 'I don't know. I don't want to let on'. 'I said mine. I'm hungry'. What they were doing [Napurrula explained], is calling each other's secret names. Another name was Yarrirnti. 'You can be Yarrirnti'. . . . He answered: 'What about you?' He then said: 'I'm Wakuwarlpa' which is a fruit like *yaakiy* . . . They were asking each other. . . . [Napurrula explained] these two *yaakiy* were asking each other's secret names and also for the secret places that they held. That is all, and then he went back – the one who was visiting went back from Wakulpu . . . to Waake . . . back to Waake. The one who was at Wakulpu stayed living there permanently. He stayed there and that is it . . . and the one who came from Wauchope . . . He was staying there where there is that house, the hotel at Wauchope . . . He went from there, from Wauchope. He went to Warnku from Wauchope. He went from Warnku to where there is a swamp and he slept there, at Wirlilunku. That is the name of a swamp where the dreaming camped . . . Then he went in at

Wakulpu for ever. He entered the ground.

The soakages of Wakulpu, Kurlartakurlangu, Wirlilunku, a swamp, Jarnapajinijini, Amarralungku, Martunkunya, Kungku, Alajiyte, Alyirre, Kunanyirre, all *yaakiy* places, Kuunali, Kulalje, Kurlalkinyje, Pwujijante, Julkarnte, Minyalke, Ngurlukurlangu, Milpajirrame, Mantakartu, Wanjimarange, Kurlalkinyje, Wilyaninye, that dreaming goes around in a circle from Wakulpu, Jurujuparnta, Pajipajile, just north of Waake, Purntunge, Kurte, Kulya, Kulaji, Kurlariji, Marunganja, Arrkipinyi, Wurnmurrngu, a soakage and Yanginmari, a rockhole on Stirling. Going west from Wakulpu yaakiy came to Lumpulumpu, on its way to Ngarnapirlapirla. Stop there we're getting too close to someone else's country.

We do that *yawulyu* for Wakulpu all the time [Nungarrayi explained]. We make the country good . . . for fruit. So it will grow up well, so that we can make it green, so that we hold the Law forever. My father told me to hold it always this way, so I go on holding *yawulyu* for that country . . . Sometimes we dance, man and woman together . . . For Wakulpu. So we can 'catch him up', 'hold him up'.

This version was told in the context of a land claim, and therefore does not violate women's privacy, but on other occasions and during ritual celebration of Wakulpu other relations and exploits of the dreamings of the area may be emphasized. Of particular importance and gravity were the songs, designs and dancing which gave ritual form to the mythological account of the going down into the ground of *yawakiyi*. His journey to Wakulpu had been a long and tiring one. Throughout, his faithful *kurdungurlu*, the two *yirpadirlpadirlpa*, (little black birds) had accompanied him, urging him on, encouraging him not to collapse before reaching his goal. They danced beside him and at his final 'going down' watched and mourned his passing. When the ritual items are rubbed clean of their designs which show *yawakiyi* and his companions, two women stand either side of the place where the ritual *kurduru* (ritual pole) was planted and as living *kurdungurlu*, re-enact the dreamtime relation of *kirda* to *kurdungurlu*.

Not all stories are of sorrow and loss. The adventures of the two grandmothers, usually played by the two Nampijinpa, are full of light-hearted fun and gentle instruction for younger women. In a

During the Willowra Land Claim Hearing (1980), Nangala explained to the court how women 'lift up' country.

favourite segment of this *yawulyu* the *kirda* dance and pick sweet fruits from the trees. They place them in their *parraja* (food carriers) which are under their arms. Several young girls who are following behind, begin to steal the fruits. The older women turn and engage in a mock fight, after which the young girls fall in behind the older women and assist them in their work. Still other stories enacted in *yawulyu* tell of encounters between the dreamings. They may recount how one dreaming looked across and saw another, how one crossed over the track of another, how dreamings met and travelled on together. In all these ways the relations between and within countries are articulated. For example, within the country of Wakulpu, the sites of Waake, Wakulpu and Karlukarlu are related as siblings. But in a song concerning rain, Wakulpu and Waake look across to Walapanpa in the south and to Junkaji in the north and call these sites 'brother'.

The relations amongst these three countries established what is known as a 'company relation', which is one of the most common links established between countries for whom the *kirda* belong to the same subsections. Often interests in a common dreaming track, such as *ngarlu* (sugarbag) for Nampijinpa's mother, *ngapa* (rain) for Walapanpa and Wakulpu, provide a further link. But relations are also forged between countries which call each other granny (*jaja*) such as between Wakulpu and Wurrulju. There are also cases where one country calls the other mother: the Nakamarra of Pawurrinji call the Napanangka of Miyikampi mother, and the Napangardi of Miyikampi call the Napurrula of Pawurrinji mother.

Where one dreaming track crosses over another, as does witchetty and rain, even though these dreamings emanate from different countries and continue onto different countries, rights in the track extend outwards from one's own country. Also through much of the marginal country of Central Australia, supra-tracks such as those of rain, kangaroo and snake forge links across vast distances, but within most countries there are also localized forms of these dreamings.

The women of Jarrajarra have responsibility for the localized kangaroo dreaming at Jarrajarra, while at Karlukarlu women hold a complex of rain dreamings for the site separate from those of rain travelling to the site. However, it is a mistake to think that localized dreamings are evidence that women's rights are conscribed by a hearth-centric interest in the *jukurrpa* master plan. As we saw, the Wakulpu women named the sites which link Wakulpu to Waake and

In the soft sand Nungarrayi traces the tracks of the mythological heroes who travelled from the country of her father to that of her mother. By encompassing the two sets of ritual items which represent sites in the different countries, Nungarrayi, demonstrates their closeness.

which they celebrate in their *yawulyu*, just as readily as they named the Wakulpu soakages where they camped.

Nungarrayi, Napurrula and Nampijinpa,[12] in retelling the story of Jarrajarra, illustrated the way in which a responsibility for a localized dreaming does not preclude knowledge of travelling dreamings for the same ancestor and for other travellers of the country:

He just stay at one place, that kangaroo . . . Yes, Jarrajarra . . . The big father kangaroo was staying at one place at Jarrajarra, and two kangaroos came from the east, his brothers, to visit him. They told him, 'Get up, get up.' He could not get up, he still stayed there. They tried to wake him up, get him to rouse up and go with them but he could not get up. He still stayed there . . . The fire came down. He was still there and the others were telling him 'Get up' . . . The fire was coming closer and his brothers were telling him 'Get up, old man. The fire's coming closer; it's coming right up,' but he couldn't get up because he had an injured back, and he still stayed there . . . he couldn't get up and the fire was coming closer and his brothers were telling him 'Come on. You've got to get up now. It's going to burn you,' but he couldn't get up because of his broken back . . . The fire was coming closer. The two brother kangaroos are sitting down now. The fire got really close, and then they did something magic, something special. They took him under their arm and they were asking 'Which way will we go' of each other, and then they went through the fire. They put the old man somewhere, some magic way . . . they went to Ngapawulpayi . . . Nyirrawirnu. Larrara, Ngapawulpayi and Jarrajarra . . . Yes, Nyir-rawirnu – then they went to see them to Yalukarnti . . . Yes, right through to Yalukarnti. The dreaming went straight through, but we leave it there . . . at Yalukarnti.

Of course much more could be said of the lives of the Karlukarlu women: I have chosen to emphasize certain aspects of their lives for the purposes of discussing land-based relations. We can see that considerations of descent, residence, marriage, place of birth and death, subsection and patrimoiety affiliation, ceremonial roles, kinship, personal skills and life histories are all important in deciphering who does what, when and with whom. The Kaytej women are a close-knit group, held together by many and diverse ties, but analyses of other desert *jilimi* and their residents would reveal a similar intertwining of cultural and historical factors.

Let me step back from Kaytej personalities and explain in more general terms the way in which the structure and organization of the *jilimi* and *yawulyu* and mythology may be used to generate a model of land tenure which accommodates change and continuity. My focus in this section remains on Kaytej but because Kaytej have interests in Warlpiri country which abuts Kaytej lands and because a comparison of similarities and differences illuminates land-based relations of the Kaytej, I refer to Warlpiri where it is useful.[13]

Kaytej country, being broken by substantial ranges, is on the whole better supplied with water than Warlpiri. It is thought of as comprising more or less discrete blocks within which there are a number of sites which tend to cluster in areas of key resources. The name of the most important of these sites is the name by which the country is known, but in some countries where there are important sites, such as Waake, Wakulpu, Karlukarlu and Warnku, the choice of one on any given occasion may depend on the perspective and interests of the speaker. Linking the sites are tracks which often converge within 'a country' rather than transversing it as do Warlpiri tracks. But generally there are both 'localized' and 'travelling' dreamings for the most important ancestors, who provide the focus of ritual activity in a country by their association and who in travelling give names to its principal sites.

The number of different levels at which one may express a relationship to country is underwritten by relations to the *jukurrpa*. Today, as in the *jukurrpa*, people may say of a site, 'It is my place'; of a country, 'This is my country from my father, grandfather, mother, aunty, uncle', of two countries, 'They are brothers, grannies, or mother'. Ancestral activity in country provides a metaphor for relations between the living: the comings and goings of the dreaming animate the landscape, infuse it with significance, and provide paths along which links between living people may be traced. Each individual has a unique complex of relations to land, its sites and dreamings, but it is the corporate nature of interests in land which is emphasized.

In the Arandic system of land tenure, people as a group are associated with a parcel of land: the relationship is then marked with a suffix which encodes the nature of the affiliation. For mother's country *altyerre* (dreaming) is affixed to the name of the country and the spiritual nature of the relation is underscored. This then becomes the name of the persons who call the country 'mother'. For father's country one affixes *arenye* (associated with) and this term becomes the name of the people who call that country 'father'. For the country of Wakulpu (Akwerlpe) the *kirda* will be called Akwerlparenye and the *kurdun-gurlu*, Akwerlpaltyerre. This mode of mapping people directly onto country is one of the differences between the Warlpiri and Aranda systems of land tenure and is indicative of the tight nature of the relationship of people to land and land to people in Aranda territory.

In the Warlpiri system of land tenure, the link between the role and relationship of a person to country is stressed in the use of kin-based terms to denote the nature of the affiliation to land. *Kirda* is one of the Warlpiri terms for father and *kurdu* the term for woman's child.[14]

Warlpiri inhabit vast stretches of sandhills where a basic problem is to achieve a balance between people and land. Knowledge must be transmitted across vast tracts of country. In areas such as these Warlpiri emphasize dreaming tracks and the interlocking nature of the tracks which criss-cross the land. People are thus 'spread out' across the land.

The sites at which tracks cross may be shared by several groups of persons who meet to celebrate rituals for the maintenance of that land. Often such meeting places are 'hand over' sites where members of one dreaming terminate their responsibility and rights in the dreaming and hand it over to the next group, which then 'carries' the dreaming to the next 'hand over' point. In some areas there are zones between countries in which sites and dreamings are jointly held. In all these ways groups may be linked across vast areas and each will know something of the dreamings of the other.

While the notion of a separately held parcel of country is not as marked, Warlpiri will speak of 'my country' and mean an area (not merely a site or track) whose boundaries are inferred rather than delineated.[15] In the better-watered areas, such as in the Lander River area, the land tenure system comes to resemble the Kaytej system which it abuts in this district. In the poorer-watered countries of Kaytej, such as the sandhill country of Etwerrpe, their system comes to resemble the Warlpiri. These differences in land tenure systems are apparent in the rituals which maintain the land, such as the *yawulyu* staged by the older women of the Warlpiri and Kaytej *jilimi* of Warrabri.

In both the Arandic and Warlpiri systems the roles, rights and responsibilities of *kirda* and *kurdungurlu* are critical to an understanding of their systems of land tenure. In Aboriginal English these terms have been given the glosses 'owner' for *kirda* and 'worker'/ 'manager' for *kurdungurlu*. The analogy is based on the cattle-station experience and is apt to mislead if taken as a literal translation. Certainly *kurdungurlu* 'work', but for Aborigines the 'work' analogy is applied consistently to the spiritual domain. Ceremonial activity is called 'business', the ritual store-house the 'office' and the responsibility to prepare correctly and to perform is 'work'. The roles are laid down by the Law.

Both Kaytej and Warlpiri state that according to the Law a person is *kirda* for one's father's and father's father's country, while one is *kurdungurlu* for the country of one's mother and mother's father. Although the words themselves are Warlpiri, they are used by Kaytej as a convenient addition to the suffix system of marking relations. Aranda appear to have taken more readily to the term *kurdungurlu* (than to *kirda*). In many cases for Kaytej it is a more precise description of actual genealogical relationships – that is, the child of a woman – than it is for the Warlpiri, for whom it frequently includes the entire patrimoiety.

As *kirda*, a woman holds certain knowledge which is encoded in myths, designs, songs, gestures and various ritual objects. These validate her rights in the country. She must perform certain rituals to uphold that trust and to transmit the knowledge. This can only be achieved with the co-operation of the *kurdungurlu* for the country for which she is *kirda*. As *kurdungurlu* are responsible for the safety of the ritual objects, for the correct performance of rituals, for the singing and painting-up, it is the *kurdungurlu* who 'wake up' the *kirda*, who opens the dancing ground and who 'lifts up' the country. *Kurdungurlu* participate in rituals for the maintenance of country and are custodians of the dreaming knowledge. *Kurdungurlu* must be present at all ceremonies and visits to important sites because it is they who keep the *kirda* 'straight' and punish them if they deviate from the business. In this role *kurdungurlu* are sometimes called 'policemen'. *Kurdungurlu* have a detailed knowledge of country from which flows their responsibility to ensure the proper management of country – that is, to see that the nexus between the use of the land and the maintenance of the land is not threatened.

The ritual roles of these *kirda* and *kurdungurlu* are essentially interdependent and complementary. 'We are level,' said one witness in a land claim and pressed his thumbs together to indicate the closeness. 'She is my boss for the secret side,' said another.[16] The interdependence of the two has already been illustrated in the personal accounts of the Karlukarlu women and in the discussion of ritual organization, but there has been a marked reluctance on the part of some anthropologists to iterpret the role of *kurdungurlu* as one of spiritual responsibility.[17]

So far I have been speaking of descent-based relations which may be tied to actual genealogies, but Kaytej (and indeed most Aboriginal people with whom I have worked) do not restrict themselves thus. While people assert that *kirda-* and *kurdungurlu*-ship to land and in ritual are descent-based, and while they may validate these claims by reference to the kin system, it may be impossible to locate this information on a genealogy. The problem is with the assumptions inherent in such anthropological tools of trade. In land claim hearings the need to locate persons on a genealogy has frustrated claimants and anthropologists alike. However, in finding ways of explaining why a person is 'of a certain country', important clues emerge regarding both the Aboriginal conceptualization of land relations and the way in which the system is maintained across space and through time.

When a person states 'I'm following my father' or 'I hold that country from my mother', these should be read as statements of kin relations and not be restricted to genealogy. A claim to *kirda*-ship from a grandfather may be from a person who was a classificatory grandfather but who, for a number of reasons, is considered to be close enough to support the claim. One may also speak of one's granny or *jaja* country (as Napurrula speaks of Wakulpu) and mean the country of one's actual mother's mother. More often one speaks of the relation as one which pertains between countries. By asserting a kin relation to that country one then may speak of 'granny country'.

In the past, climatic and ecological factors, warfare and disease may have created demographic imbalances, so that persons other than those who were actual genealogical *kirda* and *kurdungurlu* may have stepped in to play the role - the ceremonies must continue, the land must be maintained. Today many more factors disrupt the relation of people to land - migration to centres of population, work, introduced disease, massacre and forced removal, destruction of country by pastoralists, miners, urban development. Mechanisms which were once safeguards, a fail safe, have become part of the everyday working of the system. What was once latent in the structure of land relations has become consciously articulated principles.

With reference once again to Kaytej ethnography, let me explore some of the ways in which people may be incorporated within a country and its rituals. At the level of *kirda* for any given country, there may be one or more lineages each of which is closely associated with one site within that country. For example, within Wakulpu, the sites of Waake, Karlukarlu and Wakulpu itself each have such associations of persons. Within the group of persons who are 'of Wakulpu' we have therefore lineages related to subcountries. It is sufficient to state that one's grandfathers were 'brothers', or that in the *jukurrpa* the sites called each other sibling, for the subcountries to merge.

The division of labour between the siblings, Wakulpu and Waake, may indicate that the subcountries are in the process of merging or splitting. Fission and fusion of countries is possible when the major sites are thought of as siblings; where the countries are of the same section or subsection affiliation; or – and often as well – a common dreaming track may run through and link the adjacent countries. The existence of territory which is held in common between countries also facilitates such merging and shifts in ownership just as do the many levels of naming of countries. If one lineage has become particularly powerful and numerically strong, it may break from the other lineage(s); if weak, it may be absorbed. The process in the past was part of a closed system: today there are a number of new variables.

In my discussion of the *jilimi* and *yawulyu* organization, I noted that the Wakulpu women sought to incorporate the Napaljarri who, as the daughters of the Nangala, were first generation *kurdungurlu*. However, their mothers had not been *kirda* for Wakulpu and therefore their relation was classificatory. If they were to participate in the ceremonies, gain the necessary knowledge and reside in the area, within a generation these women could become known as the daughters of Wakulpu. The subsection system permits such incorporations and the extension of kin terms to classificatory relations allows that the process of incorporation will be invisible by the next generation. Little Nampijinpa's claim to be *kurdungurlu* for Jarrajarra is one such case. She is known as *kurdungurlu*, but her mother was a classificatory *kirda* by virtue of her interest in *ngarlu* (sugar bag) dreaming, which linked her father's country of Ngunulurru with that of Jarrajarra. I would like to speculate that Nungarrayi's daughter, Little Nampijinpa, will in time, become known as *kirda* for Wakulpu. This will not be because it is her father's father's country (although her father could claim classificatory *kirda*-ship as a Jangala) but because she is of the correct subsection, has the knowledge, has participated in the ceremonies and continues to reside in the country. Her genealogical relation will be that of mother's father's mother's country but, in another two decades, this could be information which is no longer the criterion of her status. As I argued in the previous chapter, it is not the depth of genealogy which is being celebrated but the rights and responsibilities in the land.

I have stressed that residence and knowledge are important factors in legitimating claims to land and ceremonial roles. What then of Big Nampijinpa's claim for Wakulpu, after her absence for a lengthy period? She has retained her status as *kirda*, but to be recognized as an authoritative *kirda* and be able to play the role in ritual, she will need to spend some time in the country.

I have been using *kirda* and *kurdungurlu* in relation to country and ceremony, but as we saw in the first chapter, in my description of a *yawulyu*, they may also be used to distinguish one moiety from the other[18].

It is at this level that persons may be incorporated and at this level that the reciprocity inherent in the division of the world into *kirda* and *kurdungurlu* is given expression. The reciprocity is not achieved through a symmetrical exchange of spouses between countries but rather at the level of subsection and moiety affiliation (see Appendix 2).

In practice the exchange of spouses is never symmetrical, for marriages are not arranged between patrilines as they would need to be for the children of the senior women of one patriline to be found in the patriline of one other group. Instead the children of the senior women are scattered throughout several other patrilines. In this way knowledge is spread and links are established from one patriline to several others. Ritual reciprocity is, nonetheless, the model which Kaytej state underlies the *kirda-kurdungurlu* relationship and one which they strive to achieve.

A further set of rights in land, not yet mentioned, are those conferred by one's conception dreaming – that is, the place near which one's mother first noted her pregnancy. To mark this relationship a person has certain rights in the rituals of the country within which the conception site is located but not in the entire country. The rights include access to ritual objects associated with the site. Although people assert these are non-inheritable rights, based as they are on pragmatics, there is a sense in which they may merge with the rights which flow through mother or father.

Of course, place of conception may be within mother's or father's country and it may be manipulated or, as with Napurrula, be within her *jaja* country and thus doubly significant. If a person lives all his or her life in the country associated with the conception site, then it may, in several generations of residence, become the country of father or mother. For example, all children born at Warrabri are considered to share dog dreaming but not all are initiated into the cult lodge associated with this mythological ancestor. However, increasingly, second-generation Warrabri residents are accepting that they hold dog dreaming in a different and more transmittable form than a conception dreaming. Certainly today at Warrabri there are fewer opportunities to adjust conception dreamings to suit the territorial ambitions of a parent than in the past.

Another strategy in the transmission and spreading of knowledge is to 'give away' or to 'lend' certain dreamings and the associated objects. In one case several Warrabri women, who were known as prolific dreamers but who had suffered severe losses and bad health, gave away some of their knowledge to an impoverished group who owned knowledge further along a shared dreaming track. The formal handing over entailed the singing of only a fraction of the songs which the other women are now said to know. Of course, many of the women had already heard and sung the songs in joint rituals with the givers, but the ceremony marked the formal handing over. It was then up to the new owners to elaborate the songs – to demonstrate their right by using the knowledge.

A further way in which knowledge is safeguarded is by a custodian passing knowledge to another custodian. The mother's people may hold songs in trust for the *kirda* if there are none of suitable age, as may the *kirda* for the *kurdungurlu*. When a person of suitable age comes along the songs and business will be passed back formally, but the person will know much already from attendance. Persons may participate in rituals by claiming rights and exercising responsibilities through any of these channels.

In the model I have proposed of the land-maintaining group we have a way of linking groups together for the purposes of ritual, land maintenance, and for the survival and transmission of the *jukurrpa*. *Kirda* to *kurdungurlu* is conceptually a reciprocal relationship: the system of mapping people onto land is overlaid with safeguard mechanisms that ensure knowledge will be preserved and transmitted. There is no need for formal rules of succession because, setting aside a demographic disaster, groups don't disappear; their membership is too widely based; there is always someone who may move into the space. This is well illustrated by the example I cited on page 51 of the killing of a patriline. At such times the system is stretched to its limits. Many people today insist that some of the 1928 massacres occurred during 'business time' and thus the toll was heavy, but there is still knowledge and the possibility of rekindling knowledge in the area. It has taken several generations and much hard work but evidence can always be re-found of Dreamtime activity if people have access to the land. In this respect the ancestral world of Kaytej is constantly being reasserted and reactivated.

Women's relation to land is one which derives from the same principles as does that of men. By exploring these land-based relations we have heard women 'speak' at the level of the structural relations between the mythological ancestors and their country. Now let us listen to them as spiritually empowered actors in their own ritual domain. Let us look more closely at the way in which women elaborate their distinctively female role of nurturer.

Women's responsibility to maintain harmoniously the complex of relationships between people and the land is manifest in the intertwining of the rituals focusing on health and emotional management. In the shift from a hunter-gatherer model of subsistence to a sedentary life style, the nature of these responsibilities has changed. Women's role in establishing and maintaining relationships between men and women through their access to and use of *yilpinji* rituals, and their role in maintaining social harmony and thus physical well-being persist, albeit within settlement structures. In *yilpinji*, as in their health-oriented *yawulyu*, women seek to resolve and to explore the conflicts and tensions which beset their communities. At Warrabri in the late 1970s, jealous fights, accusations of infidelity and illicit affairs occurred on a scale impossible a century ago when people lived in small mobile bands.[19] But today, women's role in the domain of emotional management is, like their role in the maintenance of health and harmony, truly awesome.

HEALTH

Jilimi life, as we have seen, constitutes a complex interplay between woman's need for a refuge in a strife-torn community such as Warrabri and woman's proud assertions that she is an independent member of her society. Similarly, in the domain of health, women's perceptions of their role in maintaining health must be explored within the changing *milieu* in which nurturance roles are played out. Increases in leisure time, in population density and in access to certain resources have helped to intensify women's ritual activity at Warrabri. But expanded possibilities for ritual displays and assertions of women's solidarity are not necessarily signs of an increase in women's status in the wider society of the Northern Territory.

In analysing my data, I have isolated those songs which have to do specifically with themes such as health and love as if they constituted discrete corpora. Although these songs occur within the context of *yawulyu* performances of country in general, there is some support for my classification in the practices of the Warrabri Kaytej.

Health songs which have to do with a particular condition such as a swelling, sore, pain or temperature are said to be 'properly old ones' or 'properly dear ones'. They are thus distinguished from other songs sung during a *yawulyu* performance which may have health as its focus, but which may also concern country in a general sense. These are said to be 'properly *yawulyu*'. When the women sing these specific songs for health, they bathe with water to stem swellings or fevers; they massage with fat to ease pain and weaknesses.[20]

At a higher level of generality, curing songs are specified by a gesture which involves a pushing-away action. In this action the women hold their cupped hands before themselves and shuffle the hands outwards from their bodies, thus signifying the sending out and bestowing of power. They also use this gesture when singing specific health chants and certain land songs which have to do with the restoration of well-being. It is a gesture which is said to be for those who are sick (*murrumurru*). Women therefore clearly distinguish, in several

145

ways, songs which have to do with health and curing. Similarly, *yilpinji*-associated designs, songs and gestures are distinguished within *yawulyu* performances.

Here I explore the Kaytej concept of health as one which entails the maintenance of harmonic relations between people and place. Women, as the ritual nurturers of relationships, seek to maintain and to restore harmony, happiness and thus health. Disruption of this complex of values and relationships may come in different forms. Over the past fifty years, it has been the shift from a hunter-gatherer mode of subsistence to a sedentary life style which has posed the greatest threat to social harmony and which has intensified interpersonal and sexual tensions. Some of these tensions are manifest in women's love rituals, some within the domain of health.

Aboriginal medical practice and classification of disease are sensitive to mood and situation: conflict between members of a community or transgressions of the Law are considered injurious to smooth social and religious relations. Because a healthy individual or community is one in harmony with others and with the world of the *jukurrpa*, Aboriginal health practitioners seek to maintain an existing state of good health or to re-establish harmony and thus to restore good health. Underpinning the indigenous concept of good health is an equilibrium model of society backed by the dogma of dreaming which Aborigines vehemently assert exists at the level of lived reality. As I stated in my discussion of the dogma of dreaming (p. 91), this conscious model masks the actual experience of people who, in their daily lives in a world of rapid change, are constantly engaged in power-plays and negotiations.

Kaytej women state that in the past they were competent nurturers of people and country and that this role enhanced them as women. Today Kaytej women refer to Warrabri as a 'sickness place' and comment upon the good health they enjoyed in the past. Settlement sickness is juxtaposed with bush health and women will often comment that they were never sick in the bush. Indeed, one remedy for a lingering illness is time in the bush away from the contaminating influence of the settlement.

For Kaytej there are few happy associations with the growth of Warrabri as a linguistically and culturally mixed settlement and time away from the pressures and tensions of Warrabri is beneficial. But, Warrabri is considered a 'sickness place' for reasons other than the stress of life in a heterogeneous community. It was, for instance, an unfortunate choice of a site for a settlement. Various ritual codes were violated and continued to be so following the establishment of the settlement.

As already noted, in selecting Warrabri as a site, Government officials were guided by such criteria as the availability of water on land which pastoralists might not want. Unfortunately they did not seek the permission of the Kaytej spokespersons of the country, who were affronted when Warlpiri people were moved to the settlement area. To compound the error, the unfortunate Aboriginal 'front guy' who was consulted did not have the authority to sanction Warlpiri settlement in his country and died shortly after the move. Twenty years later Kaytej Aborigines claim that he died of worry and the knowledge that he had transgressed. Warlpiri have paid heavily in cash and ritual exchange items for their residence at Warrabri and there are still disputes which erupt from the tensions between the holders of the country and the interlopers.

Unfortunately the incidents surrounding the settlement of Warrabri impinged little upon the consciousness of white officials, who continued to behave as if they were exempt from the strictures of Aboriginal law and its punishments. An oft-repeated tale, told by Kaytej with some pride, is of the policeman who attempted to rid Warrabri of its dog scourge by rounding up and removing the diseased dogs from Warrabri and destroying them some distance away from the settlement core. This violated a sacred trust of the Kaytej and Alyawarra to care for dogs and never to kill them.

Because Warrabri is dog dreaming, all children born at Warrabri have an interest in dog dreaming; the lives of children and dogs are inexorably linked. In the *jukurrpa* dogs scratched and today children also scratch. It is said, if dogs are destroyed, children will sicken and die. After the policeman had destroyed the dogs, the old people predicted that children would become ill and indeed they did.

In order to restore harmony, the men took the policeman to the bush to reveal to him something of the power of dog dreaming. As a consequence dogs are no longer destroyed by whites at Warrabri. Dogs may thus continue to scratch as do the children. Aborigines have since suggested that a veterinarian would be an appropriate answer to new health problems created by dogs.

Further tales linking behaviour, location and health concern sorcery accusations. When the Warlpiri and Warumungu were moved from Phillip Creek to Warrabri, the old people promised the Government and the mission that they would leave all their 'bad magic' behind. But, say the Kaytej, one old Warlpiri man, a Jangala, brought it with him. The Kaytej believe that Jangala's grandfather, father and now his son have all caused trouble for people. This Warlpiri power to harm is based on their rights in and access to certain mythology associated with rain dreaming.

Kaytej recount how, at Phillip Creek, Jangala had used his powers in order to reinforce his claims to certain women as wives. He threatened illness if they refused him. With an ever-increasing population at Warrabri, Jangala's scope to harm women increased dramatically. No longer content merely to harry women who stood in the correct marriage relationship to him, he extended his activities to married women and women over whom he had no claim at all. In a period of one week at Warrabri, this man was believed to have caused three women to suffer.

The first, an introspective Kaytej woman, who worked in the school, was in a very distressed state for some time. Jangala had made a pass at her at school but she had thought him merely to be a work friend, for he also held a position in the school. She then began to have recurrent dreams in which images of water appeared. Finally, on the advice of older Kaytej women, she confided these dreams to several older Warlpiri men who recognized the work of Jangala. She claimed to have no idea of the content of his dreaming nor the particular mythology but said she had faithfully recounted the story to the men who recognized its origin.

In another case Kaytej women reported to me, the man performed certain rituals which focused on the Warumungu mother of a girl he wished to marry (that is, his mother-in-law). At the same time another young Kaytej woman, whom he fancied, was suffering with a paralysed arm. Like the other woman, these two reported having *ngapa* (rain or water) dreams although each dream was different. The old Warlpiri men met and decided that Jangala should remove the evil from the women. All but the first completely recovered. She moved to Tennant Creek in an attempt to get away from Jangala after unsuccessfully appealing to her relatives at Ti-Tree, 200 km south of Warrabri, and the local Warrabri Council to assist her. When I saw her several months later, she had completely recovered. In cases such as these women are placed at a disadvantage by all male councils who do not wish to become involved in male-female affairs and perhaps lose face with their fellow men.

Women acknowledge that communities and individuals may lack good health for many reasons. At the most general level women speak of times of 'troubles' and say that if these can be ended good health will ensue. 'Troubles' may be anything from a family fight, a sudden death, an unexplained accident, a sorcery accusation or an accumulation of persistent but minor incidents or ill-fortune for a family or camp. 'Troubles' do not include issues associated with the European world such as money worries, the need for car repairs, nor a child's school performance, although people are concerned about these issues.

During a time of 'troubles' there is a moratorium on travel because it is considered too dangerous to move about until the source of the 'troubles' is located and treated. Self-criticism and criticism of the behaviour of others which may have caused the misfortune ensue. It is a time when sorcery accusations proliferate and old arguments are revived.

Thus, within the domain of health, we need to include not only the *ngangkayi* (traditional healers) but also to broaden our concepts of who are the patients and what constitute modes of diagnosis and treatment. As good health is regarded ultimately as flowing from good social relationships, it is essential that we examine how these are maintained. In the cases of the three women, the old men explained and began the resolution of the problem. It was their access to the power of certain dreamings which gave the old men the power and knowledge to act in this way.

Aborigines seem to regard most settlement hospitals as female domains – an extension of women's caring roles in the past – and in a sense this is supported by the appointment of white female nursing staff. Men may visit and receive treatment but they do not generally work in the hospitals, nor do they gather in the shade around the hospital, as do the women, to rest and exchange news. In 1977 in the hospital at Warrabri there were two nursing sisters employed by the Health Department and several Aboriginal women health-workers who were receiving literacy and basic health-care training. The degree of responsibility given to the Aboriginal health-workers depends not only on the personality, age and maturity of the health-workers and the sister-in-charge, but also on Health Department policies with regard to health worker education.

Certain literacy skills are required if Aboriginal health-workers are to assume real responsibility in health-care programmes. Frequently, young girls chosen as health workers for their literacy skills do not have the status in their own community to exercise the authority required of health-workers. Again, it is hard for older people, especially older men, to accept the authority of young white women as nursing sisters on settlements.

Through the health-worker programmes recently organized by the Health Department, older women are being given the necessary training to cope with the demands of the position. Health-worker schemes are also attempting to integrate aspects of both medical systems by demystifying Western medicine while encouraging the incorporation of Aboriginal practices. Some medical personnel are displaying a new and growing respect for Aboriginal values as they have come to realize the Aborigines' depth of knowledge and concern in times of illness.

The autonomy which women once enjoyed, however, in the domain of health has not been regained through participation in health-worker schemes. These proceed cautiously; authority and responsibility are delegated slowly. Certain critical skills are withheld, as the Warrabri people found to their chagrin in late 1977. On this occasion the Health Department in Alice Springs decided to withdraw all nursing sisters and certain medicines from Warrabri because there had been a series of attacks and two alleged attempted rapes of white women by Aboriginal men. The Health Department feared for the safety of their nurses.

During the public meeting held to resolve the matter, many old and bitter arguments were aired in public. 'We have been trained but we can't take over,' the women challenged the officials. 'We can't give injections. Our old people will die if they can't have the medicine they now need.' 'Why are we being punished?', asked one younger woman. 'What have we done? We do not rape white men. We need the medicines.' The men were more concerned to assume responsibility for the wayward youths and to assure the white officials that there would be no more attacks. The women were interested in the area for which they assumed responsibility. That they had, since contact with white Australians, been reduced to a state of dependency, and were being

150

kept there, was clear to most women that day.

Although women's role in health maintenance has been severely undermined by a century of contact with such white institutions as schools, hospitals and welfare agencies, women nevertheless have not been the passive recipients of Western medicine. They have sought to accommodate Western health practices and to elaborate old practices where appropriate and possible. However, there is no way in which women can restore the responsibility they enjoyed in the past for good health, happiness and harmony, for their independent base for action has been undermined by loss of land. In the process women's confidence that they can effectively maintain good health, has been seriously shaken. The damage to woman's self-respect has scarcely been noted by anthropologists, who have considered women's activities to be small scale and of little consequence.

Today, girls reach sexual maturity while still at school; childbirth occurs in hospital; the health of babies is monitored by health authorities. Nevertheless, at Warrabri, as soon as the mother leaves hospital, the women take her and the child away into the bush where they perform certain rituals to ensure the health and growth of the child and the renewed strength of the mother. The use of herbal preparations and plants in the childbirth rituals is the only consistent use of plants (for health curing) I observed at Warrabri. Women have extensive knowledge of plants and usage but they tend to discuss rather than use the plants. 'Aspirin and Vicks are more powerful,' they say, 'but we like to visit the country and collect the plants too.'

As neither childbirth nor first menstruation can be timed to occur in a season of plenty, as can initiation, these ceremonies have to concern those female relatives who might be present in the family camps. It is interesting to note that women state that now, as in the past, it was their 'mother's mother' who attended them in birth. For this to be so the couple must have lived with, or close to, the wife's grandmother.

In the past, formal rituals to limit the size of families were in the hands of men. In the past, however, the practice of extensive breastfeeding, the segregation of the sexes, the later sexual maturity of girls, the tolerance of a high infant mortality rate and infanticide, all supported the male ritual statements that large families were undesirable, but left the actual physical controls in the hands of women. The shift to a sedentary life style has altered many of these patterns and women are now bearing many children, younger, and closer together. Sickly children are surviving but may spend many months in hospital away from their families. They return to their communities as outsiders and perhaps with younger siblings who require attention. Younger women are beginning to seek contraceptive advice but are still somewhat bewildered by their increased fertility and fecundity.

Older women comment that the Law is no longer being upheld. In the past, children could not have been born to mothers so young, they insist. I pursued this with one close friend and asked why such young girls were having babies today. Mindful of the experience of other fieldworkers I feared a withering reply, but was told that in the past girls didn't marry until 'their breasts hung down'. 'But what about the young unmarried girls who play around?' I continued, indicating one young mother whom the women had been discussing. It was then I got the reply, 'In the past girls slept in one place and the boys in another. There was no "humbug" then.'

At first menstruation women celebrated the attainment of sexual maturity of a female child who could now assume new responsibilities. Although these were relatively small-scale rituals, they were acknowledged as areas of female autonomy and authority with special importance for members of the girl's matriline. For the mother of the girl it marked the beginning of a new stage in her role as a mother-in-law and for the girl's mother's mother, a realization of arrangements made for her daughter (that is, the mother) some fifteen years previously.

Settlement life has not only introduced new conflicts but also new constraints which have curtailed several of women's major health activities - especially those concerned with reproduction. Although crises of life ceremonies (for example, birth and menarche rituals) have been attenuated, there are other rituals, *yawulyu*, concerned with the maintenance of land relationships, in which women explicitly state their health-giving powers and responsibilities. It is to these ceremonies that women are now turning.

Over the past fifty years, women's health-oriented activities have undergone a subtle shift from those organized within the matriline and focused on the individual, to the more general *yawulyu* rituals, based on the ritual relations of *kirda* to *kurdungurlu*. The shift, like the elaboration of new functions of the *jilimi*, reflects the interaction of women's perceptions of their necessarily changing role and the con-

During large-scale *yawulyu*, children are often painted with designs which will ensure good health. Here the mother of the child 'moulds' her head with greased hands. Nampijinpa, *kirda* for the designs of Karlukarlu which the child is wearing, looks on. The lines across the stomach promote the growth of fat which is believed to be a feature of healthy children.

straints on expression of that role.

The shifts in focus, structure and content of women's health-oriented ceremonies provide valuable insights into women's role and status on settlements today. In elaborating different aspects of their ritual range, women clearly demonstrate their recognition of the nature of the problems which beset their communities. Health-related problems now occur within the context of large heterogeneous settlement communities, rather than small homogeneous family groups as was the case in the past. Today women focus on the resolution of conflict between groups rather than on the restoration of health to individuals. Women continue to shoulder responsibility for the maintenance of the harmonic relationships of people, land and Law, and today, for Kaytej women at Warrabri, the pivot of this complex of relationships is the ritual group resident in the *jilimi*. In the past the pivot was the individual within the family. Let us then look at examples of health care.

Old Jakamarra had been ill for some time, but his concerned relatives had only recently brought him to Warrabri from Barrow Creek. They hoped that the Nungarrayi (his nieces, close 'sister's daughters') could help restore the man to good health. In their own ritual area, the women prepared fat and red ochre and formed it into a ball, which Nakamarra and Nungarrayi women (that is, 'sisters' and 'sister's daughters') took to the camp of Jakamarra. After a brief discussion with the man's wife, the women massaged the patient in much the same way as does the *ngangkayi* (traditional healer). The culmination of the massage was the painting of the feet through the soles of which the illness could later leave. Although the visit lasted only about fifteen minutes, the man knew that the women were working for him before they arrived and that they would continue to do so after the visit until he improved. Later that evening he drank tea for the first time for weeks and the next day began eating.

It is not unusual for people to seek health care from professionals who do not belong to their own community. In Jakamarra's case he was closely related, but women have asked me to take them to places as far away as Areyonga, south of Alice Springs, in order to seek particularly powerful *ngangkayi* or a more appropriate dreaming for a particular condition than the dreamings they may use. Jakamarra, the women said, was cured because he heard the songs of his country sung. It was a restoration, a 'putting-in-touch-with' process, whereby he experienced, through the women, the attachment of the *ngapa* ancestors as they travelled through the country and the well-being they felt in their country. The 'daughters' were *kurdungurlu* for the country, that is, those who assist in the staging of rituals. They were therefore playing a dual role – firstly, as 'daughters' and members of his caring matriline, and secondly, as ritual 'workers' for his dreaming.

Of another Jakamarra, an unusually tall and muscular man, I was told of a time when he had been so weak he could no longer stand. All the Napanangka (his 'mothers') gathered to assist in his treatment. Together, in the bush away from the camp of the man, the five 'mothers' prepared a mixture of goanna and witchetty fat. The ritual involved singing over various pieces of hairstring which, once pre-pared, were taken to the man's camp. He was stripped and dressed with hairstring.

In retelling the story, the women emphasize that the men were powerless to do anything. 'They just sat there worrying.' The women were in charge and directed the men as to which articles of clothing were to be removed and which not. Before they began, even Jakamarra was convinced he would die. The women massaged his head, shoulders, hands and feet, and paid special attention to his navel, for which there are powerful health and love designs. At this stage the women were using fat only.

They kept vigil all night as they sang the dreaming which infuses the country with strength and colour. In the morning they again mass-aged the man but this time with a mixture of red ochre and fat. A white head band was substituted for the hairstring around his head. This was a symbol of purity as well as attractiveness. All day he lay in the men's camp. In the afternoon he began to feel better and announced that the next day he would go hunting, which he did. Everyone was happy to see him better and moving around. According to the women he is now protected from that illness for the rest of his life.

When I asked about the possibility of a *ngangkayi* treating the man, I was told that no *ngangkayi* was present at Wauchope years ago, and that in any case his condition required the treatment given by the women, specifically by his 'mothers'.

The way in which health and curing activities break down barriers is shown in the following case when women visited the men's camp and publicly viewed a naked man.[21] This incident took place thirty years ago at the wolfram mines at Wauchope. The women who cared for him were his 'mothers' within his matriline, but not related as *kur-dungurlu* as were the 'daughters' of the first Jakamarra. This care by 'mothers' was, I believe, more prevalent in the past than is now the case.

In the next case – a woman with gynaecological problems – the use of the *yawulyu* was structured differently from the two previous examples. A particular song was required and it had to be sung in the context of the country to which it belonged. The women worked from the particular (that is the condition of the patient) to the general (that is association with country) in attempting to restore health. This performance required the presence of the *kirda* and *kurdungurlu*, which was made possible by the concentration of people at Warrabri. The Jakamarra at Wauchope could not have expected to be treated by this scale of ritual because there were too few people living in the mines to be able to stage such a *yawulyu*.

Napurrula had recently undergone gynaecological surgery but was still retaining fluid and was in some discomfort. She herself was a *ngangkayi*, but it was the women of the Nampijinpa-Nangala semi-moiety who, in consultation with Nungarrayi, *kurdungurlu* for those dreamings, assisted her. All this took place in the presence of Napurrula, her sister. Women may ask each other for *yawulyu*, or for arm blood (a potent medicine), and no doubt other items to do with health, but it is generally a joint decision of the patient and the *kirda* and *kurdungurlu* to stage a *yawulyu*.

The group assembled and sang the specific songs to ease the pain and reduce the swellings. This involved two dreamings: rain, to reduce the swelling, and bush berry to impart strength. The women sang of the ancestral women who rubbed fat into hairstring to make them feel strong again. They then invoked with singing the presence of the *ngangkayi* familiar so he could enter the woman and remove the source of the pain. Once that was achieved, the women moved to rain dreaming to sing the wound shut. All the while they were massaging and painting the patient with a design which is particularly powerful in restoring good health and good spirits. Aspects of the ceremony are even considered a little provocative by the women in that the designs and songs have sexual overtones.

During this ceremony two other ailing women with longstanding conditions were painted and massaged. Children were also painted, but the major focus of the ceremony was on the pain and swelling of Napurrula. This ceremony emphasized both the caring for the patient as an individual by members of her own matriline and the structuring relationship of *kirda* to *kurdungurlu*. The children who were painted belonged to those women present at the ceremony. In some cases this meant that the children were *kirda* or *kurdungurlu* but in others they were neither. Once again I believe that in this ceremony we can see an incorporation of smaller family rituals, focused on the caring matriline, into the structure of the larger land-based ceremonies based on the *kirda-kurdungurlu* relationship.

In the next example, the shift from the family and matriline to the ritual group is complete. Although 'sisters' helped 'mothers', they referred to each other as *kirda* and *kurdungurlu*, not in the kin terms of mother and daughter, or sister to sister.

The assistance of Nungarrayi of the Karlukarlu camp is at times sought and at others she is blamed for the collective woes of camps. Her own marriage has been a stormy love-hate relationship with passionate and jealous fights. Her mother-in-law is closer in age to Nungarrayi than Nungarrayi is to her husband, who is many years her junior. It was her irresistible love rituals which brought him to her. Napangardi (the mother-in-law) is a querulous woman who constantly interferes in her son's marriage. She had been asked to leave several camps because of her temper and finally the daughter-in-law and husband moved camp to the other side of Warrabri to avoid her meddling ways.

Nungarrayi is very aware of the power and potential danger of the love rituals she owns and frequently cautions other women not to sing songs which are not correctly theirs. She herself is very careful to observe all precautions to control the powers, but her mother-in-law accuses her of starting all the fights which take place. The husband does little to check his mother and, after returning from one spree in town, accused his wife of adultery and in spite of her pleading, beat her unmercifully. She left him and refused to return until he promised to stop drinking. This he did, but women outside her group say that she is sick all the time because of his ill treatment.

Nungarrayi had been generally ill for some time and had sought assistance from the hospital, the *ngangkayi* and from women of her own dreaming group. Finally the old *ngangkayi*, a classificatory son (that is within the matriline), was called in and prescribed *yawulyu*.

It was a close daughter and a 'mother's father's sister' of Nungarrayi who told me of the beginning of her 'troubles'. Several years back when the mother, son and wife had been at Willowra for initiation business, Nungarrayi had fought with her mother-in-law and drawn blood. Napangardi took the blood in a handkerchief to several Napinjinpa 'sisters-in-law' at Willowra. (The sick Nungarrayi is *kurdungurlu* for the dreamings of these Willowra women.) The rituals which the Willowra women did with the blood are said to have caused Nungarrayi's illness. The only way for her to recover was to appease the Willowra women with a gift in exchange for the blood.

The organization which preceded the Willowra trip took over a month and it became evident that the Nungarrayi women were going to use this occasion to settle many old scores. As I have already pointed out women have restricted access to cars, so they cannot visit as readily as can men. The women maximized the opportunity to restore as many harmonious relationships as possible.

Although the two days of dancing, singing, painting, teaching and exchanges centred on the rain and bush berry dreaming of the Kaytej women of Warrabri, the revelation and gift of the knowledge of snake and honey dreamings to the Willowra women were also effected. Nungarrayi was at the centre of proceedings, but all the Nampijinpa and Nungarrayi women of Willowra participated.

The activities which could be glossed as strictly health-related were short and spectacular. Nungarrayi, after she had presented the dreamings of snake and honey to the Willowra women, also gave them the sacred paraphernalia of bush berry to look after for some years. They then painted, massaged and exorcised the spirits from her. The separation of fat and colour, as in the Jakamarra cases, was also followed by the Willowra women, but Nungarrayi assured them if their work was not good she would 'hot it up a bit' with rainbow dreaming. Once all the gift exchanges and dancing were finished the Willowra women painted Nungarrayi with a Willowra-owned design and thus completed the singing of country.

Throughout the rituals held at Willowra the organization both reflected and was spoken of in terms of *kirda* and *kurdungurlu*. In presenting snake dreaming, Nungarrayi was *kirda* to the Willowra women who were receiving it as her joint *kirda*. In fact they were also full or close sisters but that was not the aspect of the relationship which was stressed. It was not the kin relations which were important in these rituals but the power of ownership of women who also were sisters.

In presenting the bush berry ritual items, Nungarrayi was *kurdungurlu* to the Willowra *kirda*. These women were related as 'mother' and 'daughter' but again that was not the aspect of the relationship which was stressed. In giving away so much ritual property, Nungarrayi hoped that the jealous fights would cease and that her health would improve once harmony was restored.

At certain times the restoration process highlights the interdependence and complementary nature of male and female roles, as well as the accommodation of Western medical practice in restoring health. An example is the experience of a young Nampijinpa. An astute young person who enjoyed caring for other people's children, she was, she told me, terrified of having children herself. She was married to a man who already had a large family by his first wife. Her 'mothers' and 'sisters' had been concerned about her for some time because she was not eating, was listless and breathing rapidly.

The women massaged and painted her, but this was not producing the hoped-for results. The hospital had not been able to relieve the woman's symptoms either. Although at Warrabri she had the support of close 'mothers' and 'sisters', she wanted her actual mother who lived at Willowra some 480 kilometres away. The woman summoned the mother by telegram. (It is not unusual for people to travel many hundreds of kilometres to visit sick relatives or to seek attention.)

At dusk one day, at the request of the patient, the women of her 'mother's' camp held a conference. The woman was examined and it was decided that rituals of a dreaming other than those held by the Kaytej at Warrabri were needed. The 'mothers' had tried with their own *ngapa* dreaming rituals, but they now prescribed the diamond-dove dreaming of a Warlpiri Napurrula woman. It was hoped that this dreaming might be successful in restoring the woman to good health. (To visit this Napurrula meant crossing the east-west line which divides Warrabri into those who come from the west and those who come from the east. Such a crossing of boundaries is not unusual in case of illness.)

Napurrula, in consultation with the 'mothers' and 'sisters' of the patient, decided the services of the *ngangkayi* were necessary. Nampijinpa then visited the healer who examined and massaged her in much the same way as her own 'mothers' and 'sisters' had. He could find no foreign objects to remove from her body and did not draw blood. 'She needs rest and her husband', he diagnosed. The women returned to their camp, made a separate bed for the young woman and allowed her and her husband some privacy for the evening. She recovered slowly but appreciably during the following week and later sought contraceptive advice from the hospital.

In this case the authority of the *ngangkayi* far exceeded that of the normal general practitioner and certainly that available to the settlement hospital. The diagnosis and treatment involved both Western medical practice and the knowledge and care of the members of her own camp, women of another ritual group and a male *ngangkayi*. Her health was the concern of her society.

The most important criteria for selection of *ngangkayi* in Central Australia appear to be place in family and the dreamings upon which one may call. Should the first-born be a girl, whose younger sibling is a girl or a much younger boy, she will not only enjoy the unique position of the first-born, but also the investment of dreaming knowledge from her father not shared by subsequent siblings. Further, if she belongs to a dreaming which has important *ngangkayi* powers, she may well develop the skills and exercise the powers of *ngangkayi*.

One of the constraints on women who may have received or activated the latent *ngangkayi* power is their involvement in the time-consuming and emotionally demanding task of child-rearing. As with the male practice of *ngangkayi*, it is generally older individuals who practise. These women are released from mothering duties, but they are also the women whom a male ethnographer is most unlikely to contact because most of their day is spent in the single women's camp, which is forbidden to men.[22]

Further elements of *ngangkayi* practice are incorporated in women's health maintenance activities. During ritual performance women may summon the *ngangkayi* power which manifests itself as a clicking in the head.[23] Women may also carry the *ngangkayi* stones and, through the performance of their crises of life and *yawulyu* ceremonies, effect ends similar to that of *ngangkayi*. Men, on the other hand, stage resolution of conflict ceremonies which restore harmony and diffuse tensions within a community and their practice of curing and restoring harmonious social relations is also part of male *ngangkayi* practice.[24] Both men and women, in seeking to maintain health, draw on a shared set of values and practices.

When we consider the wide range of women's involvement in the maintenance of health, it becomes impossible to discuss women's activities as merely 'growing up' children and applying a few herbal remedies. Women, in order to maintain good health, are staging ceremonies which focus on health at the cosmic level of restoration of harmony and happiness. This is because women have rights in the country from which they derive power and for which they hold a sacred trust. It is this aspect of their heritage which they are increasingly emphasizing.

We need to examine women's role in health maintenance in terms of the indigenous concepts of good health and women's role as nurturer. All women's group ritual curing activities have to do with giving – with the infusing of the body with strength. Women attempt to restore a person to health by the gift of blood, fat or bodily secretions from underarm or eyes. In giving, women are once again acting out their nurturance role where love, care and power are freely given. *Ngangkayi* practice on the other hand is essentially an individual activity concerned more with the removal of foreign objects and alien forces from a person.

The role of women in the domain of health in Aboriginal society has been rendered almost invisible by the focus upon the healer and not the healed, the disease and not the context of the ill health, the magico-religious practices and not the relationships of health to other aspects of the culture. However, I suggest that women are acutely aware of the decline in physical health and the breakdown in social relationships. Fighting and drunkenness now disrupt their lives in a fashion unknown several generations ago. Women are aware that in the shift from the hunter-gatherer mode of subsistence to settlement life they have suffered. Daily they are presented with tensions and sorcery accusations on a scale which could not have been sustained in the past. They have sought to repair and restore damaged bonds through their most powerful and spectacular rituals.

This resurgence in women's ritual activity has not been accompanied by a concomitant increase in the status of women: their autonomy has been fundamentally eroded and their relationship to land dislocated. Women's contribution to the maintenance of health in the past was within the small family group and focused upon life-crisis ceremonies. It was in these rituals that women stated their importance as the makers of adult women and in their control over their own bodies. Here, then, is the physiological basis for their nurturance roles: women do give birth, they do menstruate. This power and the nurturance roles associated with birth and growth are symbolized in *yawulyu* rituals.

The nurturance role is now expressed more symbolically than it was prior to settlement life, when woman's control over the lives of the family group and bodily care and functions was more immediate and direct. Nurturance is now being stated in terms of country and relationships. This change in emphasis does not negate the self-image of women. However, it does partly explain women's low status on settlements, for the task they have set themselves and the means with which they seek to obtain harmony, are constrained by the male-oriented and dominated European controls and policies which govern Aboriginal affairs.

LOVE

During my period of fieldwork at Warrabri 80 per cent of marriages were correct within the kinship system but promised marriage accounted for only 5-10 per cent of extant marriages. How, I wondered, were the other 90-95 per cent organized? Obviously formal business contracts entered into at initiation do not organize the totality of marriage arrangements. As Meggitt[25] notes, there are three ways a man may find a wife, but there are also ways in which a woman may find a husband. *Yilpinji*,[26] women claim, is one such way. Thus both men and women seek to regulate male-female relations. Neither has total control of all the possible strategies, formal or informal: each has room to manoeuvre.[27]

What then is *yilpinji*? In discussing the range of women's ritual activity, I used the term 'love rituals' to describe *yilpinji*. While this is not incorrect, it fails to do justice to a very complex notion – just as 'dreaming' fails to capture the nuances of *jukurrpa*.

'Love' is a very poor translation of *yilpinji* but it is one that has found acceptance in the anthropological literature and been fed back into the indigenous conceptualization. It is a translation which feeds the Northern Territory male's notion of what women ought rightly to be about. For white itinerant road gangers and station hands with whom some Aboriginal women have had sexual liaisons, 'love magic' has been a smutty joke. It was something for which one could pay and then reap the results. It marked women clearly as sex objects.

Acting with the support of some Aboriginal converts, the missionaries at Phillip Creek banned 'love magic' and labelled the practitioners 'witches'. Women continued to perform *yilpinji* but connotations of love magic as the devil's work are still current at Warrabri today. For Aboriginal men these debasements of *yilpinji* as 'love magic' and classification of women as sex objects allowed them an avenue by which *yilpinji* could be defused. Thus if some whites encouraged *yilpinji*, Aboriginal men could, with this new-found male support, construe *yilpinji* as 'magic'. Aboriginal women's religion in the process was stripped of its actual complexities. Aboriginal men were able to score telling points in their ongoing tug of war with women.

Of the 300 Kaytej love songs which I collected and translated in the field, only a few contain direct reference to sexual intercourse. Major themes are longing for country and family, sorrow, anticipation, agitation, concern, shyness and display. Country is both a basis of identity and an analogy for emotional states.

By locating *yilpinji* within the context of land and interpreting the myths in terms of power symbols, I have not dwelt upon the explicit themes of sex as have some previous analyses of male-female relationships.[28] Kaytej women themselves are not explicit but employ euphemisms like 'going hunting together', or being led away by the wrist or a profane hand sign. They may dance holding a rhythm stick or bunched up skirt before them in a mock penis, but consummation is always off-stage or obliquely indicated. Had I asked specifically for love songs and love myths I am sure I would have collected fewer songs, but they would have been explicit in sexual reference. I accepted the Kaytej gloss of *yilpinji* and have a majority of songs which deal with country and generalized emotions and few which are explicitly sexual. The songs and myths have less to do with the playing out of strictly sexual relationships than with the way in which women elaborate the common core values which underpin and shape male-female values and behaviour.

Love and sex are only aspects of *yilpinji*, which encompasses the sweep of tensions and emotions engendered by male-female relationships.[29] These, however, must be seen in their cultural context where country is a major symbol of personal and social identity. Devil's Marbles and the surrounding area of Karlukarlu is a focus for rain dreaming. It is spectacular country where enormous round rocks stand in the desert. During rains numerous small streamlets run from the rocks and ridges, wild figs grow from the crevices, water collects in the rock holes and depressions high on the Marbles. The desert lives. The colours and contrasts are sudden and dramatic; red rocks and green water heavy with slime weed, tall ant hills and spinifex plains.

Karlukarlu country is extremely rich in dreaming sites and ancestral activity, but when the road was built from Alice Springs to Darwin, it was located through the very centre of the Marbles so that important sites are no longer accessible to the Kaytej. Sorrowfully the women claim that they can still hear the old people crying from the caves. This loss has meant that certain important rituals can no longer be performed but, as the area is within a day's travel of Warrabri, women may still hunt, camp and dream there. Nonetheless, by losing access to important sites where they could express their attachment and whence they can draw power, women's position has weakened.[30] One ritual object associated with this area was so powerful that it was believed that if a man came within close range, he would meet a violent death. This terminal sanction is no longer available to women. Men have, however, retained violent sanctions which they apply during initiation time.

The two inter-related myths which provide the scenario for most *yilpinji* songs, designs and performances belong to the *kurinpi* (or old women dreaming) and the *ngapa* (rain) dreaming.[31] These dreamings belong to the women of the Nampijinpa and Nangala subsections and are managed by the women of the Nungarrayi and Napanangka subsections, all of whom trace descent from the founding drama of the Stirling Swamp and Devil's Marbles area. The behaviour glossed as *yilpinji* (in myth) only occurs in the Devil's Marbles area, because, say the Kaytej women, 'Our dreaming for that area also has rainbow, whereas Warlpiri rain dreaming [further west] only has rain.' This prompts jealousy and suspicion by Warlpiri and pride for Kaytej. On settlements it provides a further wedge for men to drive into women's solidarity.

The *kurinpi* myth exemplifies the dilemma facing women: they want the advantages of children and the company of spouse, but fear the unpredictability of men and men's challenge to their independence and autonomy. Here I am discussing only that portion of the *kurinpi* myth which concerns *yilpinji*, women's claims to feelings as their right and an exploration of the complexities of male-female interaction.

In the *kurinpi* myth, two elderly, knowledgeable and respected women, known as the *kurinpi*, wander about in the Stirling Swamp naming the country and performing such rituals as are their responsibility. Their life is one of ritual observance and celebration of the bounty of their country. Their power is manifest in their ability to turn red as they rub themselves with fat while travelling from their swamp home in search of company. On their journey they meet with other travellers of the area and observe the ritual relationship of owner to worker, experience sorrow at death and come into conflict with members of the younger generation and of the opposite sex.

Once out of their swamp homeland they cease to name the country and travel more warily. They poke the ground wih spear-like sticks. As they pass through another swamp area closer to Devil's Marbles, they enter a patch of tall spear trees. Fearing that perhaps someone might see them, they clutch their ritual packages to themselves and continue. Several young boys appear and dance flanking them, just as did the *kurdungurlu* for the *kirda* in the *kurinpi's* previous encounter with this ritual relationship. The boys are carrying spears similar to the women's. The women teach the boys to throw spears in an overarm action.

The women wonder why the boys, who are also carrying ritual packages, continue to travel with them. The young boys have ritual packages such as are the right of older people. At the meeting and while travelling with the boys the women feel a mixture of shame and curiosity. Finally they reveal to each other the contents of their packages. The *kurinpi* attempt to leave, but the boys beg them to stay so they can show them everything. 'No,' say the women, 'You are too young and we are leaving.' Suddenly the boys disappear and reappear as initiated men. The women look on in amazement as these men are wearing their ritual headbands and arm bands. Again they hasten to leave and again the men beg them to stay. The women fear that these men might spear them for they now have long strong spears such as men carry. The men follow the departing women who soon leave them far behind. 'Never mind,' say the men. 'We shall sharpen our spears, harden them in the fire and spear the women when we catch them.'

The women say to each other, 'Come. Let them go their way. We have everything we need.' As the men travel they say, 'Let them go. We have all we need and can easily catch them later when we learn how to throw these spears.' As the *kurinpi* dance on they see and join another group of women who are performing *yawulyu* rituals. The men with the spears are unsuccessful in catching the women as they are not prepared to violate the restrictions of the women's ritual area.

Although the meeting with the boys has many connotations, I shall comment here only on the significance of the myth for women's perception of themselves as social actors and of themselves in relation to men. Before encountering the boys the women had never felt shame. They had confidently and authoritatively known their country and their relationship to it. The ambiguous status of the boys is compounded by their transformation, without ritual, into men. Each is prepared to respect the ritual packages of the other, but the men rather fancy the women and decide to pursue them. The women continue to display their power by the rubbing of fat into their bodies and by producing colour changes. The men decide to use force and a new technology to win the women, but are thwarted when they discover the women have sought sanctuary in the company of other women.

In another encounter of the *kurinpi* with men, they do not escape, but are overpowered. These two encounters are not considered in temporal sequence but like the women's ability to turn red and like the colours of the desert, are seen as co-existing in constant flux, deriving from an ever-shifting dynamic power on which women may draw. The two accounts are not considered as conflicting versions of the same myth but are taken rather as an illustration of the vagaries and complexities of male-female relationships.

The women were returning to the camp from a day of hunting when some men began throwing stones at them. 'What is this?' asked the women, 'We want to get food not to run away.' The women were unaware of the presence of the men. They continued home and on the way dug for grubs. One man ran after one of the women and stood on her digging stick and asked the woman for food. They felt shamed because they had never met a man like that before. He told the woman to get up and they would dig together. 'Don't be shy,' he said, 'We shall go together.' He gently took the woman by the arm and they all continued together. But as they travelled and the woman left her country behind she held back and tried to go the other way. The man crippled the woman with a spear and as she lay naked and complaining of this cruelty, he began to beautify himself so that she would love him. He brought her animal skins to warm her body and sat with her. She tried to straighten herself but it hurt too much. She looked back to her country but knew she must leave with her husband.

It is worth noting that hitherto in the myth the women are depicted as old. Here they appear to be younger, but this is of little consequence as in myth and reality older women and men court each other and younger partners. Women regard themselves as desirable regardless of age and do not have the self-image of 'old hag'.

Women's perception of men is that they are so insecure that violence is the only way they can express emotion. Roheim[32] would interpret this myth as the wild being made quiet, but if seen within the context of land and male-female power relationships, the myth argues for the importance of women's power base and acknowledges that, through marriage, men can disrupt women's ties to land. The once kind suitor who took her by the arm now spears her. Her tie to her country is also damaged. In being crippled by the spear wound the woman is also deprived of her land. In the loss of land she loses her autonomy and power base, but he gains a wife to whom he can now afford to show affection and from whom he now seeks love by beautifying himself. In her crippled state, she feels the pain, loss of movement of her own choosing and loss of land. As they continue together she sees his country, like a mirage, before her and he begins instructing her in the wonders of his country. Through men, women may thus gain knowledge of other country, but the price is high. It is worth noting that on marriage men do not succeed in carrying off young wives to another country. Frequently they take up residence in their wife's country.

In the section of the *ngapa* (rain) myth which concerns *yilpinji*, a complex series of relationships are played out. The wise rain-father, known as Junkaji, attempts to restrain his overly pretentious sons, the Rainbow Men, who come into conflict with their older brother Lightning while pursuing young girls to whom they are incestuously related. Rain's wife, as mother of the boys, finally lures them from the dangers of their exploits by feigning illness. Their duty to their mother overwhelms them and they return at the insistence of their stern father, only to die. There are important themes of father/son authority flouted and mother duty/devotion/destruction, but I shall concentrate on the aspects of male-female which are explored in the myth. In contemplating the possible outcome of their behaviour during the pursuit, both men and girls express fear, ambivalence, tenderness, aggression and insecurities.

The Rainbow Men, as older and younger brother, travel around in circles in the Devil's Marbles area from Dixon Creek to Greenwood station. Their father warns them not to venture too far but they ignore his warning. 'Rainbows should stay close to rain,' he says. 'Let Rain rain himself,' say the sons. 'We shall travel further.' They travel up so high they can see the sea. They sit on top of the clouds and display their brilliant colours. They swoop into the green water below. They hide from Rain in hollow logs and from the girls in creek beds and behind ridges.

In most of the encounters the girls, who are classificatory sisters, but not identified as younger and older, are unaware of the presence of the men who creep closer and closer to them. The younger brother warns the older not to go too close or he may frighten the girls. 'Hold back,' he warns. The older brother counters, 'Don't be silly.' To their delight the women are picking sweet fruits. 'You'll frighten them if you go any closer,' warns the younger brother. 'Wait for rain before showing yourself.' The men have rubbed themselves with red ant hill to dull their brightness so as not to frighten the girls. As they add marks to their bodies, they reflect on their own beauty and wonder if the girls will like them. 'Why don't they love us? Have we shown ourselves for nothing?' they wonder. The younger brother questions the correctness of the pursuit of the girls. 'They may be of the wrong subsection,' he suggests. 'We can take wrong skins,' says the older brother but the younger still holds back.

Finally the girls separate. One goes to dig yams, the other to swim. The older brother descends upon the girl who is digging and such is his brightness that she closes her eyes. He woos her and finally convinces her that she should accompany him. As she leaves she looks back in sorrow for her country but also like the *kurinpi*, she knows she must leave with her husband. The younger brother goes to the water where the other girl is swimming but she is too frightened to go with him and attempts to escape. He spears her in the leg and while she lies naked before him, he beautifies himself with body scars, all the while gently wooing her with tender words.

In the exploits the brilliantly coloured and ever-changing Rainbow Men are the subject of constant references. They can overpower women with their colour and thus tear women from their land. The *kurinpi* women on the other hand change colour in a way which demonstrates their power over their bodies and men. One of the stated reasons for the extreme power of Kaytej *yilpinji* is this access to colour in the rainbow myth.

In yet another encounter, the young girls, camped with their mother, leave to go in search of spring water for her. They return very tired and do not realize that men have been working *yilpinji* for them. Like most Dreamtime women (and women today) they carried their ritual packages with them but, because they were so tired, they decided to leave them behind in the camp, high in a tree. The next day they returned from hunting with two men they had met during the day, only to find their packages missing. The girls were reluctant to go with the men who then speared them. Finally, along with the mother, they travelled into the men's country.

In this myth woman's power, in the form of her ritual packages, is stolen. Her ownership of land is thus rendered less powerful through this symbolic rupture of her tie to the land.

In many of the exploits of the Rainbow Men, the girls are actually working the *yilpinji* for the men who follow them through the scrub or who are far away. In a dream a man may see his beloved wearing her *yilpinji* design and hasten to join her. As he returns to her she makes a bed for him so that they may comfort each other when reunited. 'Make my heart still,' she pleads. 'Lie with me.' Or as he travels he may hear the sound of her voice like music from afar. He may fish by throwing grass into the water to attract the fish and see his loved one instead. Or she may have prepared a ball of the green slime weed which she threw out to him from a distance and this has now reached him.

When finally reunited, he kneels before her, woos her and gently encourages her to appreciate his charms, or he makes a pillow of his woomera (spear thrower) or swishes away the flies with it. Sometimes the girl is afraid but he reassures her. In one song she lies in a tight ball but he soothes her and covers her until she relaxes. He asks, 'Do you love me? If not I shall go away forever. Please tell me.' In the women's songs a man may even feign illness in order to gain his loved one's attention and in the hope that she will eventually come to love him.

A major symbol of *yilpinji* is colour and its power to attract. In the myth the whiteness of the headband and feather twirled by the opening woman dancer is contrasted with the bursting colour of the Rainbow Men, which must be dulled with green slime weed so as not to dazzle the women. In ritual, women throw balls of green slime to attract a lover. Thus both men and women use green slime to attract. But like the men's colours the women's colours are not static. They shift and change hue. The *kurinpi* turn red, the colour of the country.[33] The Rainbow Men burst dangerously with all colours but use red of the ant hill and green from the water to dull their brilliance. Women see their own and men's colours as not fixed in a colour spectrum, but as fluid and as dramatic as the country itself, as ever-changing and as unpredictable as the outcome of male-female encounters: the dynamic of gender values is given metaphorical expression in ritual imagery.

The shining of watch bands and buckles, the sparkling of lightning, the lure of blond hair, the blackening of eyebrows and the reddened legs of women dancers, all induce a lover to notice and appreciate the charms of a possible partner. A major theme of ritual is display. Male decoration and display has found expression in terms of traditional and introduced items. The head band which the woman wears to attract a lover is pure white and shines. In song, women may refer to the head band of a man, but in reality, it is no longer made of hairstring but is a brightly coloured scarf or the fine leather band from a stockman's hat. The arm bracelets adorned with feathers, which were celebrated in song, may now be replaced by the shining watch which winks across the desert. The pubic cover which is pushed aside by the impatient lover becomes the shining belt buckle which is seductively left open but catches the sun and shines. For women depicted in myths, the digging stick may now be a shining metal crowbar, the wooden carrier may be a metal billy can. Such items glisten as women travel and attract the attention of a lover, just as bald heads are said to shine in the sun and to attract lovers. Attributes such as colour and reflection enable women to incorporate introduced items within their own world view.

The intrusion of such themes and of items often associated with a particular person has been construed as evidence of the non-religious nature of certain love magic.[34] I think it has more to do with manner in which women dream and the ever-present nature of the Dreamtime. In ritual the Dreamtime moves concurrently with the present, so the presence of introduced goods with their evolving meanings is not a contradiction so much as proof of the relevancy of the Dreamtime Law. Many of the songs belong to, or depict, actual living people and, in time, will become part of the repertoire of songs and be given a kin term, like the songs which are readily accepted by anthropologists as *bona fide* dreaming songs.

The mixture of songs suggests to me that these present-day themes are in the process of achieving a non-specificity and vagueness which other songs have already achieved. The introduced themes have a relevancy for today's world for, as one Kaytej/Alyawarra woman commented to me when I watched in amazement as money was added to a ritual exchange, 'It does not matter what it is. It is what it stands for that is important!' The accommodation of such items within ritual lulls women into believing that they have continued control over the power to attract and that this is demonstrated by successful liaisons with white men. For women this strengthens their self-image and demonstrates the power of *yilpinji*; for men it strengthens the image of woman as a sex object.

In these myths various admired female stereotypes are presented. The *kurinpi* are the ritually important women, while the young girls exude sweetness, youth and the ability to hunt proficiently. In emphasizing their desirability in ritual, women celebrate these qualities for a number of reasons. There are striking similarities between the *kurinpi* myth and the rainbow myth on which women often comment. Men are like that, they say: cruel, unsure, vain. In all cases the men beautify themselves after wounding the women. The Rainbow Men were very insecure about their ability to woo and win, so they won, then wooed. They continually ask each other, 'Will she like me? Will we frighten them?' Once they make contact there is no standard response. Contact means that the stable, symbolically-ordered positions on the sexual axis are freed and negotiable. Like the shifts in colour, men constantly shift, like the unpredictability of the country from which women draw their power. One brother uses soft words and beauty. He has been the confident one all along. The other uses physical force and soft words.

In an Aranda men's song cycle, as recorded by Strehlow,[35] the sequence of attraction, violence, consummation and travel to a new country is followed, but from the male viewpoint woman is the passionate partner - so passionate that she leaves her own country to travel with him. When sorrow fills her as she leaves, he empathizes and beautifies himself to console her. Thus men also recognize that in marriage women may lose their close tie to their land but in the songs they explain the loss as due to women's passion and credit themselves with tenderness. In Munn's[36] account of Warlpiri male *yangaridji* (closely related to *yilpinji*), the crippling is said to ensure fidelity. Uniting both the male and female versions of *yilpinji* myths are the depiction of love as crippling and the drawing on the base symbol of land which is also an actual living resource. While it is tempting to interpret the spearing as a metaphor for sex, the women explicitly rejected any suggestion of mine that the spear may symbolize penis. Strehlow's[37] translations, however, suggest that men do see spear, penis, crippling and sex as a single symbolic complex.

In all these encounters designated *yilpinji*, the men are working *yilpinji* on the women, but when these myths are acted out in ritual it is the women who are acting *yilpinji* on the men through their ownership, knowledge and access to the myth. The appropriate myth will be chosen. If duty to family and community harmony are to be encouraged, then the myth of the girl and her mother travelling with the men will be used. Even if it means loss, women assert that this is their 'feeling'. If one wishes to go, one may. If one wishes to stay, then there are other appropriate *yilpinji* myths. Women's control of feelings is established through their ownership of the myth and their right to use it in ritual. This is another aspect of women's exercise of their rights.

By evoking their control of land they may attract men. The display of powerful colour in the Rainbow Men's and *kurinpi* women's myths is given form in the body decorations and secret rituals of the women. In *kurinpi* performances women redden themselves, and like the *kurinpi*, have the power to attract and face possible violence or to escape to the closed world of women. Women's ritual practices, unlike the action of men in myth, are deemed invariably successful. In the myths men are sometimes powerful and cruel, at other times gentle and loving. These qualities are dynamically opposed to powerful, irresistible women who give the myth form in the rites. Like the *kurinpi*, women may remain apart or seek a spouse; like the girls in the rainbow myth, they may lead a man to destruction or entrance him with their sweetness. It is their choice.

The conflicts and tensions which arise when men and women must enter into direct negotiation of rights, privileges and obligations with each other may burst forth in jealous fights which are a feature of many communities; they may also find expression in the ritual statements of women in *yilpinji*. In everyday life men worry that if they really hurt a woman she may take ritual action. If a woman 'turns away' from a man she usually has good reason. It will certainly have been the subject of much public discussion. If she acts rashly she will incur the censure of other women and have no security in their camps. Women are not considered to be fickle in the eyes of men or women and if a woman uses *yilpinji* against a man he knows he has deserved it. Fights begin with accusations of infidelity (a vastly expanded possibility in settlements), not fickleness. This image, like that of magic, has been imposed on women and their highly predictable responses to maltreatment and their emotional responses have been stereotyped without consideration of their perception of their feelings or diminution of enforceable rights.

Yilpinji may be performed for a number of reasons other than that of attracting a lover. *Yilpinji* may force a wayward husband to return, remind a wife of her duty to family and country, or even repulse the unwanted advances of a spouse or lover.[38] In Central Australia the focus of *yilpinji* is the community, not the individual, for whom the ritual is performed. Both men and women respect the power of *yilpinji*. After a performance the women take great care to nullify the power of *yilpinji* by throwing dirt and cleaning away all traces of the activity. It must only bring about immediate consequences for the subject of the ritual; nevertheless there are less immediate and indirect consequences for the whole community, who benefit from the restoration of harmony and maintenance of correct marriage alliances.

Consultation before a performance is undertaken to determine the appropriateness of *yilpinji* in the particular case. I have never heard women admit that they sang for a 'wrong-way' partner although this can result if the power is not properly controlled.[39] Warlpiri women were forever accusing the Kaytej of making trouble with their *yilpinji* by the indiscriminant singing of songs. Although the Kaytej appear to exercise enormous care in *yilpinji*, the accusations have forced them to desist from using several powerful songs. Residence on the settlement has thus limited their range of expression and played a part in narrowing recognition of women's religious activities.

Yilpinji is achieved through a creative integration of myth, song, gesture and design against a backdrop of country. The circle, the quintessential female symbol, finds expression in the body designs, the rolling hands gesture and patterns traced out by the dancing feet. Certain *yilpinji* and health/curing designs are the same, because, as Kaytej women recognize, love, health and sexual satisfaction are intertwined at the personal and community level. Exclusively *yilpinji* designs concern agitation, excitement and longing. Such feelings are said to be located in the stomach which quivers and shakes like the dancing thighs of women or the shaking leaves of men's poles at initiation, or the shimmering of a mirage or the getting up of a rain-bow.[40]

In the myth women claim their right to express their feelings, ambivalent as they may superficially appear. Ownership of myth and the rights to perform rituals provide the power base for women's claims, while the content of the myths explores women's autonomy and male-female encounters. Women in the myth encapsulate two warring principles which underpin women's identity – on the one hand, there is autonomy; on the other, there is the desire for social intercourse which involves men. The myth encounters do not follow an invariable sequence, although women's loss and pain are consistently present. Myth provides an explanation for male violence but not a justification. It is more a warning of what one may expect from men and the danger of leaving one's own country.

In extracting the story line from the ritual performances and presenting it in the form of a myth which has a beginning and an end, I am doing violence to the cultural conception. My justification for such a representation is that, short of a lifetime spent as a woman in women's camps, it is impossible to comprehend the kaleidoscopic range of nuances, ramifications and elaborations of the behaviour of the Dreamtime ancestors who acted out *yilpinji* myths.

By organizing the fragments I gleaned into this form I was able, by way of clarification, to ask further questions of the women. On several occasions I have read back to the women my rendition of the myths; they have nodded assent but declared my version to be a written text which constitutes another form, one peculiar to whites. Their telling of the myth in ritual emphasizes the richness of country rather than the development of plot or character: two cultural views are thus encapsulated in 'myth as action' compared to 'myth as text'.

Country and the sites are part of a metaphysical knowledge that is totally opposed to a system which elaborates meanings and ideas about society and the significance of life through focusing on persons and their seemingly highly individual actions. Kaytej women's ritual myths look to country dreaming and other spiritually empowered events in order to discuss themselves and their relations to men and thus their position within the whole society. A group of European women or men would approach the task of explaining their position and view through a human-centred social drama.[41]

I should also point out that by presenting the myths in this form,

I am providing an overview of ancestral activity in the area which no individual woman could recite. The different dreamings are the responsibility of different women and although each is aware of the content of the Dreamtime activity and characters of others, one may only rightly speak of one's own dreamings. Because I was able to record dreamings from all the women of the Kaytej group, my synthesis is not the product of one person's knowledge and would not occur in this form. Women would correct me if I misplaced the dreamings of others but they would not comment on the content of the dreamings of others.

There are no occasions on which a woman would sit down and tell a *yilpinji* myth, although there is a corpus of songs which are glossed *yilpinji*. There are ritual practices, designs, gestures and sacred objects which are used only in conjunction with *yilpinji*, and certain conditions which are said to flow exclusively from *yilpinji*. I have put the myths together from actual performances I attended, from subsequent discussions and translations of songs and symbols, and from women's explanations of ritual action and song furnished during performance or while listening to a replay of a tape.

In *yilpinji* women not only articulate their models of social reality but also attempt to shape their worlds. This latter aspect is apparent in the way in which women comment on ritual as it proceeds. At one level they discuss the myth as I have delineated it and at another they comment on the power and efficacy of the rituals. These two levels are not always as clear as I make them appear in the analysis. They are interwoven in the seamless web of life which encompasses the now of today and the now of the dreaming.

Particular songs or combinations of songs and actions are remembered as having been sung at a particular place for the particular person and with a particular result. Two older women married to much younger men did not see the action of a man taking an older wife as duty but of a man desperately in love with an irresistible woman. Such is the women's perception of the affair. They do not see themselves as being shuffled around a circulating connubium but as capable of deciding whether or not they will go to a younger man. As women exercise wide choice in second and subsequent marriages it is hard to believe that they go to younger men merely to uphold the gerontocracy. They go if they wish. To ensure the success of the match they work *yilpinji*. The two older women mentioned above are celebrated cases of *yilpinji*, but all the women with whom I worked would admit to having used *yilpinji* to achieve results they desired and all attested to the success they had.

As songs are being sung women comment on the possible outcome of the ritual and the action in the ritual. They assert their rights to feelings. 'That is my feeling,' I have heard women say in explanation on many occasions. 'If you want to stay you may.' If a woman wants to get out of a marriage which she finds distasteful because the man is playing around, taking a second wife or acting violently, a wife may ask for her ritual group to perform *yilpinji* to make him turn away from her. These are powerful and only allowed after the women have weighed the merits of the case. However, if a woman says, 'That is my feeling,' it is respected.

In the myths the lovers are often improperly related. Roheim[42] cast *yilpinji* as a 'holiday from the rules' but in my experience, love rituals are very carefully used and then only after extensive consultation and consideration of the merits of the request. *Yilpinji* only induces certain states: it does not have the power to condone 'wrong-way' unions, which at Warrabri are rare, notorious and generally short-lived. *Yilpinji* is used to establish correct unions, and this is why it is feared by men: it impinges upon the set of relationships which men claim to control through marriage alliances. They know they cannot negate women's *yilpinji* and often do not even know they are being performed. At any time a woman may thus overturn the plans of men. Men do not attempt to prevent women from staging *yilpinji*, but rather turn to their own sphere of control of male-female relations and intensify demands in the domain of promised marriages. Women respect the marriage codes but not necessarily the plans of men. In using *yilpinji* for correct unions they are upholding the moral order without endorsing men's rights to determine actual marriages. When men claim that women use *yilpinji* for 'wrong-way' unions, anthropologists conclude that women use *yilpinji* immorally, and women's endorsement of central social values is obscured.

Women's role in maintaining male-female relationships has been misunderstood because *yilpinji* has been designated 'magic' and of concern to women only. Glossed in this way, *yilpinji* appears to be a deviant, illegitimate activity pursued on the periphery of the real decision-making domain of men. According to Kaberry[43] love magic was a safety valve and at times a form of vengeance. To Roheim[44] it was the sort of activity in which women indulged. It was magic rather than religion, because women did not have access to the Dreamtime power. Although Kaberry, and Berndt[45] have challenged this aspect of Roheim's characterization of women's lives, the designation 'magic', with all its perjorative overtones, has persisted. Love magic remains a haphazard activity, lacking any structure or purpose. It provides background noise for descriptions of the culturally-valued activities of men.

Writing of the central west area of the Northern Territory, Berndt[46] argues that the focus on sexual intercourse and reproduction in women's ceremonies is part of the general religious scheme as exemplified in the major cult theme of fertility and increase. *Yilpinji*, in Berndt's[47] analysis, is the least secret of women's ceremonies and more vulnerable to corruption than *jawalju* (*yawulyu*). However the themes, imagery, symbolism and structure of Kaytej *yilpinji* indicate that it is emotional management, not fertility, which is the major concern of women. Through these rituals Central Australian Aboriginal women work to maintain the values of their society in a distinctively female way.

Through *yilpinji* women claim to establish male-female relationships deemed legitimate by their society. This aspect of women's role has been overlooked because, as with male-oriented approaches to an analysis of health maintenance, the paradigms which have organized research within Australia have not been those designed to focus upon women as social actors in their own right. Anthropologists have too often sought an understanding of the way in which male-female unions are regulated in terms of the twin institutions of polygyny and the gerontocracy. Within the context of arranged marriage old men are depicted as allocating scarce resources and arrogating to themselves the right to bestow women's services in marriage.[48] As we have seen, this model disregards women's decision-making role in formal bestowal practices and the rights women assert and enjoy in marriage.[49] The model within which I am suggesting we analyse male-female unions is one which allows for the dynamic interaction of sexual politics and social change in desert society today and in the past. In *yilpinji*, as with formal decisions made during initiation, women clearly demonstrate that there are choices available to them and that they choose as independent members of a society which respects their views. In their opinion they are not and never were pawns in male marriage games. That the unions into which women are now entering are characterized increasingly by violence is evidence not for women's chattel status but for the changing arena in which the sexual politics of the society are being played out. Like their responses to the changes discussed in the previous chapter, Aboriginal women's response to the changing nature of male-female unions is based on an interplay between women's perceptions of their role as nurturers of relationships, and the constraints which settlement life imposes on that role.

It might be analytically convenient to postulate an opposition whereby men control the formal arrangements (that is, promised marriage) and women the informal (that is, love rituals). This, however, is not possible, for the informal and the formal are not so easily separated. Women engage in the politics of marriage arrangements and men perform love rituals. I have no data of my own concerning men's *yilpinji* at Warrabri but other anthropologists have provided important insights which indicate that Central Australian Aboriginal men seek to regulate aspects of male-female unions through *yilpinji*.[50] Although their analyses differ in certain respects, it is evident that Aboriginal men are using *yilpinji* to establish and to maintain relationships of importance to them. Like women's *yawulyu* and *yilpinji*, the themes which men explore in their *yilpinji* are consonant with their perceptions of their role and the practical situation in which marriage rules are acted out. Thus men's *yilpinji* explore the ramifications of and tension inherent in the institutions of polygyny and gerontocracy. In both male and female *yilpinji*, the ritual participants make statements concerning their role in their society in a way which illuminates the nature of sexual politics in desert society.

In this analysis of *yilpinji* I have stressed that the rituals should be seen within the context of land and as achieving socially approved ends. By denying these dimensions, anthropologists have interpreted love rituals as personal affairs. Berndt offers only fragments of love songs and so it is impossible to judge the context, while Strehlow omits the last verses of one love song because, in his opinion, they have nothing to do with male-female relations but merely name the animals the lovers meet.[51] By dismissing the context of country and attachment, Strehlow strips the songs of their real import.

I have stressed that *yilpinji* and *yawulyu* are based on women's rights and responsibilities in land. Although much has changed, Kaytej women enjoy a continuity in their relationship to land which is the basis of the strength of their assertions that they regulate aspects of male-female unions and thus maintain health, happiness and harmony.

In exploring women's mythology I have argued that women represent their world as one which is self-contained, known and secure. The authority to control this world and the power to exclude men from this domain are underwritten by the *jukurrpa*. In acting out the responsibilities the Law confers upon them as women, women engage in work which is distinctively theirs. In the past this ensured that they would be recognized as full members of their society. Today, although they continue to work in their domain - one which remains separate and distinct from that of the men - they no longer enjoy the same status as full members of their society.

NOTES

1. Transcript of Evidence 1981:192-196. This text and those which follow on pages 119, 120-21, 131-2, 136, are based on evidence given by witnesses in the Kaytej, Warlpiri and Warlmanpa land claim heard at Warrabri in 1981. I have followed the Transcript of Evidence, much of which is based on translation by Dr. Mary Laughren, but I have omitted questions asked by Counsel because the answers adequately carry the narrative. I have chosen to use this source because it was produced in a public hearing and therefore does not violate the confidentiality of more private conversations.

2. Transcript of Evidence 1980:278. This evidence was given in Warlmanpa, Warlpiri, Mudbura and Warumunga land claim heard at Warrabri in 1980. See also fn.2:1.

3. Transcript of Evidence 1981:191.

4. Transcript of Evidence 1981:196-204.

5. Bell in press.

6. See Bell & Ditton 1980:30.

7. Meggitt (1962:224) notes that men use this symbolic complex of red ochre, blood, health and strength.

8. See also Spencer & Gillen 1899:308.

9. See also Strehlow 1971:651-2.

10. See Berndt 1950:43-51, 1965:242ff.; Hamilton 1979.

11. Transcript of Evidence 1981:175-91.

12. Transcript of Evidence 1981:115-16.

13. In the course of land claims I have worked with other people who share what

we might call the Arandic system of land tenure: the Alyawarra and Kaititja claim (see Toohey 1979a); the Anmatjirra and Alyawarra claim (see Bell 1979b); the Warlpiri Anmatjirra claim (see Bell 1980b; Toohey 1980b). The model of land tenure discussed in this section is consistent with my work with these other groups.

14.   See Nash 1980:17.

15.   See Wafer & Wafer 1983:21.

16.   See Bell 1980b:6-9.

17.   For a review of the literature see Bell 1979b; Maddock 1980:130ff.; Toohey 1980a:5-6, 11-22, 1980b:12-19; Hale 1980; Nash 1980; Wafer 1980.

18.   See Meggitt 1962:69.

19.   Spencer & Gillen (1899:99), writing of the Aranda at the turn of the century, commented that sexual jealousy was not a major tension.

20.   See also Strehlow 1971:651-3.

21.   Chewings (1936:95) comments that one woman of their party violated an avoidance relationship to nurse a sick man.

22.   For instance, Meggitt (1955:377) worked closely with older men on health related matters but his data regarding women came from two informants aged 20 and 25. Unlike his male informants these women would not have been schooled in the Law. Cawte (1974:145) elicited his data concerning women from the wife of the missionary at Yuendumu and from her Aboriginal friends.

23.   See also Cawte 1974:35; Elkin 1977:23.

24.   See Berndt 1964:280; Peterson 1970a; Elkin 1977:170-71; Reid 1978.

25.   Meggitt 1962:264.

26.   The term *yilpinji* is known and used throughout the desert region of Central Australia. Berndt (1950), Meggitt (1962) and Munn (1973) use *ilbindji*, Roheim (1933 and 1974), *ilpindja* and Strehlow (1971) *ilpintja*.

27.   Hart & Pilling (1960:18) point out that the older men can not control widow remarriage in the same way they organize their infant daughters. In their view widow marriage 'supplied the loophole in the system or the cultural alternative that took care of young men'.

28.   Kaberry 1939:262-3; Berndt 1950: 36-42, 46-51; Roheim 1974:153-224, See also Berndt and Berndt 1951:148-78.

29.   Strehlow (1971:524) clearly recognizes this when he notes how old men guard their most potent love-songs from younger men who may otherwise win the hearts of young promised wives.

30.   This shattering of the nexus between land and ritual might explain why the women of whom Catherine Berndt (1950) writes appeared to emphasise sex and not emotional management. Both Kaberry (1939:256) and Berndt (1965:247) note that 'love magic' songs are said to be introduced from other 'countries'. Thus the rituals would not be located within the rights to land as are the Kaytej rituals.

31.   Munn (1973:84, 179) and Roheim (1974:155ff, 221) comment that men's *yilpinji* is connected with rain dreaming also.

32. See Roheim 1933:237.

33. Chewings (1936:66) claims red as the colour of love and joy. Strehlow (1971:471-3, 651-2) notes use of red in love and health ceremonies.

34. See also Berndt 1950:73.

35. Strehlow 1971:476-7.

36. Munn 1973:47.

37. Strehlow 1971:487.

38. See Kaberry 1939:255; Berndt 1965:243;

39. Roheim (1933:212), Kaberry (1939:259) and Berndt & Berndt (1951:240) argue that *yilpinji* may be used for 'wrong-way' partners.

40. See also Spencer & Gillen 1899:543; Munn 1973:46.

41. Berndt (1976:143) touches on this issue in his contrast between song cycles which stress sequential development and cyclical seasonal variations and celebrate themes of fertility and procreation with other less structured arrangements from Arnhem Land. The former appears more intelligible as it follows the European style more closely. It may in fact reflect the nature of the country from which it derives its power. Sequential development and a cyclical form are absent in Central Australian song cycles which I have recorded.

42. Roheim 1933:209-10.

43. Kaberry 1939:265-7.

44. Roheim 1933:208-9.

45. Kaberry 1939:188-9, 219-21, 276-8; Berndt 1965:273-81.

46. Berndt 1950:70-73.

47. Berndt 1950:30-35; 1965:243.

48. Meggitt 1962:264-70; 1965.

49. The politics of marriage is not the focus of this book but I have argued elsewhere (Bell 1980a:247) that marriage from a woman's point of view be seen as the experience of evolving serial monogamy wherein women politick to contract progressively marriages which are more and more to their perceived benefit.

50. Warlpiri men, according to Meggitt (1962:270), perform *ilbindji (yilpinji)* to speed the growth of breasts and buttocks of young wives (see also Strehlow 1971:470). Munn (1973:48) disagrees that *ilbindji* functions within the context of marriage. In her analysis this is the function of the closely-related *yangaridji* and *manguru*. *Ilbindji* concerns extra-marital sex and is glossed as men's ancestral designs and ceremonies for attracting women (Munn 1973:223). The three categories of design are, however, Munn states, imbued with a strength supposed to increase men's control over women (Munn 1973:48). Strehlow (1971:524) agrees that *ilpintja* allows old men to win not only the services of a spouse but also the fondness of a wife.

51. Berndt 1950:35; Strehlow 1971:477.

Chapter IV
WE FOLLOW ONE LAW

Women, as we have seen, are the nurturers of people and country. In their own rituals and in their daily lives they project an image of themselves as independent individuals. They display sexual solidarity. If we were to stop at this point, we could conclude that all we need to know of Aboriginal religion is contained in women's ritual. Knowledge of men's ritual world, we might suggest, merely adds a depth but does not fundamentally alter our understanding. This approach, but with male as ego, has been the dominant trend in Australian anthropology.

However, underlying male and female practice is a common purpose and shared belief in the Dreamtime experience: both have sacred boards, both know songs and paint designs which encode the knowledge of the Dreamtime. How each sex then fleshes out this common core of beliefs and knowledge is dependent on their perceptions of their role and their contribution to their society. Men's roles and perceptions have been well-documented; women's are rather less well-known. By exploring women's ritual realm, we not only gain a clearer appreciation of women's place in the society, we also bring the activities of men into sharper focus.

The structuring principles of women's rituals, their content and focus on the maintenance of social harmony, link the ritual worlds of men and women. In both sets of rituals there is a celebration of the central values of the society. Under the Law, men and women have distinctive roles to play but each has recourse to certain checks and balances which ensure that neither sex can enjoy unrivalled supremacy over the other. Men and women alike are dedicated to observing the Law which orders their lives into complementary but distinct fields of action and thought: in separation lies the basis of a common association that underwrites domains of existence. Men stress their creative power, women their role as nurturers, but each is united in their common purposes – the maintenance of their society in accordance with the Dreamtime Law.

In the *yilpinji* myths we saw that the symbolic representations of men were as cruel, unpredictable, and as challengers to women's power base in land. On the other hand, male-oriented analyses have explored in men's rituals the symbolic representations of women as the feared, the profane and the negated.[1]

In addition to symbolic representations, men and women also have a physical presence at each other's rituals. This is necessary to ensure that, as each sex elaborates evidence of the Dreamtime experience, the common core retains its consistency, and neither sex errs in the necessary and continuous process of reinvention that enables each to assert their uniqueness and unity. The sexual politics of ritual are evident on these occasions.

Each sex vies with the other in its brilliant display of knowledge. At the same time, each is constrained by the need to represent the Dreamtime experience with meticulous fidelity. Thus mixed ceremonies have the dual function of permitting monitoring of the activities of the opposite sex and of providing a forum for display of the ritual worlds of each sex. Attendance and participation, no matter how limited, at the rituals of the opposite sex allow each to obtain a mental map of the physical layout of the ritual area of the other and of certain ritual procedures. In ritual, male and female assert their unity in the Law which underwrites their separateness. For the anthropologist it allows a unique opportunity to observe and to explore, with the participants, the way in which each has portrayed its domain to the other.

What men may know of women's rituals and what women may know of men's is a delicate matter for any anthropologist to probe. Women know more of men's rituals than is made available in mixed rituals and I suspect the same is true of men. Women often indicated in their behaviour that they knew more of the content of the rituals than that which they observed, but they did not readily vocalize this knowledge. It was rather akin to the practice of not calling dead names and of avoiding certain sites which, in order to be avoided, have to be known.

Men, as well as women, face the problem of having to know what to avoid *vis-à-vis* the rituals of the other. In ceremonies known as *yungkurru*[2], men and women are able to make public statements about their own rituals and to allow the other to approach and to handle the ritual objects. This, however, is not the same as admitting members of the opposite sex to one's own sex-specific ceremonies. Kaytej women have retained control over their own ritual domain as the men have over theirs. Therefore *yungkurru* is not an opportunity for men to infiltrate and gain control of women's autonomous world. Women were aware of the danger of this and are careful throughout such ceremonies to present only a partial display of their ritual knowledge.

Because each sex has a separate and restricted area within which closed ceremonies are performed, there is little opportunity to observe the reaction of the opposite sex to sex-specific ceremonies. While I was at Warrabri, if I was working in my house with women on the transcription and translation of recordings of their closed ceremonies, I noted that men totally avoided my house and would send another woman in to fetch me if they wished to speak to me. On one occasion, however, I was able to observe the reactions of a man to a recording of women's *yawulyu* and to probe his understanding of the songs. The songs were not secret songs but they were ones which women sang in their own ritual area. This was one of the few occasions when I was able to compare men's and women's accounts at the level of the 'word'.

I had been recording and translating women's *yawulyu* songs for some time and in so doing had learnt of the constraints imposed on ritual performance by settlement residence. There were frequent accusations from Warlpiri that Kaytej had overstepped the mark and sung too far into the country of another or strayed onto the secret side of a dreaming. This is a serious charge and a slur on the *kurdungurlu* whose responsibility it is to ensure that the *kirda* stay 'straight' and don't 'run off' onto another track.

These issues (that is, correct and appropriate ritual performances) were particularly in the minds of Warrabri residents in mid-1977, because the Education Department had been recording songs and stories for use in the school. The imbalance of teaching assistants in the school ensured that Warlpiri songs were well-translated while Kaytej songs were rather more sketchily translated.

Further, the teaching assistant who had been asked to work on the Kaytej songs was not of sufficient status to know much of the dreaming Law. The Kaytej women were distressed because they felt that yet again they had been neglected and that this time it impinged on their world. They approached me and asked if I would retape their songs. They wished to sing them 'straight' and to correct aspects of the translation. One of the difficulties had been that the Warlpiri songs recorded for use in the school followed the track of a particular ancestor from site to site, whereas the Kaytej dreamings emphasized the country and its many dreamings. Thus in one Kaytej performance it was possible that several dreamings which converged on a site could be mentioned. The idea of Kaytej singing the dreaming 'straight' turned out to be vexatious. We spent many hours recording and re-recording in order to follow the travels of *ngapa* from one place to another. One Warlpiri-Kaytej woman had the clearest idea of what was required and she was delegated to edit the tape with me.

As well as the concern with singing the dreaming straight, there is always the worry that one may sing into the secret side. Although women always indicated to me when this happened in a taped performance, they did not want any such songs being available at the school. The men had also been approached for songs which could be taught to the boys and had spent much time discussing the logistics of such an enterprise. In order to vouch for the openness and correctness of the women's tape and, I suspect, so the men could find out just what the women had contributed, they decided that a man should listen to the tapes with me.

The man chosen by the women was the brother of one of my closest friends in the Karlukarlu camp. I went before the Warrabri Council to explain the purpose of my tapes and Jupurrula's intention to listen to them. He was confirmed as the correct person to listen and we began work the next day. For a week he sat and listened to the women's singing of *ngapa* dreaming. I had already translated several of the tapes but had not finished the set. After the first day, I stopped trying to marry his explanations of songs to those I had obtained from the women, or those I knew myself from the ritual instruction I had received.

When, at a later date, I was able to compare the women's comments, glosses and explanations with those of the men, I found that the common ground concerned that which I discuss below in terms of structural aspects of ancestral activity in the land, and that sex-specific explanations concerned the content of the activity and the interpretation of the songs. Men know the structure but not the details of the activities of the ancestors. It is women who flesh out and elaborate this aspect of the ancestral design.

The tapes to which we listened traced the travels of *ngapa* dreaming from the Stirling swamp area to the Devil's Marbles. On the way both *yawakiyi* (bush berry) and *wardingi* (witchetty) dreamings are encountered. Jupurrula's commentary on the tape consisted of stating to whom the song belonged, the name of the ancestor and the direction in which the ancestor was travelling. There were several songs the meaning of which he did not know. He stated they were in a language he could not 'hear'. Indeed the songs of this tape included several in Anmatjirra and Warumungu as the travels of the ancestors cut across country in which these languages are spoken. There were also place names which he could not call because at one he was 'made a man', that is, initiated, and another was the name of a now deceased man. He commented on the meaning of the words of several songs which are sung in public accompanied by graphic mimes. They are songs which children also know and enjoy.

My understanding of the common ground between the men's and women's knowledge of rain dreaming, in this instance, was limited to taped material. However, on other occasions, when I have discussed with men the country of which women had already taught me, the information men deemed significant has been in accord with Jupurrula's comments on the tapes. Men have spoken to me at the level of the structure of the dreamings. This is information which both men and women offer. They name the *kirda* and *kurdungurlu* for an area, state to which sites individuals have special rights and responsibilities and cite the nature of affiliation of such persons to the sites. They name other dreamings which crossed, travelled alongside or are in some way associated with the dreaming being celebrated. Both men and women name the particular ancestors responsible for the location and features of certain sites. For example, at Karlukarlu wild fig trees grow from the rocky boulders; these are celebrated in the women's songs and commented upon by both sexes. It is knowledge such as this which is held in common and which is transmitted in mixed and open performances. In their commentary on ritual songs women do not provide details of place, ownership and travels. Their more spontaneous comments concern the actual activities of an actor in a particular song.

Perhaps a reason for the difference between the two explanatory

Women of Erulja (Utopia Cattle Station) give evidence in the land claim for their country. In answer to questions concerning their relationship to the land, its sites and dreamings, they responded with a ritual display, which entailed painting bodies, sacred items, singing and dancing.

modes is that in a *yawulyu* performance the structural elements on which men first comment are apparent in action. There is thus no need to recite such self-evident facts. From the boards on display and the body paintings, one knows which dreaming is being celebrated. From the gestures of the dancing women, one can follow the interactions of various ancestors. It was only when listening to tapes that women would comment on the actual text of the song. This level of information appeared to be unknown to the men.

How then did Jupurrula know anything of the songs without the extra props provided by the ritual action and display entailed in a performance? One of the answers lies in the performance of ceremonies which both sexes attend. First, let us look at the role of men at a women's *yawulyu* ceremony and then at a *yungkurru* when men and women exchanged knowledge of several dreamings.

I had been at Warrabri only several months when this *yawulyu* took place. The Education Department, as part of its cultural programme, had organized a trip for Warrabri Kaytej and Alyawarra women to Neutral Junction and Ti-Tree schools. With the best will in the world the teachers had arranged a timetable which allowed the women to dance in both places on the same day. The buses arrived at Neutral Junction mid-morning and the women began the necessary negotiations and discussion with the local women before the *yawulyu* could take place. For the Kaytej women the occasion provided the opportunity to link together the *ngapa* dreaming which travels from Waake, west of Neutral Junction, to Karlukarlu, with the *ngapa* dreaming knowledge of the Neutral Junction women. The Alyawarra women were able, as *kurdungurlu* for some of the local women, to perform sections of the *ngapa* dreaming and thus to extend their dreaming range further to the north-east.

On this brief visit the women could only begin their *yawulyu* and unfortunately were unable to complete their exchange and display of knowledge of objects. The women resolved to return – and did so on two occasions a month apart. Over this period they were able to link together the dreamings of adjacent countries and to activate rights they enjoyed in country through mother, father, conception and residence. Once the women were certain that their display was correct, men were admitted.

The second visit took place two days after the first trip. Haste was necessary because the women had opened up the dreamings by singing for the various countries. To prepare their boards and their bodies, and to sing of the country, the women sat in three separate groups oriented to the country of the ritual. During the painting they intoned the songs which make the paint shine, which send out the power, and which call together all people for the display of the designs on body and boards and to witness the re-enactment of the Dreamtime experience. The Kaytej women sang of the travels of the *kurinpi* women from Stirling Swamp to Devil's Marbles, of the travels of *ngapa*. The Alyawarra women sang of their dreamings near the Kurundi homestead where the ancestral dog turned around. These were new dreamings for the Neutral Junction women who sang of *ngapa* for which some of the Alyawarra women were *kurdungurlu*. On this return visit the Kaytej of Warrabri opened the ground and called in the Neutral Junction women, who remained shy, reticent and afraid that they had little to offer next to the other two groups. Indeed,

Alyawarra women dance their dreaming into the ground at Neutral Junction.

against the vitality of the other two groups, their repertoire did appear impoverished. The Neutral Junction Kaytej suffered many losses during the massacres of the 1870s and 1920s, and the visit of their northern sisters provided an opportunity to repair, to replace and to refine their dreaming knowledge.

First, the Kaytej displayed and planted their boards, the Alyawarra followed, and lastly came the local women. The boards were then taken by *kirda* and *kurdungurlu* to each of the other groups and eventually returned to their home fire. On the return journey of each board, the other groups followed. In this way all the women literally followed the dreamings of the other and marked out the travels with their dancing feet. The singing, dancing, display and tracing out of tracks continued throughout the night; in the morning, when the most sacred songs were sung and the children's heads covered to protect them, the women removed the boards, carefully smoothed over the ground and rubbed down the boards to reabsorb the power.

In payment for the rich displays and for the hospitality of the Neutral Junction women, each group of women made presentations and counter-presentations of blankets, money, food and ritual items to the other. The Kaytej left behind several painted items for the Neutral Junction women, who spent the next month in feverish activity reconstructing their songs and designs.

On the third and final visit for this *yawulyu* sequence, the atmosphere was different. Men were now permitted into the ritual area and some Warrabri men accompanied the women on the trip. As before, the women set up three separate groups for the preparation. During this time men were nowhere to be seen. As night fell the women began displaying boards and singing the country to each other. The men could be seen some distance away in the direction of the main camp. They crept closer as the women sang the songs for all people to gather for business. They sang in all the languages of those present and of those through whose country the dreamings passed. Finally the men arrived at the dancing ground, but their view of the action was marred because the women had allocated them a position on the other side of the substantial woodpile – a woodpile provided by the Neutral Junction men.

The Neutral Junction women had a wider vocabulary of songs and board designs on display than on the previous occasions and the men were very approving. The Alyawarra women were particularly admired by the`men for whom that dreaming was held through their fathers. A small group of men retreated some distance, held a conference and suggested to the women that, in payment for the display by the Alyawarra women of country they had not seen for many years, they should dance their section of rain dreaming. The women of Neutral Junction said this was the first time many had seen this dance. It also allowed their own women to extend and confirm their knowledge of the rain dreaming they held. The men hurriedly painted, then danced, carrying painted boards before them. The women sang them from the dark into the light of the fire so that the boards could be seen. After the men had finished, the women continued singing until dawn when exchanges again were made.

This occasion is remembered by men and women alike as a highly satisfactory display and exchange. Men expressed no resentment at the treatment they received from the women, only pride and pleasure at seeing the country so well cared for. The way in which the Neutral Junction women were able to reconstruct their dreamings and to perform with such confidence is a further illustration of the structured potential for change inherent in the dogma of dreaming.

The exchange between men and women in the Neutral Junction *yawulyu* was brief. Only once while I was at Warrabri did I observe a more lengthy ceremony in which men and women exchanged knowledge and displayed objects to each other. Spencer and Gillen[3] do comment on the presence of women at men's ceremonies. They also mention that women actually saw the sacred objects when they were brought to the women's camp – an occurrence which confounded them.[4] Kaytej insist they have always performed *yungkurru* (which they consistently translated as 'young man ceremony'), that the last time they performed this *yungkurru* for *yawakiyi* was just after the Darwin cyclone (December 1974), and that *yungkurru* have always entailed an exchange of ritual objects, songs and designs by men and women.

In the *yungkurru* I observed in June 1977, both men and women prepared material separately in their own ritual area and then jointly displayed and exchanged their knowledge and expertise in an open public area. In so doing each was able to display to the other their elaborations of the common core of beliefs and values of the shared dreamtime heritage. While demonstrating their unique contribution as men and women, each was also able to monitor the content of the ritual world of the other. In the *yungkurru*, as in other ritual situations, there was a clear distinction between what women and men knew, what they admitted to knowing and what they were prepared to show to each other. In separate areas men and women prepared their songs, designs and boards and allocated ritual roles. When they came together they brought but a fraction of the knowledge which had been celebrated in the preparation, but each knew something of what had happened in the restricted 'work' areas of the other.

In the display to each other and in their separate celebrations, men and women emphasized their ability to establish relations across space and between people through the use of Dreamtime knowledge in the form of songs, designs and ritual roles. The portion of their heritage which women brought into the open area was a special rendering of their world in a form deemed suitable for men. Similarly the men brought into the public arena a presentation which they deemed appropriate. These displays hinted at, but did not flesh out, the contents of the myths which underwrote the dreamings being performed.

The *yungkurru* discussed here lasted for over a week and culmina-
ted in a visit to Hermannsburg for the centennial celebrations of the
establishment of the Lutheran mission. Earlier in 1977, an ex-
Hermannsburg man had taken up residence at Warrabri and established a country and western band which quickly gained him the support of many young people. Initially he was also popular with some
older people because he was familiar with white ways and appeared
as the prophet arising from the masses. But no one person can remain
in favour with all groups of Warrabri for any lengthy period and it
soon became evident that he must choose or be chosen by one of the
factions. He chose and was chosen by Kaytej.

To demonstrate his allegiance, he painted an enormous back-drop
canvas of the rocks at Devil's Marbles which he displayed at his con-
certs. The Kaytej, after a period of assessment, decided to teach him
something of the country of Wakulpu. Through his Arandic mother
he was able to forge links with a Kaytej Nampijinpa. For a period
all parties were satisfied that he was a true 'son'. His country lay to
the west of Wauchope where *yawakiyi, ngapa* and *wardingi* dreamings
were active.

The negotiations for the trip to Hermannsburg were complicated
and involved many persons with diverse interests. The ex-
Hermannsburg man suggested the trip as part of a cultural exchange
with the mission. The proposal was greeted warmly by the Kaytej and
coolly by the Warlpiri, who subsequently made access to the one community bus awkward. The women immediately began to prepare for
yawulyu but the men decided that they too should perform and that
the man needed some ritual instruction if he was to be 'theirs' at Hermannsburg. Finally the decision to stage a *yungkurru* was taken
jointly by men and women. This was essential because a high level
of co-operation between the sexes was necessary to stage the
yungkurru.

One old Jampijinpa had sought further knowledge of the dreamings
of the country between Walapanpa and Wakulpu from Nungarrayi,
to whom much had been revealed in a dream many years ago. Finally
she agreed to show it and to pass much of it on to him. The ancestor
in the dream had empowered her to transmit this knowledge, but she
also sought to incorporate more senior men within the country of the
dream, because too few men were prepared to shoulder the responsibility for maintenance of the country. 'I'll sing it and paint it,' she

agreed, 'and then you'll know it.' In this way she was able to incorporate new ritual 'bosses' and to revitalize the activity of the Wakulpu area.

In explaining to me the decision to stage a *yungkurru*, the women stated that the men were a little jealous of them. Women had been stealing the limelight and it was time for men to display their expertise. Throughout the *yungkurru* the tension between male and female ritual worlds was evident, but in these sexual politics the men rarely had the upper hand. When the men were somewhat tardy in beginning, the women reminded them of their resolve to be 'level' with the women. The men regrouped and danced. On another occasion the women refused to complete their dancing because the men were not fully participating. (I have seen this happen on other ritual occasions also and at times women have brought the action to a halt.)

During the preparations for the *yungkurru*, the old Jampijinpa asked one woman details concerning the travels of *yawakiyi*. 'Don't ask me,' she replied. 'I am a woman.' She, only half an hour before in the women's ritual area, had been discussing the travels of *yawakiyi* and teaching other women. All she would show to the man was the designs she had elaborated. When women were dissatisfied with aspects of the male performance, they said so. They accused the men of just sitting and listening and, several months later, dismissed a male request for more *yungkurru* with exactly that charge.

Yungkurru, women said, was the boys' equivalent of *yawulyu*: a 'young man ceremony'. But the 1977 *yungkurru* lacked young men. The ex-Hermannsburg Jangala was forty and the only other young man who consistently received instruction was the adopted son of one of the *kirda* for *yawakiyi*. The adoptive father sought to teach his 'son' something of his dreaming. Both men were given instruction at the structural level of dreaming knowledge of the country of Wakulpu into which they were being inducted. This knowledge was imparted by both men and women. The view of the *jukurrpa* presented in the *yungkurru* was one in which the independence and interdependence of the sexes was clearly marked.

It also became evident in the course of the week-long celebrations of country that women not only were able to direct men, but that they were also often the initiators of ritual action. The world on display for the 'young men' was one in which men and women exhibited their special skills but one ultimately maintained through the complementary nature of male and female roles. The *yungkurru* was not an occasion for the negation of women as mothers, sisters or wives, but rather a very busy period – full of serious discussion, co-operation and negotiation between men and women, between *kirda* and *kurdungurlu*.

While *yungkurru* must have 'young men' to instruct, I suggest there is another equally important purpose in staging a *yungkurru*. In order for men and women to share and jointly maintain their Dreamtime heritage, there must be opportunities for each to view the ritual activities of the other. There must also be times when men and women make public not only who is *kirda* and *kurdungurlu* by virtue of descent, but who has gained the knowledge and expertise to act out the ritual roles of *kirda* and *kurdungurlu*. The *yungkurru* provided such an opportunity.

While discussing health ceremonies (p. 158), I mentioned a resolution of conflict ceremony wherein the women of Warrabri presented ritual knowledge and objects to the Willowra women in exchange for the restored health of a Nungarrayi. One consequence of that exchange was that the Willowra women extended to the east the dreamings they could legitimately celebrate, besides confirming the closeness of the ritual roles of the Warrabri and Willowra Nungarrayi, Nangala, and Nampijinpa as *kirda* and *kurdungurlu* for *ngapa* and *warnajarra* (two snakes) dreamings.

FIGURE 1

The Yungkurru Relationships

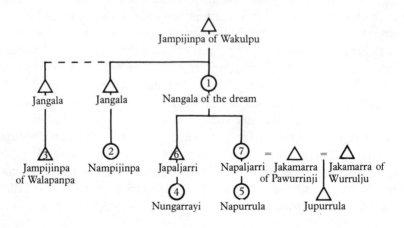

194

A similar end was achieved in the Neutral Junction *yawulyu* and in the course of the *yungkurru*. The dreaming range of one Jampijinpa was extended to the east while the ritual roles and relations of a Napurrula and Jupurrula were confirmed and two Jangala were incorporated. Central to this process was the dream of Nungarrayi, the men's desire to learn about it, and the women's resolve to incorporate senior men within the complex of *ngapa* and *yawakiyi* dreamings of the Wakulpu area.

During the *yungkurru*, a particular set of relations to a now deceased Nangala was stressed by all participants and ritual roles were allocated accordingly. This may be followed on the genealogy of Figure 1.

The Wakulpu Nampijinpa (2) were the daughters of the brother of the Nangala(1) (that is, nieces and joint *kirda* with the Nangala). The Jampijinpa (3) who sought instruction was the child of one of the classificatory brothers of the Nangala (1). He stressed the closeness of the sibling tie between the Nangala and his father. The relationship of the Nungarrayi (4) to the Napurrula (5), while appearing more tenuous, was consolidated during the *yungkurru* and is now accepted as a relationship sanctioned by the *jukurrpa*. The Nungarrayi, as we have seen, held Wakulpu as *kurdungurlu* through her father (see p. 119).

Napurrula's Warlpiri father's country, Pawurrinji, lay to the northwest, but she was *kurdungurlu* for the country of Nungarrayi because her mother was the sister of Nungarrayi's father (6). Although both Napurrula and Nungarrayi celebrated the dreamings of both parents, the country of Nungarrayi's mother and Napurrula's father lay some distance from where the women had lived much of their lives – that is, in the Wauchope/Devil's Marbles/Greenwood Station area. The relationship to country which they stressed was to the country of Napaljarri (7) and Japaljarri (6) – Nungarrayi's father's *kurdungurlu* country and Napurrula's mother's country. From these full siblings they traced back to Nangala (mother of these siblings), to the country for which Napurrula's mother and Nungarrayi's father were *kurdungurlu*. Napurrula called this country her *jaja* country: Nungarrayi claimed it as *kurdungurlu*. This was the country for which the Karlukarlu Nampijinpa were *kirda*. Thus the Nampijinpa, Napurrula and Nungarrayi were related directly to the Nangala and, as we saw (p. 111ff), co-residence had strengthened these relationships besides providing opportunities for continuity of ritual renewal of the land of their ancestors – in this case the Nangala's.

Throughout the *yungkurru*, Nangala was symbolized by a decorated *kurduru* (ritual pole) which was placed in the centre of all the displays of the men's decorated boards. It was she who provided the unity for the ritual participants – the dreamings of *ngapa* and *yawakiyi* and also the link between *yawakiyi* dreamings to the east and west of Wakulpu. This was achieved by the actual location of her dreamings, through her instructions during her lifetime to the Napurrula (5) and through the revelations of her Jampijinpa (3) father to Nungarrayi (4) in the dream.

Some twenty years ago, Nungarrayi dreamed of her father's mother's deceased father, Jampijinpa, referred to here as 'of Wakulpu' to distinguish him from Jampijinpa of Walapanpa, who lives at Warrabri and participated in the *yungkurru*. This Jampijinpa had revealed to Nungarrayi songs, designs and ritual procedure for his country, where the complex of *ngapa*, *wardingi* and *yawakiyi* dreamings are intertwined. This dream was central to the *yungkurru*, for it provided the *jukurrpa* sanction for the shift in emphasis of ritual relationships of the Nungarrayi and Napurrula, and the opportunity for Napurrula's half-brother Jupurrula and Jampijinpa of Walapanpa to be incorporated within the country and bestowed with important ritual status.

Through different channels each of the participants was able to establish a link to *yawakiyi* dreamings and therefore ritual status in the country of the Nangala and Jampijinpa. In the Alyawarra four-section system, the subsections of Nangala-Jangala and Napurrula-Jupurrula merge as Purla; and Nakamarra-Jakamarra and Nampijinpa-Jampijinpa merge as Kimarra. Thus the dreamings of the Nangala may be said to belong to the Purla/Kimarra patrimoiety (see Appendix 2). In establishing her relation to the Nangala/Jampijinpa *yawakiyi* dreaming, the Napurrula turned to the Alyawarra system.

This was possible because she had been incorporated within the Alyawarra *yawakiyi* dreaming in a ceremony. The Alyawarra *yawakiyi* ancestor was Purla/Kimarra, a different *yawakiyi* from the Kaytej and Warlpiri *yawakiyi*, which was Jangala-Nangala and Jampijinpa-Nampijinpa. The former was known as a 'dry' *yawakiyi* and in ritual designs was represented as red. The latter was represented as black and known as the 'cheeky' *yawakiyi*.

In the Alyawarra ceremony, Napurrula had been brushed down with leaves (as are sacred objects and persons on the first occasions of display) and shown red *yawakiyi* designs by the men. Although she is now said to 'know' this business, she may not yet sing of it or speak of the mythology, but she was empowered to use one of the designs during the *yungkurru*. By conferring this dreaming on her, the Alyawarra claimed her as an eastsider (her status had been ambiguous because of her Warlpiri father) and through her linked the 'dry' *yawakiyi* to the 'cheeky' *yawakiyi*. Her rights in the black *yawakiyi* were of long standing. As a child she remembered her mother's mother, Nangala, performing maintenance ceremonies for *yawakiyi*. Permission to pick *yawakiyi* was withheld until *kirda* and *kurdungurlu* had undertaken certain tasks in the country. One important ritual act was for the *kirda* to paint a *kurduru* (ritual pole) with the black juice of *yawakiyi* before the *kurdungurlu* visited the *yawakiyi* 'secret place'. Nangala had painted the Napurrula and told her to follow this *yawakiyi* of her *jaja* country because her father's country was too far away and was to be 'left alone' for a period of ritualized mourning after the 1928 massacres. To strengthen the claims, Napurrula's conception dreaming was in the country of Nangala. To mark this tie her mother's mother's brother had conferred a special name on her. During the *yungkurru* she played an important role in preparation and display of *yawakiyi* and thereby confirmed her ritual status. The Nungarrayi provided special instruction for her and announced 'Now it is your dreaming, you carry it on for me.'

The Jupurrula's link with *yawakiyi* was traced through both father and mother. Through his father he was *kirda* for *wardingi* and thus knew songs and designs for *yawakiyi* and of the rituals for Wakulpu. Through his mother and mother's mother he had similar kinship claims to those of the Napurrula. During the *yungkurru* he executed important ritual tasks in preparation and display and it was he who delivered the speech which made public the set of relations and ritual roles being celebrated in the *yungkurru*. The speech was simultaneously a mark of his status and a claim to status.

The country of Walapanpa, which Jampijinpa held from his father, was linked with the country Wakulpu and Waake by the activities of the *ngapa* ancestors. During the *yungkurru*, this Jampijinpa was given instruction by Nungarrayi and his dreaming range was extended from

197

Walapanpa into the country of Wakulpu. He had rights to participate through his relation to *ngapa* dreaming, but in the *yungkurru* he learnt more of the activities of *yawakiyi* and Wakulpu.

It is apparent in ceremonies such as the *yungkurru*, the Neutral Junction *yawulyu*, and many others I have recorded, that ritual allows people to exercise their responsibilities and thus to make public their rights in country. In their rituals the Warrabri Kaytej are maintaining a living system which can accommodate such realignments as those described here and in the section concerning the *jilimi* residents.

The first step taken by the women was to prepare the ritual objects and rehearse the ritual business for the ceremony. Each afternoon, on six consecutive days, the women sat in the shade of their ritual storehouse to grease and red-ochre hairstrings, boards and sticks, to paint their bodies and the boards, to bleach the head bands, to sing of country and to discuss the dreamings to be celebrated. On the first day they spread out the entire contents of their ritual storehouses and arranged each set of objects according to dreamings and sites. Thus objects associated with *yawakiyi* and *ngapa* were placed in separate stacks: one for Wakulpu, one for Waake and another for Karlukarlu.

The *kirda* and *kurdungurlu* for each discussed together which objects needed repair, what needed remaking, what should be taken to Hermannsburg and what should be left. Some objects they with-held: 'Leave them till next time,' Nungarrayi said.

The final decision of the senior women was that a new board should be made, a Nangala for Wakulpu, and that the Jupurrula, who was *kirda* for the *wardingi* dreaming which crosses *ngapa* and *yawakiyi*, should be asked to assist. He did cut the wood but for a number of reasons it was not fashioned into a *kurduru*. The women also planned to take two of their existing *kurduru*, one for Wakulpu, and one for Ngapajinpi, to Hermannsburg. Ultimately rather than appear too 'showy' and provoke jealous fights, they took only one board. The women decided, however, that the men should display three new boards: two for Wakulpu, and one for Ngapajinpi. These would be the 'brothers' of women's objects. (In fact the men made five new boards at Warrabri but only transported three of these to Hermanns-burg. At Hermannsburg they made a further three of local wood for public display. These were then left at the mission.)

After the women's decisions regarding the production and display of boards had been made, they were communicated to the men who waited at the edge of the *jilimi* area. The women immediately began greasing and measuring hairstring and preparing the central ritual item. This *kurduru* had been cut in Wakulpu country several months before by the Napurrula who had fashioned it. As the women worked, the *kurdungurlu* softly intoned the myth of the travels of *yawakiyi* and *wardingi*, both of which change colour as they travel along. *Wardingi* changes from white to red as witchetties do after rain, and *yawakiyi* changes from red to black. '*Yawakiyi* also needs rain,' women explain, and thus rain dreaming is also celebrated. The initial reddening of the *kurduru* was said to be for the *wardingi* and Alyawarra *yawakiyi*.

In the preparation of these objects it was apparent that the *jukurrpa* was both present and past. The *kurduru* was prepared and spoken of as a person. It was adorned with headband, feathers and body design; it was called *kirda* for the country but was also spoken of as aunty, granny and sister in an affectionate way. While painting the *kurduru*, the women sang of how in the *jurkurrpa* the young girls (Nangala) stood up and showed themselves at Devil's Marbles. This, they said, was just like the *kurduru* now.

The women sang of the name for the *kurduru*, Junkaji, of how he turned from *yawakiyi* to *ngapa*, from an old man to a young man, of how he stood up and observed all the ancestral activity of the Jampijinpa brothers in the area of Wakulpu. 'Follow Waake, Wakulpu and Junkaji,' he sang in various languages. *Junkaji* showed himself wearing various designs: he instructed others to show the straight-line design of Ngapajinpi (the lightning design which runs straight down the *kurduru*). He then sang the *yungkurru* songs for the display of the designs. In the preparation the women also sang of the way in which the ground vibrates as the dancing feet approach and how leaves rustle and then part, as if in a dream, to reveal the designs. Later, during the performance, when the men and women sang in unison for the actual display of the men's boards, it was these songs which were sung.

The women always distinguished between the *yungkurru* songs of Jampijinpa of Wakulpu and the *yawulyu* songs of Nangala also of Wakulpu. The former concerned display, the latter concerned the mythology. In the dream Jampijinpa had instructed Nungarrayi in the use of *yungkurru* songs and told her to take the business to the 'ring place', to build a *jungkayi* (bush shade) facing north for the men, and to hold the boards high above her head so that all could see. She was

Little Nakamarra and Nungarrayi watch as Napurrula shapes the wood from which she will make a ritual *kurduru* for the Wakulpu *yungkurru*.

then to make everyone sit down, as had the *kurdungurlu* birds at Wakulpu, to wait for *yawakiyi*. This display is marked with sorrow, for he shows himself only to die. The *kurdungurlu* for *yawakiyi* sang of the travels of the little birds who accompany *yawakiyi* and watch as he goes down at Wakulpu. Thus, in the singing, the women celebrated the interdependence of the roles of *kirda* and *kurdungurlu* and the inter-relations of the dreamings of *ngapa*, *wardingi* and *yawakiyi*. The *kurduru*, Nangala, symbolized the unity of this complex relationships and roles.

The actual ritual procedure of the displays which followed the preparation conformed to the instructions of Jampijinpa of Wakulpu. A group of women sat at the *yungkurru* ground to sing of the travels of *yawakiyi*, *wardingi* and of the travels of *ngapa* from Walapanpa to Wakulpu. These were songs which had been taught to Nungarrayi and Napurrula by their sibling parents. The men sat some distance away, where they were preparing their boards, and also sang of the travels of *yawakiyi*. They had prepared two boards, one of *yawakiyi* in red and one of *yawakiyi* in black. In each the little birds were flanking the travels of their *kirda*. The women sang of the impending display and were joined by the men who also sang, 'Listen for the dancing feet', 'Watch for the parting of the leaves'. At last the Nungarrayi appeared in the distance, carrying Junkaji high above her head as Jampijinpa had instructed. The *kurdungurlu* flanked her and swept the paths clean with leaves. Once she had planted the *kurduru*, she invited the Nampijinpa and Jampijinpa to approach it, but the men held back. The men then planted their boards on either side of the women's *kurduru*.

Napurrula presented the Junkaji *kurduru* with a stone from west of Wauchope, and Jupurrula made a speech about the unity of the dreamings. At this point the Hermannsburg Jangala arrived and was told that all those boards were of his country. Throughout, the Jampijinpa of Walapanpa was extremely emotional and, at the conclusion of this segment, he asked me to replay the section where the women had sung of his country. It was well into the night. The women returned to their ritual area where they slept and the men began discussing who should be invited for subsequent performances and revelations.

The next day the preparations continued. The men borrowed wool from me and began spinning 'hairstring'. After several hours' work with the wool the Jupurrula declared it a mess – which indeed it was – and passed it to his wife, who was the daughter of one of the senior Nampijinpa and therefore *kurdungurlu* for Wakulpu. The men spent the rest of the day working on the planks of a tea chest to make their boards and the women worked on the designs of their headbands. In both exercises the ways in which a limited set of symbols may be combined were apparent. The men's boards showed the line of *yawakiyi's* travel to Wakulpu, the small birds, the lines made by *wardingi* as he travelled across and with *yawakiyi*, the water hole at Wakulpu, the clouds which Junkaji saw at Walapanpa. The women used the same set of symbols as well as the round Devil's Marbles' design and the straight lines of Ngapajinpi. The Jupurrula drew the straight lines of *wardingi* and the meander line of *yawakiyi* on a piece of cardboard and gave it to his wife and sister. The women then rearranged the symbols to produce ten different headband designs.

On each subsequent day the men and women brought something new to the *yungkurru* ground; the women brought one of their *ngapa kurduru* on which they blew water before dancing; children were introduced to each of the new boards; Nungarrayi, Nampijinpa and Napurrula spent many hours leading the younger girls around the boards and *kurduru*; the men painted new boards and displayed them in the way Nungarrayi had related. They included details from the Jampijinpa's dream of how men must cut the fluff of certain grasses in order to decorate themselves properly. The displays, singing and designs continued to stress the inter-relations of the travels of *yawakiyi*, *ngapa* and *wardingi*, the sites of Waake, Wakulpu, Karlukarlu and Junkaji and the roles of the participants. Men and women continued to discuss which boards would be taken to Hermannsburg and which left behind. The women told the men not to show too much. 'Leave something for next time,' they cautioned. This of course was the position the women themselves had adopted.

When the men and women actually performed at Hermannsburg, it was short, intense and spectacular, but there was no hint of the way in which the dreamings had been woven together, nor of the negotiations which had taken place. The women painted and sang of their dreamings at Devil's Marbles. These were open songs of the humorous exploits of two old women, but they gave no hint of the complex of dreamings women own or those they had celebrated in the previous week.

202

Napanangka, *kurdungurlu* for Wakulpu, carries the men's boards on which are depicted the tiring journey of *yawakiyi*, as he neared Wakulpu. The faithful bird companions are represented by the dots on either side of the track.

The women danced around the men's boards which were already in place and then retired to sing for the men who were preparing to display more boards as the Jampijinpa had instructed. The women sang of the board they had decided not to show and of the 'sparking' of lightning at Junkaji. When the men were ready, the fires were built up and the women sang the men from the darkness to the light. The women flanked the men's dancing in of the new boards, danced around the boards, then removed them to return them to the men's shade. They danced holding the boards aloft so that all could see. 'Play with them,' the men shouted to the women. 'These are your dreamings now.'

Had I only observed the performance at Hermannsburg, where the ritual roles had already been sorted out, the displays perfected and the exchange of knowledge completed between men and women, it might have been possible to conclude that women were playing a supportive role. Like Spencer and Gillen, I might have expressed wonderment at the sight of women handling the male boards, but not speculated further. However, I had been able to observe, participate and record over a period of a week. To me it was apparent that in this *yungkurru* woman's ritual contribution to her society was critical to the continuity and renewal of the complex of land/people relationships. As the central focus and unifying force of the ceremony the Nangala was both a kinswoman and a symbolic representation. The *jukurrpa* sanction for the ritual action was provided by the dream of the Nungarrayi, in which her father's mother's father had not only revealed to her the structure of the inter-relations of the dreamings of his country, but had also instructed her in the way in which men and women should display knowledge. In the *yungkurru* men and women did indeed exchange knowledge in this way and in so doing shared the Dreamtime experience of the country of the Jampijinpa. The interdependence of male and female was strikingly apparent in the negotiations during the ceremony. The women needed men within their ritual group; the men needed the knowledge to back their claims to rights in the country.

Like most desert rituals I have recorded, the *yungkurru* and *yawulyu* discussed in this section were multi-purpose rituals. At one level the ceremonies provided the opportunity to establish relationships across space and to confirm the ritual status of the participants. It provided an opportunity to incorporate persons and to extend the range of one's knowledge and therefore rights. Men and women played distinctive roles, brought into the public arena but a fraction of the knowledge each celebrated separately, and acknowledged the contribution of the other. When the women picked up the men's boards at Hermannsburg it was with the knowledge that they had been instrumental in making this 'their country' and that they retained control of their own ritual world.

MAKING YOUNG MEN

I now wish to turn to women's participation in men's ceremonies, in order to explore women's role in and perception of initiation. Woman's ritual contribution to her society is not negated during initiation; rather, it provides a further occasion on which women affirm the importance of their active role in perpetuating the values of the *jukurrpa*.

One conceptual difficulty has been that woman's participation in initiation has been analysed in terms of her kinship to the initiate rather than in terms of her relation to the *jukurrpa*. Once the ritual correlates of kin roles are recognized, however, it is evident that these complement, extend and overlap with those of the men, to provide an avenue through which women assert their enduring role as nurturer of people and relationships within the context of affiliation to land. Thus 'sisters' and 'aunts' (that is, 'fathers' sisters') become joint *kirda* with the initiate as members of his patriline. 'Mothers' become the *kirda* for the boy's *kurdungurlu* country; the 'mothers-in-law', as members of the opposite patrimoiety, become *kurdungurlu* to the 'mothers'.

In allowing that women's ritual roles pervade the domain of initiation and structure much of their behaviour both at the intitiation ground and in their own separate camps at initiation, I am shifting the perspective from which women are seen as members of the boy's kin group[5] to one in which women are seen as ritual status-holders in their own right. In this approach, marriage arrangements become an integral part of the initiation for, like the act of circumcision, they are hedged in by ritual politics and serve to create new webs of relationships within the society. Thus, as well as documenting women's ritual role at initiation, I am also seeking to reintegrate marriage arrangements within that complex of rituals associated with initiation. These include men and women of various ritual statuses politicking to achieve both personal ends and favourable alliances between families and countries.

Through their ritual participation in segments of male rituals, through their own *yawulyu* staged independently of the men during initiation, and through the control they exercised over certain key decisions associated with initiation, women demonstrate some of the checks and balances which they may apply, even in the men's most glorious moments. Rather than a time when old men make unequivocal claims to control over women and youth, we find that initiation, like other rituals, is a time when women may make certain statements about the importance of their role in the presence of men. The right to make these statements reflects the complementary nature and negotiability of male-female relations.

Given the sexual politics of the society and the claims which men make at initiation, it is hardly surprising that male-oriented anthropologists who concentrate on male activities at initiation remain only dimly aware of the importance and the nature of women's contribution. As well as the obvious sex bias in reporting initiation, there is also the more difficult conceptual problem to be faced: if women are not negated as persons at initiation, how then are we to characterize initiation? How are we to assess and analyse the different perceptions and meanings that men's and women's worlds lend to their respective roles in initiation? Let us then look at women's activities during initiation and at what initiation achieves, what men and women seek to gain by participation and how these findings may be best assessed. In this way we find clues to the more general problem of characterizing women's role and status in a sex-segregated society.

Without doubt initiation is a time when the whole society pauses, when all resources are directed to the making of young men. However, while old men 'make' boys into young men through the ritualized death and rebirth of circumcision, and thereby celebrate the role of spiritual procreator, old women organize the feeding and nurturing of the boys, sit in all night vigils with the boys, stage *yawulyu* which celebrate the continuity of land and people associated with the boys, and nominate the mothers-in-law for the boys. In this way, women do not play a new role at initiation but rather continue to maintain the balance and harmony between individuals, families, groups and land. Women make manifest their rights – which flow directly from the *jukurrpa* – by providing the links between groups through marriage, by their ritual incorporation of outsiders, by their extension of knowledge through ritual action and, at initiation, by nominating the mother of the girl who the boy may ultimately marry.

In this discussion of the complementary nature of male and female worlds, I juxtapose the men's circumcision of the boy with the women's nomination of the mother-in-law. Both activities are acknowledged as key events in initiation ceremonies; both serve to crystallize male and female roles; both are political acts based on the ritual rights, responsibilities and ambitions of the participants. Therefore, while at initiation the values of the society are writ large, it is a *complex* of values which is celebrated.

I had many things to unlearn before I could begin to understand women's role at initiation. Also I had to learn much of community structure and family relations before many of the women's answers, when they started to come, constituted a coherent statement of women's role in initiation.

In the course of anthropological training I had been introduced to the literature regarding male initiation and although I had deliberately avoided viewing films of male secret-sacred material and the like, I still had a mental map of the activities associated with initiation. At first it seemed I knew more than Warrabri women were prepared to vocalize of certain aspects of the male activities. I lived in fear of using male-specific phrases or indicating in some way that I knew what was going on at the men's ground. Slowly and painfully I learnt that not only should I suppress most of what I had learnt but that, if I was to understand how women thought about initiation rituals, I had to begin from a new starting point.

I learnt that my knowledge was structured around events which were not of prime concern to women and certainly not the focus of their ritual activity. My knowledge of the male role and his perceptions of the female role were thus real obstacles which I am not sure I have yet completely transcended. I have however concentrated on the aspects of initiation which women told me were important and on which they lavished much time and consideration.

Over the Christmas holiday period of 1976-7, 1977-8 and 1979-80, I was able to observe and participate in three initiation seasons of Warrabri Warlpiri and Eastside Aranda. The east-west division of the

Warrabri population was starkly drawn. Warlpiri congregated at their ground on the western limit of the settlement while the Arandic east-siders, the Kaytej and Alyawarra, congregated to the extreme east. The first initiation cycle began shortly after I arrived at Warrabri and left me more confused than illuminated. While the anthropological portrayal of the men's role was confirmed in men's actions, I could not reconcile what I had seen and heard from women with Meggitt's[6] depiction of women's role. Parts of the ceremonies were familiar (such as when the 'mothers' carry the boys on their shoulders to the area where they are fed), but women appeared to be more involved than I had been led to expect; their activities were more structured and their attitude more reflective. Above all there appeared to be a high degree of co-operation between the sexes, more marked in the eastside initiations than the westside Warlpiri. I attempted to reconcile my mental map with my field data but my questions were answered with blank stares, embarrassed silence or shrugged off as nonsense.

My ignorance during the first round of initiations of all the actual relationships between the ritual participants certainly led me to ask questions which were either irrelevant, shameful or immediately marked me as an outsider white fella. I found that many of the questions I asked concerning the identity of participants and their relationships could not be answered; for example, the names of initiates cannot be spoken by women from the time of their capture to the time of the 'finish up' business described below.

Further, different sets of relatives were scattered in special purpose camps and difficult to locate: 'mothers-in-law' were under a speech taboo and, along with 'mothers', restricted to the area of their particular camp. I participated in one initiation cycle (which lasted over ten days) without knowing the identity, other than 'skin' terms, for the men and many of the women involved. At the time I felt as if the women were being pushed back and forth from camp to dancing ground in a totally insensitive way. By the next year, when I knew the participants and the overall procedure, the participation became a pleasure with much to speculate about, prepare for and discuss.

Some 'facts' still remain unknown. My blunder with the use of the English word 'bullroarer' had been a salutary lesson, but I persisted with Warlpiri dictionaries. I once tried to elicit the names of various nights of dancing and the participants: immediately one younger woman warned me in English, 'We can't say "initiation".' Ultimately by listening to women's conversations, I learnt the word for the period preceding the circumcision, but I stopped asking questions.

The Warlpiri women were interested to tell me about the night when 'the firestick was passed', but little else, except that I was welcome to attend and that I was 'a big help'. I decided to wait until the next year when I would know more of the people and their affiliations to land. At an eastside initiation, the Kaytej and Alyawarra, with whom I began to work during the first initiation period of 1976-7, sensed my frustration and gave me sound anthropological advice: 'Watch us, follow us, only go where your 'sisters' go, move with others, never alone. We'll explain it all to you afterwards,' they promised, 'all about the white fluff, the running-away and the finish-up.' Again I translated this within a male-oriented world: the only one for which I had a framework. Thus the 'white fluff' became the down of the men's body decorations, the 'running away' the time when women hurriedly leave the ground while men swing menacing bullroarers, while the 'finish-up' became the re-integration of the boy into the community at the completion of his bush exclusion. Fortunately I didn't ask questions based on these suppositions, for to have done so would certainly have set back my search for understanding even further.

The sequence of events described to me had nothing to do with the act of circumcision but, rather like the Warlpiri women's interest in the firestick, concerned key moments in the nomination of the mother-in-law. Only after I had attended and participated in another season of initiation was instruction offered. By then I had learnt how people were related, which country was which, and that women were not the pawns in male games but rather, daughters of the dreaming who proudly and forcefully made decisions concerning their lives and heritage. The instruction I was given during this second round of initiations centred on the role of 'mothers', 'sisters', 'aunts' and 'mothers-in-law' and the countries represented in the *yawulyu* rituals of these women.

The general structure and sequence of events at initiation are well-known to all women. When the boys will be caught, when women will dance, when men will dance, and when visitors from other places will arrive are all important events which affect all women and which are discussed at length in the women's camps. Actual ritual roles and ritual procedure, however, are not discussed openly. The role of a mother, a mother-in-law or a sister at initiation is known through participation in that role. Thus in order to learn the different roles which women play at initiation I had to participate in those capacities. I was fortunate to have been present at sufficient initiations, twenty in all, to have participated in all the major female roles. Where I was able to be present more than once, I was given extra instruction.

The way in which I was taught of the content of the ritual roles was the same way in which my teachers had learnt. Their knowledge of initiation was role-specific and built up over participation in successive initiations. The problem is that when one participates as a mother, one has limited access to the activities of the mother-in-law. This was one of the difficulties I confronted in the first season of initiation I attended: I simply did not know where people were or who they were. By January 1980 when I attended my third round of eastside and westside initiations, I knew much more of the country and the people. Also I had had time to reflect upon my data.

It was an important occasion in many respects. I had been invited by a woman whom I called 'mother' to attend the eastside initiation of her brother's son. This Penangke was a close friend with whom I had worked, camped and travelled and from whom I had learnt much over a period of four years. Because she was my 'mother' and teacher, I was able to ask her questions which would have been impossible to ask of a 'sister' or 'mother-in-law'. As my 'mother' she taught me the importance of 'growing-up' people and country. She was concerned for me to understand the purpose of the initiation and its importance for her and other women. She explained how in initiation people are 'turned around': that is, transformed from one sort of relative to another. I had heard men say this in relation to initiation when they had commented that women were 'turned around' to become mothers-in-law, but my 'mother' explained that boys were 'turned around' into men by the work of the 'sisters', 'mothers' and 'mothers-in-law' during the entire period of initiation, not just in the period preceding circumcision.

With this knowledge I was considered informed: I was red-ochred from top to toe and propelled into ritual action which I had previously only observed from a distance. Afterwards the women said, 'Now do you know the answers to those questions you were asking last time?' Did I? I certainly knew there was more to being a mother than preparing food. The eastside men thanked me for participation, as had the westside men in previous years, and commented they were proud of their 'sister' who sat all night or danced all night, as was the case. It was, they said, 'a big help' and from then on the families of those boys have treated me with special care and affection. My own son had been 'claimed' by the eastside Alyawarra men in the throwing ceremony (see p. 214) three years before, and his maturity now became the subject of mild joking amongst men and women. From asking questions I was being asked questions: Would I hold onto him? Who would push him out? Who would catch him? It was time *I* began to consider such questions.

Although many decades separate Spencer and Gillen's and Strehlow's observations from mine, the Arandic initiations I attended in the summers of 1976-7, 1977-8 and 1979-80 had much in common, in terms of male activities, with the Arandic circumcision ceremonies outlined by these early anthropologists. Similarly, but more strikingly, the male role in the westside Warlpiri initiations I attended closely paralleled those Meggitt witnessed in the 1950s. Regional variation in both Aranda and Warlpiri initiations – a feature noted by Spencer and Gillen with reference to the northern Aranda, and by Meggitt with reference to the Warumungu influence on Warlpiri at Phillip Creek – partly accounts for the differences between our observations.[7]

We also need to note the nature of the changes in the world of Alyawarra-Aranda and Warlpiri outlined in Chapter II. Perhaps two of the greatest changes in initiation are the shortening of the period of bush exclusion for the novices (in order to meet the requirements of white educationalists) and the absence of an extended 'bush tour', in which boys are shown and taught of country.

At Warrabri I had a unique opportunity not only to note variations within Alyawarra-Arandic and Warlpiri ceremonies but also to observe and to probe the differences between eastside and westside ritual practice. No Kaytej initiations took place during my stay at Warrabri, but my Kaytej women friends participated in eastside initiations as close relatives of the Alyawarra boys who were initiated. On one occasion, westsiders who were initiating a lad who held country which was jointly maintained by Kaytej and Warlpiri, were assisted by several of the lad's Kaytej 'sisters'. All preparation was undertaken in the Kaytej camp and the women only joined the westsiders for the dancing. On all other occasions Kaytej stressed their

Arandic heritage.

Because my focus is on women's ritual worlds, a thorough exploration of differences and variations between eastside and westside initiations is outside the scope of this work. However, in order to explore women's ritual role and contribution during initiation, it is necessary to sketch the structure of initiation for Warlpiri and Aranda as I have come to understand it. Although my discussion of eastside initiation is based on Alyawarra initiations, the data also apply to Kaytej, who share most of the initiation procedures outlined here.

Firstly, there are similarities between the two cycles which point to critical aspects of women's role and status in initiation. Secondly, the descriptions of Spencer and Gillen, Strehlow and Meggitt - while consonant with my observations and understanding of male roles and perspectives during initiation - contrast directly with my understanding of women's role and perceptions. Meggitt treats women's participation as peripheral to the main purpose of initiation, while Spencer and Gillen admit to being at a loss to explain women's presence and access to certain objects.[8] Not one of these anthropologists records women's views on the male initiation rituals and neither records women's perceptions of their own ritual activity during initiation.

This outline of initiation is not intended as a full description of all the events, decisions and negotiations which occur during this time of the year. I have chosen to focus on certain aspects of initiation – aspects which women themselves underscored as important - in order to dispel a few misconceptions about women's role and status during initiation and to highlight others. In particular I wish to illustrate the way in which women's independent ritual life continues to provide a context for women's action and decision-making and how these ritual activities integrate with those of the men. Certain decisions, such as the choice of circumcisor, are taken independently by the men; others, such as the nomination of a mother-in-law, are taken independently by the women. But these choices and decisions are interwoven in the ritual action of both men and women so that action moves back and forth between men and women. Much is subject to negotiation, for young men cannot be made without the co-operation of women, and men recognize this. Finally, in this outline of initiation, I hope to show that a fixed model of man-to-man ritual negotiations is inappropriate. Men and women, young and old, engage in ritual politics and express preferences in diverse ways.

The initiation season at Warrabri usually coincides with the school holidays, although this constraint bears more heavily on Warlpiri than on the Arandic eastsiders at Warrabri or the Warlpiri at Yuendumu and Willowra. It is probably yet another example of the way in which Warrabri Warlpiri have come to accommodate white institutions. Warlpiri begin in November and continue through until February-March; eastside initiations tend to begin after the Warlpiri in January and to run until March-April. Aranda aim to coincide with the stand-down period in the cattle industry and the height of the holiday season when Europeans are thin on the ground.

Within the family camps, husbands and wives discuss the forth-coming initiation season. A mother's decision that her son is ready must be secured before any plans can be made. She assesses his maturity, both physical and emotional, and the availability, or possible availability, of potential mothers-in-law that coming year. Generally there is agreement between a couple and negotiations begin with the 'mother's brothers' for the Warlpiri, and the older 'brothers' for the Aranda.[9] At times women will withhold permission and this is respected by men. I have seen this occur, and so, Mary Laughren tells me, has she at Yuendumu. Ultimately, however, a mother will agree because it is in her interests to have adult sons.

The timing of an initiation is a nice example of the politics of ritual decision-making. Women should appear reluctant to lose their sons; they should cry and worry for their safety. In practice, boys have usually been living in all-male peer groups for some time and are the bane of everyone's existence, mothers included. A mother should mourn the loss of a son – but in fact she gains much through the initiation of her son: a relationship with the woman he calls mother-in-law and whom she calls *wankili*; a new status both as *ngarrka parnta* (man-having), as one who has reared a son to physical and emotional maturity, and an entitlment to access to ritual knowledge. While women joke about holding their sons until they are too old for initiation, they also state that boys should be 'pushed out' before they are too heavy to pick up. This may be because women must carry their sons on their shoulders during certain period of initiation.

Today Warlpiri boys are being initiated younger in an attempt, it seems, to quieten them down.[10] Alyawarra initiates were on average several years older than Warlpiri boys, a fact which probably reflects both a difference between the two initiation procedures and the differential impact of the changes of the last century on Alyawarra and Warlpiri. Women often object that a boy is too young and may even seek the co-operation of school authorities. Because after initiation boys attend school irregularly (although they are returned to the settlement in time to resume school), schools are sometimes sympathetic to this appeal.

In 1977 my son was quite unexpectedly grabbed, along with several of his 'brothers', and thrown into the air by Alyawarra men. They regarded me very seriously as they did it and the women encouraged me to participate in the 'sending of the power' hand action which they were employing. From then on matters concerning the readiness of my son for initiation were discussed with me by women and instruction was begun in how I should plan the timing of his initiation.

This Arandic mode of marking ceremonially the initiates for future years by the 'throwing up in the air' ritual is described by Spencer and Gillen[11] as a separate ritual for the Finke Aranda. In the Alyawarra-Arandic initiations I saw at Warrabri, it was incorporated into the week of ritual activity which precedes the actual circumcision of the boys (not the ones who are thrown). The throwing in the air is an indication that there are many more young boys to follow the present crop, that the boys thrown are entering a new period of their lives and will soon be initiated, and that they should begin to absorb the power of country – a strengthening process welcomed by youth, women and men alike. On the second last night of the initiation the young boys are thrown high into the air by the assembled men and then bounced onto the painted shields on the ground, while all the women stand, motioning upwards with their hands and trilling. Afterwards the men, seated within the men's wind break area, paint the boys with simple white-line designs.

Generally several boys of the same 'skin' are initiated at the one ceremony. Women are happy to see a large assemblage of people, because it provides greater scope for their political dealings in finding a suitable mother-in-law and an opportunity to extend and share the range of their ritual knowledge with other women. A large gathering also means the presence of many classificatory relatives for each of the boys, with the possibility of staging a big show and of thereby establishing for the boy a wide set of age-mates.

Where an initiation will be held is subject to many factors. In the past they were held on the country which was celebrated in the rituals associated with the initiation. Today much of the ceremonial activity occurs on the settlements within walking distance of the main camps. Ritual instruction is thus becoming increasingly separated from actual country. For Warrabri Warlpiri this presents a greater problem than for other Warlpiri who are closer to their own country (Willowra or Yuendumu Warlpiri for example). Further, because a woman must be present to be nominated as a mother-in-law, the staging of ceremonies at places such as Warrabri has ramifications for marriage. Warrabri Warlpiri, for example, with their choice limited to those Warlpiri present, must enter into less than correct marriages or marry eastside women. All these options are exploited.[12]

While Warrabri Warlpiri tend to be initiated at home, Aranda travel many miles to initiate, even beginning in one country and finishing up in another. This reflects both their greater mobility between station and settlement and their proximity to their own country. Over the past few years the larger ceremonial gatherings associated with Alyawarra initiation have tended to occur at Warrabri. On the one hand, there are practical advantages to Warrabri. The store can provide, in theory at least, for larger numbers than can a cattle station store - and the politics of the relations between cattle station managers and Aboriginal workers are changing rapidly. On the other hand, the eastsiders of Warrabri are beginning to take a new political stand on the ownership of the country and are turning to the rituals associated with initiation to stake their claims to the area.[13]

Like the decision to initiate or not in a particular season, the catching of the boys who are to be initiated is one where normative statements need to be balanced against actual behaviour. Men say the capture is a surprise which frightens, shocks, causes women to hide their heads, young boys to quiver and quake, and younger children to believe they will be beheaded if they look up. In fact, everyone knows ahead of time who will be taken and about what time the catch will occur. The boys can only be caught when all is ready for the initiation to begin and to this end mothers often keep their sons by them so that they are available for the catch. Men pass this off by saying women are trying to shield their sons.

While the fiction must be maintained that the catch is a surprise, it cannot be too much of a surprise, and in fact one genuine surprise catch I saw - the Warlpiri grabbed an Alyawarra boy - aroused the

Alyawarra to righteous indignation backed by serious sanctions. Some warning is necessary because the red-ochred captors, emitting blood-curdling cries to alert all to their presence and the need to hide, immediately parade the boys through the camps. For several hours before a catch, if it occurs in day time, older women will be found sitting quietly in their camps waiting. They forgo hunting or shopping, for the danger of being on the wrong side of the red-ochred men is too grave.

After the catch, both Warlpiri and Alyawarra women dance briefly at a 'half-way' initiation ground. Because the procedure is so different in each case I shall treat them separately, beginning with the Warlpiri. As soon as the cries die down, the Warlpiri 'mothers' emerge and follow in the direction of the cries to a ground that lies between the camps and the main initiation ground used later in the week. There the women dance on the ant hill 'to soften the soil', then return quickly to their camps; they do not emerge again until evening to join in the action with the men. In their own camp – which is often a special-purpose camp constructed on the initiation side of the major camps – the women prepare their ritual paraphernalia, their elaborate body paintings, and the feathers and food for the evening.

This is the first occasion on which women paint-up specifically in connection with initiation and a clear hierarchy emerges. The designs of the mother (that is, those of the country for which the boy is *kur-dungurlu*) are widely used, the mother reserving the most spectacular for herself. Her actual daughter, the sister of the initiate and one who shares the boy's ritual affiliations, is given special attention during the ritual preparation and, while she is expected to work as *kurdun-gurlu* to her mother, she is also given instruction. On later occasions, the visitors from whom a mother-in-law may be chosen are singled out for special attention, and the country of the boy's patriline is celebrated. But on this first day it is clearly the mother who is in charge.

That evening the women wait until they are called down to the ground. They take their swags and rest nearby until called over by the men. Fires are lit by the women, one for each boy, and the women sit in groups behind their own fire. The men send small concave boards to the mothers, who 'hold' them until the end of the ceremonies. During the night the men sing of the travels of the two kangaroos and the women dance, following the songs. 'Mothers', 'mothers-in-law' and 'fathers' sisters' dance in the middle, while 'sisters' and 'mothers' mothers' dance to the side. The 'sisters' dance with a side-ways action and call out to the 'brothers', while the others dance in a tight formation with the fire stick. At dawn the women farewell the boys and leave.

During a Jungarrayi initiation in the 1977-8 season, I shared a swag with a close 'sister', a Nungarrayi, who as each song was sung began to whisper to me of the meaning of the words, which she claimed to have learnt from her father. I have not had the opportunity to compare these interpretations with those offered to a male anthropologist, but it seemed to me she offered full details of the purpose and intent of the kangaroos, the direction of their travels and the places they visited. Finding someone whispering explanations in my ear during a night of dancing became a familiar mode of instruction from Warlpiri. Women spoke of things which they would not or could not discuss away from the action. Alyawarra women on the other hand were more concerned that I should simply be present, for then I would 'know'.

For Alyawarra boys the men manufacture less of a surprise, and throughout the initiation period all parties stated they were – and they appeared to be – well-informed as to what would happen next. The men's ritual storehouse is just visible from the women's *jilimi* and the women can see the comings and goings of the men between it and the initiation ground. All around are the leafy poles of the initiation ceremonies of previous years as reminders of the boys made into men. The whole atmosphere in the camps is one of a dearly awaited and cherished time of year when, although much hard work is required, many families can congregate and share ritual business.

Unlike Warlpiri initiations, which are large sprawling affairs with a momentum of their own, Alyawarra initiations are very tight family affairs where there is a clear notion of what is correct and much criti-cism if this is not realized. Women will leave the initiation ground if they are dissatisfied, or refuse to dance if the ground is not cleared properly. Such things happen rarely because Alyawarra men and women, while fulfilling their own sex-specific tasks, remain in con-stant communication with each other throughout initiation.

The action following the catching of the Alyawarra boys is a good example of this level of co-operation and of the difference in atmos-phere between westside and eastside initiations. Usually the boys are caught mid-morning, there being no real fear on the part of the Alyawarra that whites may stumble upon the red-ochred party. From their camps the women watch as the men prepare for the next stage of the ceremony. Finally, an older brother calls out to the women that all is ready for them. The women of the mother's *jilimi* then come forward in a wide line and place bags of flour and hair-string on the road leading to the initiation ground. Two older brothers come forward and take the flour to the group of men who have returned from the nearby ground. The 'sisters' of the initiate then go straight to the camp of the mother of the future mother-in-law of the boy. They dance on the way and when they reach the camp they pick up the girl and call out 'la-la-la'. They then take her to the mother of the initiate, who holds on to her in the front row of the group of assembled women.

The party of men and women then proceed to the ground. The men carrying flour lead the way, under the guidance of the 'older brothers', while the women, with the mother and mother-in-law in front, follow. 'Sisters' call back and forth to the 'brothers'. The women are supervised by a senior 'mother's mother' who acts as mistress of ceremony throughout the coming week of ritual business. As they travel, the party pauses, the men place the flour between them and the women, the women dance briefly, and then the men retrieve the flour and continue on their way. When they arrive at the ground, which is east of the camps, the flour is put on the ground in front of the waiting party of men, who place emu feathers on top of the pile. The women dance briefly and retire to about fifty yards away. From there they watch the 'older brothers' dance and accompany the performance with the upward cupped hand action of 'lifting up the business' and 'sending out the power'. The latter gesture is often used by women in their own ceremonies, but the former is specific to male initiation. Women sometimes noted that the way in which they 'lift up' the ceremonial activity is similar to the 'growing up' of children and the 'coming up' of a mirage on the horizon. After the third man has danced they return to the main camp.

The nomination of the mother-in-law is a decision which all agree is a woman's decision and specifically that of the mother, who must like the person chosen. Men ponder aloud who will be chosen and although there are obviously limits within which the mothers will choose, the actual decision is not known until morning. Ideally the girl should be under twenty, not yet married, or if married, have no children. It is an opportunity, really the first in the context of initiation, for a young woman to play an important role and she must therefore be someone who is willing to learn. Some girls are never chosen because they marry, absent themselves at the time when mothers-in-law are being chosen, or are just too busy 'playing around'. Therefore, although a mother may wish to choose a certain girl and have discussed the matter with the girl's mother, the girl may exercise her options by being sick on the day or merely absent. (This is a tactic also employed by Warlpiri women on the night when mothers-in-law are nominated in the Warlpiri ritual cycle.)

These considerations reflect personal preferences, but there are important factors of ritual and country which guide women in their choice. As one woman explained to me, 'We have to keep the families straight.' Women are engaged in the process of establishing and maintaining reciprocal links between groups. In women's discussions of initiation they imply that marriage exchanges achieve this end (see Appendix 2).

The evening of the day of the ceremony in which the mother-in-law is nominated further demonstrates the joint responsibilities men and women share in initiation. At dusk the women proceed to the initiation ground, where they sleep until about midnight. On the call of *'wadja'* they move to where the men are assembled at a small windbreak. On each side of the 'mothers' and 'mothers-in-law', who dance in a tight formation in the middle, the 'sisters' and 'mothers' mothers' dance with limp arm and a special sideways knee-jump step. The 'sisters' call out across the space and are answered by the 'brothers'. The mothers dance, holding the 'mothers-in-law', who are said to be 'hanging on' for support. As they dance their dancing feet make a track towards the men similar to the east-west groove made by the male *kurdungurlu* through the initiation ground.[14]

At about 1 a.m. several of the men light a fire to the west behind the women. The women then separate in two groups on either side of the ground, a blanket is placed on the ground in front of the men, and shields, painted with the country of the mother, are laid on the blanket. The mother and mother-in-law then sit facing the east on one blanket. A 'brother' brings a firestick and gives it to the mother, who passes it to the mother-in-law, while the 'sisters' hold a torch to light the mother-in-law's face. The 'mothers-in-law' and 'mothers' dance together briefly and then a 'brother' puts white fluff on the mother-in-law's head. The 'sisters' then take up a position between the man and the mothers-in-law, and remain there for the rest of the evening, twirling a small head scarf (in the past, a bunch of tails from a marsupial possum). Calls echo back and forth to the 'brothers', who answer *'wadja'*. At dawn, when the men announce they are ready, messengers are sent out who then escort the boys, arm in arm, to the blanket. They sit down before the 'mothers-in-law', who rub their ochred bodies against the boys.[15] This was explained to me as being a parallel to the *yawulyu* practice of women rubbing sacred objects over their bodies to absorb their power. The boys are then taken to a cleared space near the men, where the women fall upon them, while the men recite a couplet about growing hair (i.e. maturing).[16] The women then depart, 'mothers-in-law' being supported by 'mothers'. The 'mothers' and 'mothers-in-law' prepare separate camps: the latter, who are considered to be in an extremely dangerous state, look to their own mothers to feed and care for them. Movement is restricted for 'mothers' and 'mothers-in-law', and the latter are under a speech taboo until the 'finish up' ceremony. 'Mothers' are required to be red-ochred from this time until after the circumcision and to sleep near the initiation ground.

It is apparent from this description that the role of 'sister' as *kurdungurlu* is critical to the ritual action; indeed the dedication with which a 'sister' dances for her 'brother' is always the subject of comment and something for which a 'brother' must show gratitude in later years. Warlpiri 'sisters' also work, but they do so by preparing tea, transporting it to the initiation ground and calling out all night. These differences are marked in what women call the 'half-night' dancing which follows the first full night for Warlpiri and Aranda.

After the first full night of dancing there is a break of several days which, the Warlpiri say, allows the men to 'find' the new initiation ground and which the Alyawarra women say is long enough to allow the leaves to dry on the break which the men construct at the new initiation ground. For Alyawarra it is also a time when visitors begin arriving from faraway places. 'Family' is stressed throughout and the 'visitors' who arrive to witness the event, to share and extend the ritual range of countries celebrated, are called 'the strangers'.

The real influx, however, does not occur until later in the week. Women also begin stockpiling food during this period. In the Warlpiri camp there is discussion about when the dancing will resume, how long it will last, the need to be finished before the next pay day and the influx of drunks. All women discuss the weather (both heat and rain are regarded unfavourably), the condition of the dancing ground, the people who will visit, and their stocks of fat, ochres and feathers.

Warlpiri women wait in their camps until they are called down to the initiation ground. Each night they prepare the tea and damper and each night they paint up. During every Warlpiri initiation I have attended there has been at least one occasion when, although the women were ready, the men called off the night's dancing. Women grumble but take no further action. The initiation ground is out of sight and it is difficult for them to determine whether or not the postponement is for ritual reasons or others, such as the presence of drunks. While the Warlpiri often continue despite interruptions from drunks, eastside women refuse to dance if disrupted in such a way. Neither eastside nor westside women felt constrained to attend every night's dancing, although a woman who never attends is called lazy.

The *yawulyu* which Warlpiri women staged prior to these 'half-nights' of dancing (from dusk to 9 p.m.) emphasized different lines of descent and countries. I have already discussed painting up of mother's country on the first night. On subsequent nights the 'sisters' of the boy display the designs of their *kirda* country. In this they are assisted or led by the 'fathers' sisters' with whom they are joint *kirda* with the boys. Women who are visiting from other countries are incorporated at the level of patrimoiety or semi-patrimoiety and thus are able to extend their knowledge and ritual range. For Aranda, where the mother of the mother-in-law and the mother of the boy are in the same semi-patrimoiety and therefore potentially joint *kirda* for a country, or *kirda* for countries in a 'company relationship', the women's ceremonies at initiations are a chance to affirm and establish ties of affinity and ritual roles of *kirda* and *kurdungurlu* (see Appendix 2).

For Warlpiri women these *yawulyu* have an added importance. In their painting-up and discussions over this period, the range of possible mothers-in-law is narrowed down and finally the mother makes her preference known by the order in which the women are painted. The mothers-in-law must fulfil certain requirements but these are not as clearly articulated as they are by the Alyawarra. Warlpiri do achieve a balance between countries and families in the exchanges, which are a consequence of initiation promises, but my data for them are drawn from extant marriages. In the Aranda case I am drawing

221

on actual initiations I witnessed or on direct statements from women. During the dancing of these 'half-nights', the women dance in different formations as they follow the travels of which the men sing. As each new song is begun the dancing revives, until the last song when women say it is 'nearly time' and prepare to leave. When the last song is sung, some return to the main camp while the mothers go to a nearby special-purpose camp.

This quiet and informed retreat of Alyawarra women is in direct contrast to that of Warlpiri women, who leave amid cries and the howl of bull-roarers. There is also a marked difference in the way in which women approach the male ceremonial ground. Warlpiri women are called through in stops and starts, whereas Alyawarra women wait within earshot of the men and then proceed directly to the ground. Dragging leaves and calling, the 'mothers' run through the initiation ground of the previous year where the leafy poles are still standing, then walk down the centre of the new initiation ground, where the male *kurdungurlu* have prepared a long east-west groove. This leads from a single fire at the west end to where the men are seated at the east end. 'Mothers' and 'mothers-in-law' dance along this line to the place where they state the boy is 'damaged' (that is, circumcised). The leaves which the women drag are placed on the men's wind-break. When visitors arrive they, too, are required to 'open the path' by dragging through leaves.

While the initiate of the eastside ceremonies is absent during this period, the Warlpiri lad is present throughout and it is to him that much of the women's attention is directed. After each night of dancing the Warlpiri women take the boy to a clearing some fifty to a hundred metres away, near the main camp, where they feed him. He is carried aloft by 'mothers', who then sit with the boy on their lap while the 'sisters' feed him and the 'father's sister' performs certain rituals to ensure his growth within the country which she and the 'sister' share with him. There is a clear statement here that the affiliation to his mother's country and the role he will play as *kurdungurlu* is interwoven with his responsibility to his *kirda* country. In many respects these rituals evoke the symbolism of birth which, like the feeding of the boys, is an exclusively female activity. There are the smokey leaves and the exhortations to grow strong. It seems to me also to be an indication that women are co-operating in the symbolic rebirth of initiation. A 'sister' stands at the edge of the group of women and calls back and forth to the men. When the women are finished the boy is returned to the men by the 'sisters' and all the women hurriedly return to camp.

Although the Alyawarra women do not engage in a feeding ritual with the boys, they do have a night which achieves the same ends. At the conclusion of the 'half-nights' (usually three or four), and when sufficient 'strangers' have arrived, the boy is ceremonially returned to the initiation ground. Following further ritual (described below), the 'mothers' and 'mothers-in-law' sit in an all-night vigil with him.[17] During this night, when the naked boy sits clasped on the lap of the mother, with his mother-in-law seated behind, it is clear that he is being claimed as the child of women: that women bore him and women will marry him.

Before women engage in this vigil there is the 'getting of the somebody' ceremony by the men, when firesticks are whirled into the air.[18] Women are present throughout and thus although the 'somebody' is the father-in-law and probable circumcisor of the boy, the women continue with their care of the boy and statements that they have chosen a mother-in-law. Women state emphatically that the 'somebody' is not of the same family as the mother-in-law they have nominated. We have therefore an interesting conundrum. If the mother-in-law and father-in-law are not husband and wife, does the boy have two possible marriages lines? Both will be within the same semi-patrimoiety but may be of different countries. I tried to elicit terms distinguishing a marriage which was the result of the nomination of a mother-in-law as against one resulting from the nomination of a father-in-law, but I met only with puzzlement. 'It depends if she likes him and he likes her. It depends where they live,' was all women would say. Using my genealogies I explored the puzzle with women whose marriages were said to have been arranged and which entailed an age difference between husband and wife great enough for the marriage to be the result of mother-in-law bestowal as described here. Again I met with shrugs. I tried with the young women whom I knew had been nominated and who had daughters. This was more promising but women wisely said, 'Who knows what will happen tomorrow? People are getting lazy.' It remains a puzzle but one which I think illustrates that all is not fixed, that there is room for choice, even for youth, since the widest possible range of people is implicated through ritual action.

The penultimate night of initiation for Warlpiri women is when the choice of mother-in-law is made public to the men. Throughout the 'half-night' dancing the 'mothers' have danced with the firestick, which a 'sister' rekindles each night; on this occasion the mother passes it to the mother-in-law, who then dances holding it. Although the range of possible women is known, the actual woman who will contract to provide a daughter is not nominated until about 2 a.m., during the women's dancing. Since it must be a woman who is present, women will often say they were intended, but were not chosen, because they fell asleep and did not dance, or because they were ill and did not attend. There is much speculation about who will be passed the firestick, and different reasons are advanced in support of different choices. Once again women insist it is the mother's choice and that both personal and ritual considerations are important. The mother of the mother-in-law may support her daughter by her presence, but her role is not institutionalized as it is with the Alyawarra.

The women's responsibility to dance is taken over by the men on the final night of initiation, when the leafy poles are paraded, the choice of circumcisor is made public, and the boy is actually cut. For Warlpiri women this is an occasion to enjoy spectacular male theatre and then to retire early; for Alyawarra women it is another all-night stand which involves further action from them. This night is well-documented and I do not intend to further discuss the male role.[19] Rather, I wish to illuminate the role played by women.

During the dancing with the long poles, the 'mothers' and 'mothers-in-law' are seated, facing the dancing, in the middle of the group of men, while 'sisters' assist in the stripping of the poles. After, the women retire to a nearby camp where they wait until just before dawn. Calls echo back and forth, the vibrations as the poles hit the ground are felt and the calls of *'wadja'* rend the air as the hairstring is unwound from the boy. Bullroarers can be heard.

On a signal from the men that the boy has been cut, the 'mothers' and 'mothers-in-law' move quickly to the men's wind-break. The leafy poles, almost completely stripped, are now in two long rows running from the single fire to the ground where the women danced. The women run the length of the ground to the waiting men, whom they rub against, breast to back, and brush down with leaves. The men click their fingers and assure the women that the boy is all right. The women then run back to the place where they have danced, to the place where they say the 'damage' was caused. Here they kneel and rub out the traces of the dancing feet. 'That,' one woman said to me, 'is the main thing.' The 'mothers' then escort the 'mothers-in-law' away to a secluded place where they remain until the 'finish up'.

I have only seen this ritual with Alyawarra, although Warlpiri women tell me they have a 'finish up'; the only Warlpiri ceremony I have seen entailed a rather casual exchange of clothing between the 'mothers'. For the Alyawarra of Warrabri, the 'finish up' occurs within a week of the actual circumcision. The women say the 'mothers-in-law' do not like being away from the camp for long periods and the children of other women who are with them want to return to the settlement.

On the appointed night, at dusk, the 'mothers' sit in a semi-circle facing east. The boy is brought and placed in front of them. A 'sister', with the firestick hidden behind her back, approaches from the north and plants the stick. The 'mothers-in-law', bearing gifts, then appear from the north and run around the assembled group. The 'mothers' place food on the ground in front of them, which is then distributed to the 'mothers-in-law' under the supervision of a 'mother's mother'. All the while the 'mothers' clap in the 'hollow lap' style used during certain of their own rituals. (One hand is cupped in the lap and the other cupped hand is brought down on it to make a 'clop' sound.) The 'mothers-in-law' rub against the boy's back and then turn around to rub the 'mothers' breast to breast. Together the women blow out the firestick. In this action the boy is said to be 'turned around'. He is now a young man. He now has a mother-in-law, not just a 'cousin'; he now has responsibilities to these women which are of a different order from when the women last sat with him. From then on all taboos on speech and movement are removed. The women have 'finished up'. They have played their part in making a young man.

The role I have outlined for women at initiation is one which entails both separate ritual action and co-operative ventures for which women are essential. There is room for male-female negotiations, and key decisions are by no means the prerogative of men. Women are continuing to assert their importance as nurturers of central relationships, but they do so within the context of their affiliation to country and are guided by their ritual responsibilities. They are not merely members of the boys' kin group, they are also descendants of the *jukurrpa*. Male ritual action at initiation does not negate or undermine that relationship.

My depiction of women's role is a far cry from the image of terrified women running away from men who make total claims to women during initiation. In fact, women are also engaged in the business of making young men but in a distinctively female way. The feeding, the vigils, the choice of mother-in-law, all indicate that women continue to care for the boy's well-being. The *yawulyu* and ritual action suggest that women do so on the basis of their relationship to the dreaming. The use of designs, the rubbing of bodies, all indicate that women are not subsumed by men but themselves help to transmit the power of the *jukurrpa*. The choice of mother-in-law points to the continuing importance of women's decisions in maintaining society.

Meggitt's analysis of initiation focuses on the way in which men are establishing relationships with each other in a ritual context. Strehlow's interest in *tjuringa* ownership leaves women as the cooks and keepers of the home fire. Spencer and Gillen are at a loss to explain the presence of women during initiation, although they do allow that women have a role. The role I suggest women play at initiation is consonant with the image of themselves women project in their own ritual and with the sexual politics of a sex-segregated society. It also completes the model of women's ritual domain which I have been constructing throughout the book.

Not only has the sex of the fieldworker obscured the importance of women's ritual role in male initiation, so also have the questions ethnographers characteristically have asked. As I explained earlier in this section, I had to learn how to ask questions; I was 'turned around' and refocused. While the accepted frameworks explain male dominance of women and children in terms of the gerontocracy and polygyny, I have argued that women are not pawns in male marriage games and are not the uninitiated of their society.

We have seen that women are autonomous, independent ritual actors who actively participate in the creation, transmission and maintenance of the values of their society. These values do not constrain woman to the domestic round of child-rearing and limit her contribution to her society to economic considerations. Aboriginal women are the proud nurturers of people, land and the complex of relationships which flow from the *jukurrpa*.

NOTES

1. Roheim 1933; Hiatt 1971; Munn 1973; Bern 1979a, 1979b.

2. *Yungkurru* appears to be the Warlpiri pronunciation of the Arandic *ingkura*. Spencer and Gillen (1899:271ff) write of *engwara*, Strehlow (1947:100ff) of *iŋkura* and Alyawarra women at Warrabri also use *ingkura*. Although in different orthographies, it is the same term and refers to a final, or near final, stage of male initiation. The *yungkurru* I saw in 1977 was not associated with initiation ceremonies. The only resemblances of the *yungkurru* to the *ingkura* were that, like Spencer and Gillen's (1899:324) ceremony, *yungkurru* is a way of introducing change while maintaining tradition and like Strehlow's (1947:100) ceremony, the *yungkurru* focused upon an important totemic site. It is not unusual for Warrabri Kaytej, although members of the Arandic language family, to use Warlpiri forms. Women often use *yawalyu*, not the Arandic *awelye*, but this glosses the same ceremonies. I have not been able to find a reference to *yungkurru* in Warlpiri vocabularies or from field linguists (Laughren, personal communication). Thus although I can find ceremonies of the same name in the literature I can find none which is similarly structured. I am therefore left with *yungkurru* as the Warlpiri form which glosses a ceremony which is not described in the literature.

3. Spencer & Gillen 1899:350.

4. *Ibid.*:367-8.

5. See Meggitt 1962:284.

6. Meggitt 1962:281-316; 1972.

7. Spencer & Gillen 1899:261; Meggitt 1962:284-90.

8. Spencer & Gillen 1899:366-7.

9. See Meggitt 1962:281; Spencer & Gillen 1899:218.

10. See Bell & Ditton 1980:27.

11. Spencer & Gillen 1899:214.

12. See Bell 1980a:247ff. In the case of children with dual subsection affiliation (that is, children of second-choice marriages), initiation is sometimes used to 'straighten a skin' and to confirm the boy as correct in the mother's line or father's line. A certain amount of politicking occurs between mother's family and father's family to have the 'two-skin' boy initiated within a particular country, though the father's side are by no means the foregone victors.

13. The country is said to be Kaytej but the present owners are all Alyawarra speakers. Two such statements are not inconsistent with each other but I think that as the Alyawarra are numerically strong in the area they are protecting the rights of the closely related and intermarried Kaytej against possible takeovers or extension of dreamings to the Warlpiri. This is done by activating and consolidating their knowledge of the area in the necessary and continuous process of reinvention.

14. See Spencer & Gillen 1899:219.

15. *Ibid.*:244.

16. I have been told that boys crawl between mother's legs at this stage in a mock

birth but I have not seen it myself. Like the use of ant-hill it is a matter which requires further gentle investigation but it does appear to indicate that 'birth associated' symbols in initiation are a continuation rather than a negation of women's reproductive role.

17. See Spencer & Gillen 1899:238.

18. See Spencer & Gillen 1899:365.

19. See Spencer & Gillen 1899:240ff; Meggitt 1962:301-3.

Chapter V
THE PROBLEM OF WOMEN

In the field we meet with actual women who may well not agree with popular anthropological characterizations of their lives as impoverished and male-dominated. The women with whom I worked would not have endorsed Lloyd Warner's[1] statement that women make little sacred progress through life but remain largely profane; nor Kenneth Maddock's[2] that women's ceremonies are small and personal; nor Nancy Munn's[3] that their interests are conscribed by the life of the camp; they would not have recognized themselves as the 'toothless old hags' of C. W. M. Hart and Arnold Pilling's[4] studies.

Over the past forty years, since Phyllis Kaberry's pioneering work with Aboriginal women, few anthropologists other than Catherine Berndt and Jane Goodale have lifted their voices in protest at the characterization of the Aboriginal women of Northern and Central Australia as the pawns in male games and the uninitiated of the society.[5] Then, in the late 1960s and 1970s, feminists looked anew at 'the case of the Australian Aborigine' and found evidence for dramatically divergent analyses.[6] Although many scholars have felt confident to categorize and label Aboriginal woman's contribution to and place in her society[7], few have examined her life as she perceives it, or, having documented her values, perceptions and activities, they have failed to assess their 'findings'.[8] How are we to conceptualize women in Aboriginal society?

In the preceding chapters I have teased out the strands of the social fabric of desert life and suggested that a re-weaving, which accommodates women as social actors in their own right, is timely. The task is complex and compounded by the poverty of the ethnographic data concerning women. Although I now have many answers to my questions regarding the nature and structure of women's rituals in Central Australia, others remain unanswered. Let me then return to the broader issues which my analysis raises for those who seek an accurate portrayal of desert society and those who would probe the 'problem of women'.

In exploring women's rights and responsibilities in land, the nurturance themes celebrated in ritual, and women's power to exclude men, I have argued that women's self-perceptions of autonomy and independence are neither fantasy nor nostalgic longings for a bygone era. But women's perceptions of themselves *do* present an analytical challenge to anthropological models which purport to characterize male-female in terms of male dominance. I have suggested throughout that our understanding of woman's contribution to her society has been constrained by male-oriented models within which our questions are located. Instead, I have begun with an examination of women's power base and then looked again at the nature of the relation between the sexes and of desert society itself. I have shown women to be social actors in their own right but I have also demonstrated their structural importance.

New understandings emerge when women are allowed to speak. Without a knowledge of the complexities and richness of women's ritual world, our ethnographic understanding of desert society is impoverished. Too often we have taken male ritual activity to be the totality of the religious experience in Aboriginal society. The vital and complementary role of women in maintaining the *jukurrpa* heritage is thus obscured. It is through the co-operative endeavours of both women and men that the *jukurrpa* is maintained across space and through time; it is women who keep the land alive and nurture the relationships of the living to the *jukurrpa*; it is through the links established by women that knowledge is transmitted and ritual reciprocity established; and it is through women's interactions with the country that the *jukurrpa* is reaffirmed and activated. That desert society is a living, vibrant, dynamic culture is apparent when woman's ritual contribution to her society is explored.

While my ritual analysis focused on the Kaytej women, I located it within the context of women's lives at Warrabri and within the wider society of Central Australia. I have argued that male-female relations are in a constant state of flux and that the impact of the changes of the last century has been devastating. The separation of the sexes, I suggested, was not a solution to the tensions engendered by male-female relations, it merely re-ordered certain aspects of these relationships. Underlying male-female domains there remains the unresolved tension *between* men and women. Woman's role in the maintenance of harmonious relationships has been taxed, eroded and usurped in a century of white colonization of desert lands. Thus while men and women have remained separate, the evaluation of their activities by the wider society of Northern Australia has changed as has the relation *between* the sexes. That this process is complex is clear from the different responses of women at Warrabri.

One important question posed by my analysis is how to evaluate women's power base and exclusion of men. I have throughout this book avoided speaking of sexual equality or inequality because I believe these concepts distort our understanding of male-female relations in desert society. I have not argued that women's autonomous ritual life is a challenge or a threat to the consolidation of a male power-base. Instead, I have allowed that both men and women strain to consolidate their position and that this is evident in the way in which women extend their dreaming range and organize ritual relationships. It is the settlement life style which is the greatest impediment to the consolidation of women's power.

I do not claim to understand fully all there is to know of women's lives; I was not socialized within that culture but rather came to learn as an adult woman from another culture - that of post-World War II working class, white Australia. However, I do think I came to appreciate what it means to be a woman of my age and perceived status in an Aboriginal community in the late 1970s. Because my teachers were patient and dedicated to teaching me 'straight', I learnt to see much through the eyes of Aboriginal women. What I saw was a strong, articulate and knowledgeable group of women who were substantially independent of their menfolk in economic and ritual terms. Their lives were not ones of drudgery, deprivation, humiliation and exploitation because of their lack of penis and attendant phallic culture, nor was their self-image and identity bound up solely with their child-bearing and child-rearing functions. Instead I found the women to be extremely serious in the upholding, observance and transmission of their religious heritage. Religion permeated every aspect of their lives - lives which were nonetheless full of good humour and a sense of fun. Why then have Aboriginal women so often been cast as second-class citizens? Was the problem located at the level of ethnography or of anthropological model-making? Were these women deluding themselves? Was my vision in some way impaired?

In discussing my incorporation into women's worlds in the field,

I argued that age, sex, marital status and length of stay in the field were critical factors in assessing access to information: factors which not all anthropologists have considered worthy of anything other than passing anecdotal comment. My responses to fieldwork and to my 'findings' were shaped by the fact that I came to anthropology in my thirties, with one career behind me and that, on the way, I had begun to reflect on my own position in society. My children were, and continue to be, two of my greatest fieldwork assets. Being able to return to the field over a period of seven years has greatly deepened my understanding of women's changing role. Let us then speculate about how these factors may have affected the fieldwork of several anthropologists who have worked with women.

Geza Roheim must have presented an enigma to the Luritja and Aranda women with whom he worked in 1929. Here was a male fieldworker asking questions about sexuality and dreams. Within culturally defined limits, sex is discussed in desert society, but in a special joking fashion when men or strangers are present. It is not, therefore, surprising that Roheim learnt much of the profane love magic and little of the emotional management discussed in Chapter III. Roheim admits that when he asked an older woman to explain song words, she hushed him, saying 'Who were these *mamu* [demons] women who told you this? They must have been mad to sing this in the presence of a man.' [9] Older women are the ones with access to the deeper meanings: the younger women know little. It is as if a male ethnographer only sought information from uninitiated males. Roheim therefore learnt little of the religious significance of women's ceremonies and concluded that women were without support from the supernatural world.

As a young single woman, Phyllis Kaberry would have been told about those things which were appropriate for her age (if the comments of my older friends are any indication). Further, in an area where the recent dislocation had not yet allowed women time to adjust to different 'country', the 'nomadic' style of Kaberry's fieldwork may have masked the nature of the changes in women's ritual lives. [10] Similarly, Jane Goodale, as a single but adult female, admits that at first she was an enigma to the women who had to teach her basic skills. Only quite late in her fieldwork did they comment that she was no longer like a white woman. [11] In discussing her return to Tiwi, after a lengthy absence, she speculated how their perceptions of her may have changed; indeed, when I visited Jane Goodale in May 1981 on Melville Island, it was apparent that she had become a Tiwi sage. Younger women would ask her what the old people would have done or said in various contemporary situations.

Catherine Berndt was the wife of a fellow researcher who was interested in men's business. Once again, if the women with whom I worked were any indication, at first she may not have been told things which it was improper for a man to know. Certainly in the years of her research, Aboriginal women must have changed their perception of her as she matured and no doubt have been prepared to discuss matters appropriate to her perceived status.

Isobel White, as an older woman with adult children, and in lengthy contact with the Yalata community of South Australia, has been in a strong position to document and reflect upon the changes in women's lives. In comparing our fieldwork experiences, we have found many similarities in the direct and often disarming way in which women have chosen to represent and to share their ritual world. To be fondly called 'old woman' is a mark of respect, we found.

But when we step back from the field situation and the role of the anthropologist and look at the way in which women have been depicted in the Australian literature, we find that the theoretical pre-occupations, context of fieldwork, research design and the nature of the discipline in Australia have all conspired to relegate women to a marginal position within Aboriginal society and within the discipline. Whether or not this characterization is accurate is another question of both empirical and theoretical import to the problem of women in general and to my enquiry into desert society and Aboriginal women's rituals in particular.

Glancing at the presidential address to the Australia and New Zealand Association for the Advancement of Science (A.N.Z.A.A.S.) in 1935, we might conclude that it is not for want of encouragement that women are absent from the ethnographies. In his historical résumé, A. P. Elkin[12] cautioned that:

We anthropologists, therefore, must take care lest, as a result of our scientific urge to systematize whatever we study, we abet this dehumanization of a living people ... women could prevent us from doing this; the wives and daughters of station managers, settlers, and officials should be encouraged to carry on the work of

Mrs Parker and Mrs Aeneas Gunn, while specially trained women who go out to do anthropological work amongst the aborigines should work consistently through the native women, not to find out what a male worker can better ascertain through the men, but to get a real understanding of childhood, motherhood, the family, and women's place in society.

Few women, however, seemed anxious to take advantage of such encouragement. In fact Catherine Berndt[13] suggests that women such as Daisy Bates and Olive Pink were a potential hazard who did Aboriginal women a disfavour. Those who evinced a more positive approach were few. Phyllis Kaberry and Catherine Berndt were the only two female anthropologists who published in-depth studies of the lives of Aboriginal women during that early period. (Although her fieldwork was undertaken in the 1950s, Jane Goodale's work did not appear until 1971.) Other women, such as Diane Barwick, Fay Gale and Marie Reay, in their work on assimilation, migration and urbanization have offered important insights regarding the lives of Aboriginal women.[14]

The state of the discipline is well illustrated in the report of the '1961 Conference on Aboriginal Studies' held in Canberra, where women appear in the section devoted to 'Special Problems', along with 'Notes on Psychological Research' and 'Tribal Distribution and Population'.[15] Marie Reay[16], at that conference, made an urgent plea for comparative research on the social position of women and outlined some of the severe practical handicaps facing women anthropologists.

At the 1969 A.N.Z.A.A.S. Congress in Adelaide, thirty-four years after Elkin's plea and eight years after the Canberra Conference, Catherine Ellis organized a symposium 'to counteract earlier misconceptions and to give airing to more recent scholarship'.[17] A decade later this remained the standard reference. Further conferences, symposia and texts are needed which examine the directions in which the study of women has moved within Australia and within world anthropology.

A workshop organized to focus upon 'Aboriginal Women's Changing Role' during the 1980 A.N.Z.A.A.S. Congress held in Adelaide partly filled this lacuna.[18] A shift of emphasis and focus was apparent as Aboriginal women, who were clearly in charge, spoke forcefully of their lives as women and Aborigines. The sessions were structured so that Aboriginal and white women gave papers on the first day and on the second and third days the Aboriginal women held closed workshops. When, on the afternoon of the third day, the Aboriginal women reported back to the session, it was poignantly obvious that they had important matters to discuss and that their sense of political action was astute. Again and again during the three days I asked myself, just where had anthropologists been looking all these years? How could they have missed so much?

In part the answers lie in the nature of development of the discipline of anthropology in Australia. Aboriginal society was not systematically studied until two Oxford scholars, Baldwin Spencer and W. E. Roth, began their scientific fieldwork in Australia during the late nineteenth century. Previous data relied upon the casual observations of early explorers and settlers or the collation and compiling of data by well-educated professional men who dabbled in anthropology as a hobby. Even when the detailed research began, the methodology was more of an armchair variety where speculation abounds: intensive participant-observation fieldwork - which has come to characterize the practice of anthropology and which may have highlighted women's role - was not undertaken.

Day-to-day life, wherein theory could be tested, was spurned as phenomenon worthy of enquiry. This was illustrated nicely by Baldwin Spencer's co-worker Francis Gillen, who noted in his diary of camp jottings of 1901-2 that, 'The morning was wasted through the natives being engaged in a squabble arising out of slander spread by one woman against another.' [19] It is too simplistic to say that it was the preponderance of male researchers which prevented women from speaking in the ethnography; it was also the orientation of the discipline. Gillen's notes show that women themselves were not invisible.

Of course these were men of the Victorian era and their own model of femininity is evident from their notes and their published work. It was a model wherein the epitome of all civilization was their own social order with its domestication of female sexuality.[20] All other sexual values and sexual orders were held to be primitive, lacking the hallmark of civilization. Such an analysis obviously has attractions, because fifty years later the eminent British anthropologist E. E. Evans-Pritchard[21] was still extolling the virtues of Victorian womanhood as a standard against which to measure other women's position. It is little wonder then that the independent and, to the Victorian eye,

wilful ways of Aboriginal woman, received scant recognition in ethnological debates. In behaving in such an untamed fashion she was
merely demonstrating her uncivilized and uncultured primitiveness.

Another factor which for many years kept women's activities well
in the background was the scientific orientation of the University of
Sydney's Department of Anthropology. Established in 1925 and
financed by government grants and Rockefeller funds, the Department set out to train field officers and to record the culture of Aborigines before it disappeared. Aborigines were regarded as interesting
subjects for testing theories of group marriage, totemism and kinship
models. Because the research was predicated on a 'salvage' rationale,
little interest in the history of Aboriginal societies developed.
Research focused upon formal structures such as kinship systems,
religion and social organization. Women were assumed not to reflect
upon such matters and their views were neither sought nor recorded.
The 'domestic' realm of family, child-rearing and food-gathering was
taken to be their lot.

Australian anthropology bears very much the stamp of British
anthropology as a result of the appointment of individual professors
and their theoretical interests. The founder and first Professor of
Anthropology in Sydney, A. R. Radcliffe-Brown, was a student of the
French sociologist Émile Durkheim and the English ethnologist
W. H. R. Rivers. For these men, women's self-evaluations were not
central to an understanding of society. Durkeimian dualism (the
sacred-profane dichotomy), with its view of women as the profane,
existing only to highlight the importance of men in the moral order,
has permeated Australian anthropology. In such a scheme women
have no religion, only magic. This has been a hard yoke to throw off.
In analyses that posit such constricted contexts, however stridently
or positively women assert the validity and uniqueness of their world
view, they are treated as mute or socially disruptive. The way in which
women have either been excluded or ignored is well illustrated by the
major debates concerning conception beliefs, local organization and
marriage which have erupted in Australian anthropology.

Working with Tiwi, albeit one on Melville Island and the other
two on Bathurst Island, Jane Goodale and the C. W. M. Hart and
Arnold Pilling team depict Tiwi marriage in quite different, though
not necessarily incompatible ways.[22] Similarly, Annette Hamilton has
questioned Les Hiatt who worked in the same areas as she did in

Arnhem Land.[23] Both Hamilton and Goodale illustrate that the received male truths based on data gathered by men from men, about women's lives, may not be a lived reality for women. For various reasons, the models which inform women's behaviour are not proffered by men.

Certainly the nature of marriage arrangements in Aboriginal society has not been ignored, but women's role in establishing and maintaining marriages has been neglected or relegated to the domain of the secular.[24] It is the way in which solutions are sought which has rendered women inarticulate in the ethnographies. What may a woman say of her role which will strike the anthropologist as affirming her importance if she has already been type cast as a pawn in the games of the polygynous gerontocracy?

One of the continuing debates in Australian anthropology concerns local and social organization. Nicolas Peterson and Mervyn Meggitt[25] recognize the importance of women in group composition (men desire 'access' to their 'services'), but in such analyses women still have the status of objects. Unless women are accorded the status of joint owners and managers of country and ritual along with their male kin our understanding of group structure will be skewed.

At the core of the debate concerning the nature of the land-owning group in Aboriginal Australia is the patrilineal, patrilocal, territorial exogamous horde of Radcliffe-Brown.[26] The level at which this model may be said to exist, its fit with empirical reality and its universality have all consumed many pages of anthropological texts.[27] Writing of Central Australia, Meggitt emphasized the fluidity of Warlpiri social organization, while Strehlow depicted the Aranda as having a land-based kin-group class system of *njinaŋa* (father-son) sections.[28] Underlying these contributions to the debate is the desire, not always made explicit, to isolate groups and to attach a function which can be specified as spiritual, economic, or marriage-contracting. In my portrait of Aboriginal women's social and ritual organization I have not sought the discrete land-using or land-owning group, but rather the ritual land-maintaining group which encompasses many overlapping ties and claims to country.

The core of the land-maintaining group – in my case the Karlukarlu and Wakulpu women – is composed of people who trace their relation to land in two distinct and complementary ways.[29] The group living in the *jilimi* is a localized socio-ritual group held together by cross-cutting ties of land, family, personal history, and the common assertion of rights and responsibilities in a particular tract of land. Underlying this group is a balance between the interest one has in one's mother's country and the interest one has in one's father's country. However the group of women living together in a *jilimi* share the maintenance of certain dreamings and therefore have a common function.

In Chapter II I described the articulation of women's ritual organization with land tenure systems in terms of a ritual division of labour of *kirda* and *kurdungurlu*. Women, I also claimed, are of critical structural importance in the establishment of links between groups. However, writing of Ngalia Warlpiri, Meggitt states that endogamous generation moieties organize women's ceremonies.[30] These ceremonies, Meggitt contends, are 'not seen as part of the dreamtime ritual life', and further, such is their ignorance that women believe men's ceremonies are organized in endogamous moieties too.[31] Munn, working also with Ngalia Warlpiri, found no evidence of endogamous generation moieties but rather that ownership of designs was channelled through affinal ties.[32] Women, Munn stresses, lack corporate group membership.[33]

Herein lies the most important ethnographic difference between my work and that of Munn and Meggitt – the organizational structure of women's rituals. Our differences however, must also be seen within the wider context of our divergent analysis of women's role and status in general. Meggitt's and Munn's location of women's ceremonies outside the sphere of spiritually-empowered rituals is consonant with their analysis of the role and status of Aboriginal women in general. In exploring women's domain, both Meggitt and Munn focus on the *absence* of certain elements. In Meggitt's[34] analysis, women lack direct access to the *jukurrpa*; all relations are mediated through men; in rituals of initiation women participate as kin not in ritual roles; women possess only a 'bipartite' psyche whereas men enjoy a 'tripartite': an all-important patrispirit is added to the matrispirit and conception dreaming which both sexes possess. Similarly, Munn describes women's domain in terms of their limited and conscribed interests of camp and family and the absence of such symbolic complexes as the line/track/travel or meander line/snake/penis.[35] In Munn's analysis women are concerned with the micro-temporal, with heterosexual reproduction, and themes of intra-generational moment. Men, on the other hand, are concerned with the macro-temporal, the trans-generational, and spiritual reproduction within the patrilineal descent group.[36]

My own experience is at odds with these portraits of women's world. Aranda women do have line designs which encode information about the travels of the ancestors. They also share with Willowra Warlpiri the meander line to depict the travels of *warnajarra* (two snakes). Both Aranda and Warlpiri women have a variety of ritual objects which represent the person/place/*jukurrpa* complex and are a symbol of the corporate nature of the ritual land-maintaining group. Are we looking at regional variation? Are the differences evidence of rapid social change? Or is the difference partly one of orientation of the ethnographer?

Even if we could dismiss the differences by answering all three questions in the affirmative, we would still be left with the discrepancies between Meggitt and Munn themselves. Both undertook field-work in the mid 1950s with Ngalia Warlpiri. I would like to suggest that the apparent confusion concerning *yawulyu* structure reflects, in part, the upheaval in the lives of Warlpiri, but in a special way. The Warlpiri of Munn's study had only recently been settled at Yuendumu in the 1950s and the women had not yet had time, through interaction with the country, to explore fully and to confirm to the point of consensus, the nature of ancestral activity in the area. Without this knowledge they could not assert their rights and exercise responsibilities in land through the performance of large scale *yawulyu* where ritual *kirda* and *kurdungurlu* must be precise. This may also account for the apparent paucity of women's ritual activity and women's reluctance to stage 'bush *yawulyu*'.[37] The 'necessary and continuous process of re-invention', described in Chapter II, had reached a low point, but twenty years later women could act with confidence in the roles of *kirda* and *kurdungurlu*.

Perhaps there was a reluctance to stress these ritual roles, but why then did Meggitt find endogamous generation moieties and Munn affinal ties? Both Meggitt and Munn elicited information without witnessing a secret 'bush *yawulyu*'.[38] It is possible that women stressed the kin relations of mother and daughter in their discussion with Meggitt. As I have stated this is the kinship correlate of the ritual roles of *kirda-kurdungurlu* and is important in the transmission of knowledge, the application of designs and the positions of dancers. Could it be that in describing their ritual organization the women explained mother-daughter dyad in terms of endogamous generation moiety affiliation?

What then of the ties of affinity in Munn's work? Munn[39] observed the painting dyad as comprising sisters-in-law, but this fits with my experience of the *kurdungurlu* as members of the opposite patrimoiety. Further, as I have argued, *kurdungurlu*, with the advantage of residence in a country, have greater opportunity for ultimately assuming the role of ritual *kurdungurlu*. Sisters-in-law are such persons.

Thus I am suggesting that both Meggitt and Munn may have been confused by their data because neither actually witnessed ceremonies and because the women themselves had not yet organized their ritual ranks in that 'country'. To this I would add that ritual activity intensifies the larger and more permanent the *jilimi*. Two decades after Meggitt and Munn's fieldwork, the women of large long-established *jilimi* have the necessary numbers and knowledge to articulate clearly in their *yawulyu* their structural relations to land. They also have more reason to incorporate persons in these roles because the base of the *jilimi* is wider than was the case in the past.

Because women's ceremonial life has not been seen as a key to understanding relations to land, the rights channelled through women have been inadequately explored. The *kurdungurlu* have been cast in an essentially mundane or person-oriented role which provides support in a complementary, but secular fashion, to the spiritually-empowered patriclan.[40] Yet the spiritual basis of the *kurdungurlu* role is clearly marked in the use of suffixes such as *altyerre* (dreaming) by Aranda for *kurdungurlu* country, and in the role of *kurdungurlu* in country and ceremony. The tendency to view the patriclan as the location of spiritual responsibility, while treating relationships which flow through women as secondary and secular, has been a major obstacle to gaining a clear understanding of women's relationship to land and the dynamic nature of land tenure systems.

Overall, we may conclude that the 'problem of women' has been a non-issue in Australian anthropology because the development of the discipline precluded any interest in a field which may have raised 'the woman question'. The philosophical underpinnings, notions of sexuality and female stereotypes based on Western experience, led early fieldworkers to see Aboriginal women as deprived and devalued by their culture. The big issues to which anthropology directed attention were those which cast women as 'the other'. Those women who sought to work with Aboriginal women and to interpret their lives more sensitively have done so within this oppressive framework.

Within Australia the tendency has been for male fieldworkers to study male institutions and subsequently to offer analyses which purport to examine the totality of Aboriginal society. Evaluation of female institutions has been based too often on male informants' opinions, refracted through the eyes of male ethnographers and explained by means of the concepts of a male-oriented anthropology. Thus statements concerning the role and status of women are formulated within the context of a male ideology, which means they can only rarely be reconciled with the behavioural patterns of Aboriginal women in desert society. In a sex-segregated society, women can most easily be studied by another woman, but funding more female fieldworkers will not necessarily ensure that Aboriginal women's perceptions are explored: we also need theories which allow that Aboriginal women create their own social reality.

The problem of theorizing about male-female relations has been tackled from within three different frameworks, each of which has generated different questions and thus produced different answers. The first which I shall call 'Man Equals Culture', is, as we have seen, the most consistently worked out and certainly the most popular. It reinforces cherished notions of how the world is constructed. The second, an 'Anthropology of Women' presents an ethnographic challenge to the 'Man Equals Culture' approach, but may be easily dismissed or subsumed. The third, which I am calling 'Toward a Feminist Perspective', is the only real challenge to the first. It has produced more questions than answers, but it does bring the burgeoning corpus of feminist scholarship to bear on the problem of women.

These three organizational frameworks are akin to Kuhn's[41] notion of 'a paradigm' which predicts a problem or a set of related problems that the community of practitioners then sets out to solve. But, as Kuhn makes clear, one cannot move easily from within one version of the paradigm to work with another, as to do so involves something of the magnitude of a gestalt switch. Although the various practitioners of one paradigm may use the same vocabulary, the conceptual baggage which adheres to a term varies radically between paradigms. For example, if politics is defined as a male domain, then it is difficult to document the activities of women politicians as anything other then deviants. However, if politics is defined as including sexual politics, that is, the power relations between men and women, both men and women can then be depicted as politicians.

Armed with diverse theoretical weaponry such as Marxian class analysis, Lévi-Straussian structuralism, Durkheimian dualism, and psychoanalysis, the practitioners of the 'Man Equals Culture' paradigm have sought to explain women's secondary position in terms of economic markers, in the realm of symbolism, social organization and kinship. They have cast women as the profane, the 'other', the devalued, the wild, the feared and the excluded, the substance of symbols but never the makers of their own social reality, the exploited and dominated, but never the decision-making adult.[42] As ethnopsychiatrist John Cawte so gaily puts it, women are 'feeders, breeders and follow-the-leaders'.[43]

Geza Roheim[44] looked to the realm of myth to explain men's fear of women and argued that these rites are their means of maintaining their superiority. Women, he contended, had no religion, no corporate ceremonial life, only personal magical practices. This, as I argued in Chapter III, skewed his understanding of women's love rituals. Roheim's particular version of the psychoanalytic approach, although crude, has provided insights which have been refined and were popular again in the 1970s.[45]

Perhaps the most sophisticated and well worked out analysis of the adherents to the 'Man Equals Culture' paradigm is the symbolic analysis of Munn.[46] Like Roheim, Munn takes the male-female opposition to be a fundamental starting point in any analysis of Aboriginal society, but Munn's concern is with the socio-cultural order whereas Roheim's is with the individual psyche.

The second paradigm is closely related to the first, the practitioners working on a particular theoretical issue, begin with the assumption that women also have rights, opinions and values and that these are not exactly coincidental with those of the men. This type of research makes a chink in the doctrine of male dominance, it becomes apparent that it is not as complete as we once thought; nevertheless, as long as we insert certain qualifications, the model will more or less suffice and the data on women will illuminate the institutions of marriage, kinship and social structure.

For example, in her extremely detailed and rich portrait of Aboriginal women, Kaberry was able to challenge several of Roheim's grosser misconceptions about the function of the women's religious life; to offer a counter to Warner's assertion that women make little sacred progress, but remain wholly profane; and to indicate that Ashley-Montagu's case for ignorance of physiological paternity did not apply to women in the Kimberleys.[47] Yet, many of Kaberry's most important observations concerning the nature of women's ceremonies have not been fully explored. Kaberry's[48] critically important observation that men represent the uninitiated at women's ceremonies remains buried beneath a pile of studies of secret male cults, totemism and kinship which assume that the male view is the only important perspective.

Like Kaberry, Goodale chose to organize her data within a life-cycle framework which, while providing a sympathetic portrait of women's lives, sidestepped certain critical issues concerning the way in which men evaluate women's activities. However, Goodale does tackle this problem in her final chapter where she sets out the difference between male and female world-views. Tiwi women are unusual in that they are initiated at the same ceremonies as are the males, pass through the same formal procedures and are not excluded at any stage during the ceremony.[49] Like the women of Kaberry's study, Tiwi women are substantially independent economically whilst being ritually dependent.

Both Phyllis Kaberry and Jane Goodale went into the field to study women and worked mainly with women informants. In their depictions of women's role and status, both stress women's importance, their equality in some fields and their near equality in others.[50]

The women who have published in-depth studies of women have been, I suggest, constrained by theoretical perspectives developed to focus on men as the leading and most interesting social actors. There was little impetus from within Australia to develop frameworks within which women were deemed of anthropological interest as social actors. While Elkin was encouraging women to document the lives of Aboriginal women, male fieldworkers who thanked 'my wife who collected material from the women' were laying the foundations for future research in Australia.

Catherine Berndt[51] was able to identify innovatory and destructive forces at work in the West-Central Northern Territory, but she admits that her research was incomplete because of the demands of her wider research project on contact. On the basis of her extensive data on women's ceremonies, Berndt also explored the relations between the sexes in terms of complementarity and a 'two-sex model' and for this reason her work spans paradigms two and three.[52]

The third paradigm is that of feminist social scientists who question the origins and mechanisms of the all-pervasive and hitherto persuasive cultural dogma of male dominance. Perhaps, they suggest, it is not an enduring, timeless, constant which regulates male-female relations in Aboriginal society. As yet this framework has produced more questions than answers and, in the Kuhnian sense, we are still at the stage of having too many anomalies to be satisfied with earlier paradigms but do not yet have a sufficiently elegant structure within which to analyse our new data. The old paradigm is under threat: an anthropology of women is not a satisfying alternative, but in feminist debate we find the 'problem of women' re-defined and re-evaluated.

From different perspectives and from within different intellectual traditions feminists seek the origins and mechanisms by which gender hierarchies and such cultural dogmas as sexual asymmetry are established and maintained. Feminists have flirted with various analytical modes from Freudian psychoanalysis through Marxian models to structural symbolism. They have declared themselves to be outside the discipline and to present a major challenge to those interested in overhauling the discipline.

Problems of definition, methodology and epistemology confronted by feminists in the 1970s and 1980s are neither new nor the prerogative of anthropology. Waxing and waning according to the interests of the day, concern with the place of women in society has moved in and out of mainstream anthropology. Certain nineteenth-century Marxist and liberal activists regarded 'the women question' as central to an understanding of the market economy and capitalist mode of production. By the early twentieth century, studies of female roles and status had become a matter of cross-cultural analysis which drew upon the insights of psychoanalytic theory. Notwithstanding, in 1956 Evans-Pritchard[53] could speak still of the 'position of women' as a peripheral problem which scarcely warranted serious anthropological consideration.

But from the mists of motherhood and celebration of 'feminine roles' of the post-World War II years came a new awareness of how anthropologists have neglected women; Edwin Ardener's[54] analysis of

Bakweri rituals attributed to the 'problem of women' a new significance. Feminist anthropologists went on to explicate the problem in analyses which diversified, specialized and challenged the received wisdom of a mainstream anthropology long committed to understanding society almost exclusively in terms of kinship, social structure, culture theory, ritual and economy.

The present women's movement embraces diverse perspectives, paradigms and programmes: from Shulamith Firestone's radical re-reading of Freud and her revolutionary solution, to the more measured reinterpretation of Juliet Mitchell; from the search for egalitarian society by Eleanor Leacock to the explorations of sexual asymmetry.[55] In the new feminist anthropology, attention has turned to the insights of ethnological studies with its refutation of the 'man the hunter' dominance theory,[56] and to the reformulation of structuralist, cognitive and psycho-anthropological models.[57] Thus women are offering diverse solutions to the 'problem of women' and drawing upon different conceptual frameworks in their attempts to understand the role and status of women, both today and in the past. The emphasis on 'women' as the unit of analysis immediately propels us into cross-cultural and cross-temporal analysis and it is in this area that women are attempting to establish new models.[58]

There is, however, no consensus on how best to attack the problem. Feminists dispute whether the major task is to seek the origins of sexual inequalities or the mechanisms which perpetuate them.[59] They are further divided according to their political stance, which often complements their commitment to a particular mode of analysis.[60]

In reviewing the feminist literature on the 'problem of women' rather coolly and cynically, one might reduce to two the choice of frameworks within which to analyse women's status: first, the 'evolutionists' who offer romantic reconstructions of a long-lost past; second, the 'universalists' who seek ahistorical formulations from contemporary male-female relations which are then overlaid on past regimes and applied cross-culturally to suit the purpose of the analysis. Uniting both approaches is the stated concern of feminists to develop analytical tools which are free of male bias and pejorative overtones. Each is concerned to measure the status of women and to speculate as to the mechanisms which constrain women. Evolutionists argue for qualitative changes which have transformed the alleged sexual egalitarianism of band society; universalists posit the public-private dichotomy as a universal to explain what they take to be another universal: sexual asymmetry. All are agreed that anthropology is shot through with androcentrism; that there is a profound reluctance on the part of the discipline to come to terms with the social contribution of women to their society and to develop theories which accommodate women as social actors in their own right.

In general, feminists agree that it is no longer possible to take female roles as a reflex of biology or of some hypothesized 'natural order'. In their explanatory prescriptions and in their political rationale and platform feminists differ about how we should conceptualize the problem. Evolutionists insist that to focus on the universality of sexual asymmetry is to ignore the material conditions of dominance and the historical transformation of female roles. However universalists insist that a glorious past is wishful thinking: change can only be based on an understanding of the present social order so that then it can be dismantled or modified.

Feminists have indicated important areas of enquiry but the extreme separation of the sexes in desert society represents an analytic challenge which I suggest is best met in the first instance by increasing our ethnographic understanding of women's domain. We need to explore the possibility that qualitative changes in the relation between the sexes may have occurred during the past century. We cannot begin with a static model of male-female: we know too little of the female half of society to argue for male dominance as an enduring, timeless reality. We need to be clear regarding the nature of woman's contribution to her society, her rights and responsibilities, before we endorse one particular model of male-female relations. The recognition that male-female relationships are not rigidly fixed and that women may develop their own power base, leads us to an analysis of the power differentials of male-female in Aboriginal society.

Writing of male-female tensions, Annette Hamilton has suggested that women's secret ritual life represented a serious threat to the 'consolidation of male dominance', not because of any 'coherent ideological opposition expressed within it', but because its 'mode of organization provides a structural impediment'.[61] Underlying the contrasts between the sexes she[62] argues that there is:

> a well developed organization that can best be understood as a dual society . . . I suggest that these two systems are, in the Western Des-

ert as a whole, in a situation of dynamic disequilibrium, whereby the men's domain is intruding into the women's through ritual transformations and through the strengthening of male links between generations as a result of changes in the system of kinship and marriage.

It is in the shattering of the ritually maintained nexus of land as resource and spiritual essence that I have located a shift from female autonomy to male control, from independence to dependence. Thus while Hamilton and I are concerned to explore the changing nature of the relations between the sexes from an historical perspective, we have focused upon different institutions and sets of relationships employing different conceptions of time and place.

In Hamilton's analysis of change in Western Desert society, where endogamous generation moieties organize ritual life, men may infiltrate women's hitherto autonomous worlds by undermining the mother-daughter tie, a central relationship in women's ceremonial life. However, ritual organization in Central Australia emphasizes the relation of person to place in terms of two distinct and complementary lines of descent – one through the father's patriline (*kirda*) and the other through the mother's patriline (*kurdungurlu*). Furthermore, Central Australian women have a wide range of ritual items which symbolize their relation to land and *jukurrpa*. The population-intensive settlement life-style has allowed women to consolidate these relationships and, through ritual, to forge new links with other women.

Obviously if women held they were independent while men insisted they were subservient and the male claims were backed in terms of their control over women's domain, then we could suggest the women are not facing the harsh reality of life and that they are using ritual as an escape mechanism. This line of analysis I found hard to sustain in my fieldwork because women do have an independent base which is respected by men. Further, in the rituals jointly staged by men and women, men's respect for the independence of women's worlds is amply demonstrated. Finally, in the rituals associated with male initiation, an occasion when male control of women is said to be manifest, I found women to be engaged in key decision-making which affected both ritual procedure and the aftermath of initiation. Further, their initiation-associated rituals celebrated woman's ongoing role as nurturer of people, relationships and land. Thus, women's ritual domain is not subsumed by male ritual activity during initiation.

My focus on ritual brought forth rich data which bore directly upon both the ethnographic and theoretical levels of understanding women's role and status in desert society. It also led me directly to consider the nature of social change and sexual politics. In the dynamic interweaving of these two critically important factors in the lives of Aboriginal women in Central Australia, today and in the past, lies the means of reconciling women's claims to independence and autonomy with anthropological models which characterize women as the dominated and oppressed.

In Aboriginal society both men and women base their claims to status within their society on their direct access to the *jukurrpa*, but each then elaborates their rights and responsibilities within separate domains. An understanding of sexual politics therefore must be based on knowledge of the power base of each sex and the way in which male and female domains are connected. A corollary to this argument is that the separation of the sexes does not solve the tensions engendered by male-female relations: it merely orders certain aspects of the sets of relationships within and between the domains of men and women. Our understanding of sexual politics within Aboriginal society is skewed because we have inadequately explored the nature of women's power base. By setting up a framework for understanding women's rituals which relates the tensions of sexual politics to the far-reaching impact of recent social and cultural changes, I have depicted the relation between the sexes as an ever-shifting, negotiable balance. Women's rituals then become both an element in the balance and an indication of the state of the balance.

In ritual the Law is made known in a highly stylized and emotionally charged manner: the separation of the sexes, so evident in daily activities, reaches its zenith. Ritual may therefore be considered as an important barometer of male-female relations, for it provides, as it were, an arena in which the values of the society are writ large, where the sex division of labour is starkly drawn and explored by the participants. It was in ritual that I found men and women clearly stating their own perceptions of their role, their relationship to the opposite sex and their relation to the Dreamtime whence all legitimate authority and power once flowed. However, while women and men today, as in the past, maintain separate spheres of interaction, the evaluations of their respective roles and their opportunities to achieve status have fundamentally altered during a century of white intrusion into Central Australia. Men and women have been differently affected in the shift from a hunter-gatherer mode of subsistence to a sedentary life-style on large institutionalized government settlements.

Within the historical context of Aboriginal society, the maintenance of male-female relations entailed a continuing dialogue which allowed women to participate actively in the construction of the cultural evaluations of their role in their society. But today, as members of a colonial frontier society, Aboriginal women no longer participate as equals in this process. Women's solidarity and autonomy are being eroded and devalued. They are constrained and defined by the male-dominated frontier society as a necessarily dependent sex. The interrelations between the sexes are thus no longer shaped predominantly by the set of male-female relations of Aboriginal society; the new forces of the wider colonial society affect them too. The activities of men and women within this new order are differently evaluated and different opportunities for participation are available to men and women.

In seeking to understand the changing role and status of Aboriginal women I found it necessary to explore not only the basis of female autonomy and solidarity within Aboriginal society, but also to allow that their claims to autonomy and expressions of solidarity now occur in a vastly changed and changing *milieu*. 'Male dominance' may appear to be a satisfying explanation of the relation between the sexes, and its persistence through time is well documented, but I suggest that we look anew at the historical record of the past century. There we find evidence of a shift in the relative negotiating powers of men and women. The material conditions of women's existence have changed dramatically and some of these changes are, I believe, reflected in ritual, both in terms of the way in which new ideas are incorporated within the Law of the dreaming and in terms of the opportunities to stage rituals. The loss of land over which to forage constitutes more than an economic loss, for it is from the land that Aboriginal people draw not only their livelihood but also their very being. The mining and pastoral industries have alienated the best lands, so that Aborigines must live herded together in controlled settlements which, like Warrabri, are poised on the margins of what was once their traditional country.

In Northern Australia the incoming whites have brought new ideas and resources. These have been differently exploited by Aboriginal men and women. Women were disadvantaged from the outset because of the white male perception of them as domestic workers and sex objects. Aboriginal men have been able to take real political advantage of certain aspects of frontier society, while Aboriginal women have been seen by whites as peripheral to the political process. Aboriginal women have thus lost valuable ground as negotiators with equal rights. Their separateness has come to mean their exclusion from the white male-dominated domains whence new sources of power and influence now flow. There was no place within the colonial order for the independent Aboriginal woman who, once deprived of her land, quickly became dependent on rations and social security. Thus, while I am in agreement with Berndt and Berndt[63] that Aboriginal women enjoyed privileged access to the hearth and home of white frontier society, I am suggesting that women's status was not enhanced within this domestic and sexual context. On the contrary, in white society, women lost the bargaining power they enjoyed in desert society.

Some Arnhem Land specialists regard my claims to women's high status in the Central Desert region with open amazement. I vividly remember as a very new post-graduate student at the Australian National University, Canberra, one learned academic telling me that my trouble was that I didn't believe women could be oppressed. When I returned from the field and began enumerating the institutions and rituals which women controlled and maintained, our discussion continued. 'But,' he countered, 'they don't have sacred sites.' 'Yes, they do,' I assured him. 'Well,' he said in triumph, 'they don't have incised boards.' 'Sorry,' I replied. 'In that case,' he observed, 'they got the anthropologist they deserve.'

Certainly I was extremely fortunate to undertake my first in-depth fieldwork amongst such women as the Kaytej of Warrabri, but fieldwork further north in the Roper River region, the Victoria River Downs, the Daly River and North Eastern Arnhem Land has led me to see continuities rather than radical discontinuities.[64] In each of these vastly different regions, there is a separation of the sexes. However, the basis of the separation, the content of male and female domains, and the nature of the links between the two vary in significant ways as we move from the desert to the lush north. But that is another book.

Husband and wife, on a trip into the country of Pawurrinji for which they are jointly responsible, Jakamarra as *kirda* and Napaljarri as *kurdungurlu*. Together they decide on the location of a site by indicating the direction in which the dreaming travelled.

NOTES

1.   Warner 1937:5-6; see also fn.1:9.

2.   Maddock 1972:155. Maddock's intensive fieldwork was undertaken in Southern Arnhem Land between 1964 and 1970 and focused upon the Jabuduruwa – a regional cult of great significance to men. His generalizations concerning women are often treated as if they were an accurate assessment of gender values throughout Australia; for example, see Collier and Rosaldo 1981:305.

3.   Munn 1973:214. Munn's work is discussed below p. 238-40.

4.   Hart & Pilling 1960:14. Their monograph, *The Tiwi of Northern Australia*, was published eleven years before Jane Goodale's *Tiwi Wives* appeared. The potential for debate raised by the differences in the findings of these fieldworkers has not yet been fully explored. See below p. 236-7.

5.   Kaberry 1939; Berndt 1950, 1965, 1970, 1979; Goodale 1971. See also fn.1:10, and below p. 242-4, for a further discussion of the work of these women.

6.   White 1970; Leacock 1978; Hamilton 1979; Cowlishaw 1979; Bell & Ditton 1980; Collier & Rosaldo 1981.

7.   Meggitt 1962; Maddock 1972; Munn 1973; Bern 1979a & b.

8.   In her exploration of gender values, Isobel White provides a resolution of what she terms 'the paradox' of Aboriginal women's status. Catherine Berndt (1970:44) has proposed a model of the relation between the sexes in terms of domestic, economic and religious domains within which links of marriage and descent and relations of dominance and authority are articulated. This organizational device allows Berndt to discuss the interpenetration of the spheres of male and female action. Berndt (1970:41, 1979:34) emphasizes woman's importance as an economic producer and the brakes which women thus may apply to male ritual activity. A question mark remains, though, in respect to the relation between male and female ritual domains (Berndt 1970:44).

9.   Roheim 1933:218.

10.   Kaberry 1939:xi.

11.   Goodale 1971:xvii-xviii.

12.   Elkin 1935:197. From 1933 to 1956, as Head of the Department of Anthropology at Sydney University, as Editor of *Oceania* from 1933 to his death in 1979, and as author of authoritative texts on Aborigines, Elkin exerted enormous influence on the growth of the discipline of anthropology in Australia.

13.   Berndt 1963:335.

14.   Barwick 1970; Gale 1972; Reay 1963b.

15.   Sheils 1963:viii.

16.   Reay (1963a) notes that to Daisy Bates (1938) and K. Langloh Parker (1905), Aboriginal women were not of central importance. In Ursula McConnel's (1930) reports on the north Queensland Wikmunkan, women's status is not a critical issue and the survey by C. P. Mountford and Alison Harvey (1941) of women's lives in northern South Australia is very brief.

17. Gale 1970:1. Betty Hiatt (Meehan), Nicolas Peterson, Isobel White and Annette Hamilton contributed papers on the role of women in traditional society, Diane Barwick one on social change and Catherine Berndt an overview.

18. Gale 1983.

19. Gillen 1968:147.

20. See Fee 1974:101.

21. Evans-Pritchard 1965.

22. Goodale 1971; Hart & Pilling 1960; see also fn.5:4.

23. Hamilton 1970b. Fieldwork with Pitjantjatjara in South Australia in the early 1970s, with Gidgingali speakers at Maningrida in Arnhem Land in 1968-9 has provided the data base for Hamilton's anthropological writings. Hiatt 1962, 1971, also worked at Maningrida and has written extensively on various aspects of Aboriginal society, including local organization and ritual symbolism.

24. See Lévi-Strauss 1949; see also Bell 1980a.

25. Peterson 1970b; Meggitt 1962:50.

26. Radcliffe-Brown 1930-1931:35, 1954, 1956; Berndt 1957.

27. Stanner 1965:10; Hiatt 1962:286; Berndt 1957:347.

28. Meggitt 1962:51; Strehlow 1947:139-50, 1970:98.

29. My contention that the core population of the *jilimi* reflects ties to land is supported by O'Connell (1977:121), who says of the Alyawarra of McDonald Downs that the women of the *Alugera (jilimi)* were related as father's sister/brother's daughter, mother/daughter, mother's sister/sister's daughter. In terms of ritual relations we see that these women are *kirda* or *kurdungurlu* to each other but that yet again it is their kin ties which are emphasized by the ethnographer.

30. Meggitt 1972:74, see also 1962:189-90 and Appendix 2.

31. Meggitt 1972:74.

32. Munn 1973:37.

33. Munn 1973:36, 213.

34. Meggitt 1972:73, 78.

35. Munn 1973:213ff, 127-8.

36. Munn 1973:214.

37. Munn 1973:41 (fn.)

38. Meggitt 1962:189; Munn 1973:41.

39. Munn 1973:36-7.

40. Pink 1936:300-304; Strehlow 1947:124, 132; Meggitt 1972.

41. Kuhn 1970:43ff.

42. Roheim 1933; Warner 1937; Hiatt 1971; Maddock 1972; Munn 1973; Cawte 1974; Cowlishaw 1979; Bern 1979a, 1979b.

43. Cawte 1974:140.

44. Roheim 1933, 1974.

45. Firestone 1971:46-72.

46. Munn 1973.

47. Kaberry 1939:188-9.

48. Kaberry 1939:221.

49. Goodale 1971:338.

50. Goodale 1971:xxiii. Goodale claims that her work is mainly descriptive and limited to the Tiwi, but comparison with mainland Aboriginal studies is enlightening. The nature of Goodale's debate with Hart and Pilling is reminiscent of Kaberry's challenges to Warner and Roheim. See also Rohrlich-Leavitt *et al.* 1975:110-26.

51. Berndt 1950:9-10.

52. Berndt 1965:265ff, 1970:49. Berndt (1965) has also explored the complex relation between the sexes and men's and women's deep attitudes to their respective ceremonies. Berndt (1965:265) asserts:
    The ceremonies emphasize both differences between the two sexes and complementarity: they are dissimilar, but interdependent . . . Spatial withdrawal, temporary segregation from members of the opposite sex, is a means of achieving a close end: closer proximity, closer intimacy.

53. Evans-Pritchard 1965.

54. Ardener 1975. In 1968, as a tribute to his former teacher, Audrey Richards, who had worked on female puberty rites among the Bemba of Uganda, Ardener took a new look at his material on the rituals of Bakweri women living in Cameroon. Although his analysis has been critized, it remains influential.

55. Firestone 1971:46ff.; Mitchell 1974:346-50; Rosaldo & Lamphere 1974; Leacock 1978.

56. Slocum 1975; Tanner & Zihlman 1976.

57. Chodorow 1974; Ortner 1974.

58. Edholm *et al.* 1977; Begler 1978.

59. Rosaldo & Lamphere 1974:1-7.

60. Edholm *et al.* 1977:101.

61. Hamilton 1978b:2; see fn.5:23.

62. Hamilton 1979:xx-xxi.

63. Berndt & Berndt 1964:441-2.

64. Bell 1981a & b, 1982a & b.

APPENDIX 1 *

THE WARLPIRI ORTHOGRAPHY

	bilabial	alveolar	retroflex	lamino-palatal	velar
stop	p	t	rt	j	k
nasal	m	n	rn	ny	ng
lateral		l	rl	ly	
trill, flap		rr	rd		
glide	w		r		y

vowels i, a, u; ii, aa, uu

THE ARRERNTE AND KAYTEJ ORTHOGRAPHIES

Arrernte (Eastern Aranda)

	bilabial	alveolar	retroflex	inter-dental	lamino-palatal	velar
stop	p	t	rt	th	ty/j	k
nasal	m	n	rn	nh	ny	ng
nasally-released stops	/pm	/tn	/rtn	/tnh	/tny	/kng
lateral		l	rl	lh	ly	
flap, trill		rr				
glide	w		r		y	/h

vowels	front	central	back
high short		e	we
high long	i		
low long		a	ew

The slash / indicates Kaytej additions.

Kaytej

vowels	front	central	back
short	e		we
high long	ey		ew
low		a	
diphthong	ay		

*I gratefully acknowledge the permission of the Institute of Aboriginal Development, Alice Springs, to reproduce this material from the *Sourcebook for Central Australian Languages* (1981) compiled by Kathy Menning and edited by David Nash.

255

APPENDIX 2

KINSHIP

To explain kin terms to me women would offer English equivalents, but these always had to be qualified because of the differences between the kinship system of the Aborigines of Warrabri, which is of the type referred to in the anthropological literature as Arandic,[1] and those of white Australians. The comparison of systems was instructive: it forced me to re-examine the range of kin terms available to English speakers and increased my admiration for those Warrabri women who spoke of their social organization in such a clear-headed and reflective way. For the benefit of the non-specialist reader, let me draw out several of these comparisons between what I shall call 'my kinship system', that of English-speaking Australians (and, I am assuming, that of many of my non-specialist readers), and the Arandic, the system which is shared by all of the four major language groups of Warrabri.

Within my kinship system I trace relations lineally. I think of family as linked through my mother's line or my father's line and down through my own children. I make a basic distinction between my blood relatives (consanguines) and my in-laws (affines). In the Arandic system, too, these distinctions are made, but within each category further distinctions are drawn. For example, four lines of descent, one from each of the grandparents (that is, father's father, father's mother, mother's mother and mother's father) are distinguished terminologically. In English, I need to speak of maternal or paternal grandparents to make this distinction. In the Arandic system, each of the lines has a particular set of rights and responsibilities in respect of land, marriage arrangements, and ceremonial organization, and different rules of behaviour apply to each. For instance, one may engage in obscene joking with one's mother's mother and her brother but not with one's father's mother. From one's mother's father flows the responsibility of *kurdungurlu* but from one's father's father that of *kirda*.

Kin terms, which within my system I would reserve for lineal relatives, in the Arandic system are applied collaterally, that is, by extending outwards to include people such as second and third cousins. This is best understood by comparing the use of the terms mother, father, aunt and uncle at the upper generation level; of the terms brother, sister, cousin at the level of ego, and of the terms daughter, son, nephew and niece at the lower generation level.

In my system I call my actual genitor 'father' but in the Arandic system, all my father's brothers, my maternal grandfather's brother's sons, and my great grandfather's son's sons would be called by the term for father. Similarly I would extend the use of the term 'mother' to my actual mother, all her sisters, my maternal grandmother's sister's daughters and so on. At any generation I can extend outwards and trace up or down the generations. In Aboriginal English all one's father's brothers are called 'father'; the term 'uncle' applies only to mother's brothers. In my own kinship system, 'uncle' includes both mother's brother and father's brother. Similarly, in Aboriginal English, 'aunty' applies to father's sisters, not to mother's sisters.

When we go down a generation to our children and the children of our siblings, in English we speak of son, daughter, nephew, niece. Siblings call each other 'brother' and 'sister', while the children of siblings call each other 'cousin'. In the Arandic system, there is no distinction drawn between the children of siblings of the same sex: I would call my own children and those of my sister by the terms for 'child'. This word is different from the term by which brothers would call their collective children. In the Arandic system, the term for 'niece' and 'nephew' is reserved for the children of my brother and he in turn reserves that term for my children.

The way in which the children refer to each other follows on from this: my sister's children and my children would call each other 'brother' and 'sister', as would the children of two brothers, but my children call my brother's children by the term for 'cousin'. In the anthropological literature, this distinction is known as that between parallel cousins (the children of same-sex siblings) and cross cousins (the children of different-sex siblings). In addition to all the above distinctions within the Arandic system, one also distinguishes between older and younger siblings and, once again, one behaves differently to each of the relatives.

FIGURE 1

Warlpiri Kinship Diagram (from a man's perspective)[2]

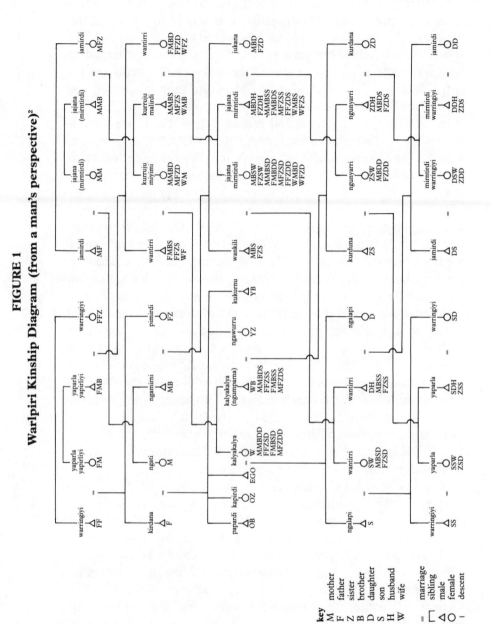

key
M mother
F father
Z sister
B brother
D daughter
S son
H husband
W wife

= marriage
⌐ sibling
△ male
○ female
- descent

FIGURE 2
Warlpiri Kinship Diagram (from a woman's perspective)[3]

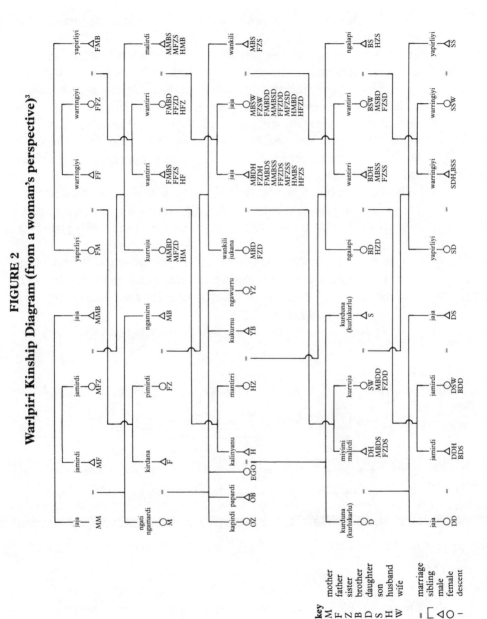

key
M mother
F father
Z sister
B brother
D daughter
S son
H husband
W wife

= marriage
⌐ sibling
△ male
○ female
- descent

THE SUBSECTION SYSTEM

Various categories of kin are grouped together to form three major cross-cutting divisions of the society: generation levels, patrimoieties and matrimoieties. In the first division, people distinguish between one's own generation – in which are included all siblings, one's grandparents and their siblings, and one's grandchildren – and the other generation, in which are one's parents and their siblings, that is, all one's aunts and uncles, and one's children and all their cousins. The system folds back on itself, so that great-grandparents are in the same category as one's parents and one's great-great-grandchildren are in the same category as one's self.

In the second division of the population into patrimoieties, all persons who trace relationships patrilineally are within one patrimoiety, and all those who trace relations patrilineally from one's spouse (or potential spouses) are in the opposite patrimoiety.

The third major division is that of the matrimoieties. Within one's own matrimoiety are all the persons to whom one is related through the matriline and in the opposite matrimoiety are all those who are related matrilineally to one's father.

If we draw these out we can see that the society is divided into four:

FIGURE 3

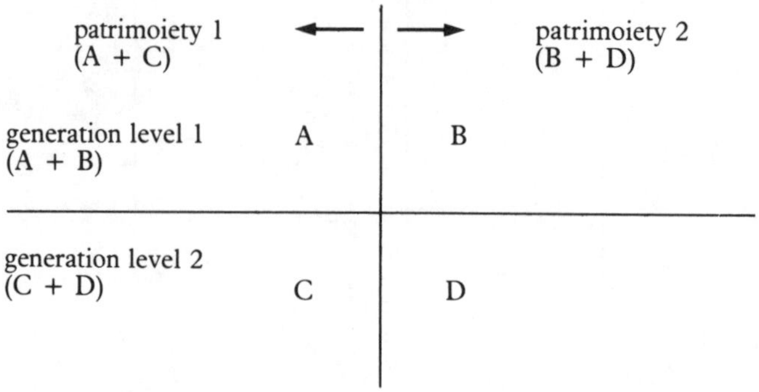

	patrimoiety 1 (A + C)	←	→	patrimoiety 2 (B + D)
generation level 1 (A + B)		A	B	
generation level 2 (C + D)		C	D	

Alyawarra speakers use a four-section system, the terms for which are set out below on the grid, formed by placing generation levels onto patrimoieties.

FIGURE 4

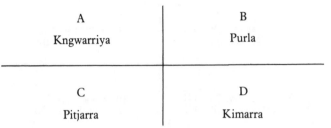

A	B
Kngwarriya	Purla
C	D
Pitjarra	Kimarra

In Eastern Aranda, Kaytej and Warlpiri, each of the sections is further divided into two to give eight subsection terms. These are listed below. Warlpiri: N for female and J for male form.

Alyawarra	*Kaytej*	*Aranda*	*Warlpiri*
A. Kngwarriya	Apenangke	Penangke	Japanangka
			Napanangka
	Kngwarrey	Kngwarraye	Jungarrayi
			Nungarrayi
C. Pitjarra	Kapeje	Peltharre	Japaljarri
			Napaljarri
	Apengarte	Pengarte	Japangardi
			Napangardi
B. Purla	Pwerle	Perrwerle	Jupurrula
			Napurrula
	Thangale	Ngale	Jangala
			Nangala
D. Kimarra	Akemarre	Kamarre	Jakamarra
			Nakamarra
	Mpejan	Mpetyane	Jampijinpa
			Nampijinpa

The terms may be organized in different ways to illustrate different aspects of the groupings. When organized as above (Figure 3 and 4) patrimoieties and generation levels are apparent but matrimoieties are not. When the latter are emphasized, correct and second-choice marriage partners are evident. Below in Figure 5, using Warlpiri terms, persons in A may marry B: the first choice is $A^1 = B^1$ and $A^2 = B^2$ and second choice is $A^1 = B^2$ and $A^2 = B^1$.

FIGURE 5

A			B	
J/Napanangka	A1	=	Ju/Napurrula	B1
J/Nungarrayi	A2	=	J/Nangala	B2

C			D	
J/Napaljarri	C1	=	Ju/Nakamarra	D1
J/Napangardi	C2	=	J/Nampijinpa	D2

On different occasions women would emphasize different aspects of the subsection system and, in a way, one had to learn to think of the division in three dimensions. David Nash[4], in his 'flip card' ready reckoner of the subsection system, comes closest to presenting information concerning generation levels, matrimoieties, patrimoieties and first and second choice marriages, in a form which allows all the data to be given equal weight. (I have included this for those who wish to be further teased by the intricacies of the system.)

Certainly it is possible to play computer games with the system and no doubt its intellectual elegance was an attraction to Central Australian desert peoples when they decided to adopt sections and subsections. Meggitt[5], in the 1950s, estimated that the Warlpiri probably had sections for about 150 years and the refinement of subsections for 100. The skin system fits well onto the Arandic kin system and this no doubt facilitated its adoption. In other areas, where there is a lack of fit between the two, the adoption of the skin system has been short-lived or caused confusion in matters of social classification.

People move back and forth between skin and kin systems in explaining their relationship to land, to *yawulyu* and to each other. Where precision is required, women would normally turn to the kin system, but the broader more inclusive categories of the skin system allow marginal relatives to be gathered in and allow certain categories of kin to be collapsed into one. This flexibility provides a mechanism whereby continuity may be asserted in the relations of person to place, and thereby present no threat to the notion that land/people relations are fixed.

The subsection system is, as Meggitt[6] points out, 'a summary expression of social relationships that may sometimes be practically

Appendix 2

FIGURE 6

Skin Names Flip Card Ready Reckoners

Warlpiri

Side 1   Side 2

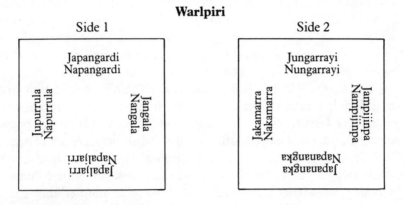

Directions
Glue side one to the back of side two
Father: flip towards or away
Mother: rotate 90° clockwise
Spouse: flip and rotate — 90° clockwise first choice marriage
                        — 90° anticlockwise second choice marriage

Kaytej

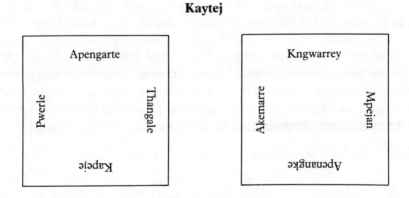

directions as for Warlpiri reckoner

useful but just as often is dangerously ambiguous': a Jupurrula could be my 'father' who should be treated with respect, but had my 'daughter' married a Jupurrula (her second choice after Jungarrayi), I would call that man 'son-in-law', and he would stand in an avoidance relationship. There is a big difference between calling someone 'son-in-law' (*miyimi*) and 'father' (*kirdana*). Both had the same 'skin', but the behaviour expected of a 'son-in-law' was not that expected of a 'father'. Thus men would distinguish between being my 'father' or 'son-in-law' by a second-choice marriage of my 'daughter'.

I was also taught to distinguish between those I called 'son' and those I called 'father-in-law', both of whom fell within subsection, Jungarrayi. Usually this was reckoned on the basis of seniority, so the elderly Jungarrayi I called 'father-in-law', while younger men I called 'son'. However, there was a grey area in which men aged about twenty-five to thirty-five would make decisions, not entirely unambiguously, as to what I should call them. As their 'mother' they could ask me for food, as a 'daughter-in-law' they could instruct me.

In a similar way, women would distinguish between being my 'sister-in-law' and my 'granny' (father's mother), both of whom were Napaljarri, but each involved relationships which required different behaviour. My 'mothers-in-law' and 'daughters-in-law' also fell in the same subsection, that of Nangala, but once again I had to learn how to distinguish. From my reading of the literature I had expected my 'sisters-in-law' to be my close friends but all the Napaljarri, my potential 'sisters-in-law', were of the granny generation. Their brothers were men I was allowed to call 'husband' (not father's mother's brother, as one would expect) but these women, most of whom were older, traced the relationship through actual kinship ties to make me of the grandchild generation. They were my 'father's mothers', not my 'husband's sisters'. Thus the Napaljarri were the women with whom I, as a member of the Nakamarra-Napurrula *kirda* pair, called 'mother' of my dreaming.

COUNTRY RELATIONS

The way in which descent-based relations are traced from country may be represented in the following way:

Appendix 2

FIGURE 7

Descent-based country relations

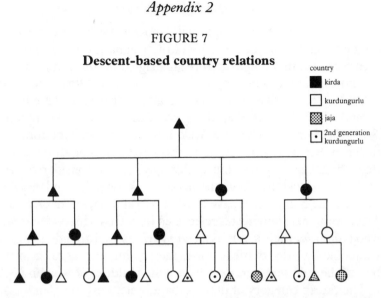

country
■ kirda
□ kurdungurlu
▨ jaja
⊡ 2nd generation kurdungurlu

From Figure 7 we can see that a woman shares her responsibility as *kirda* with her 'sisters', 'brothers', 'fathers', 'fathers' brothers and sisters' and 'fathers' fathers' brothers and sisters', and so on back through the patriline, but this is not the way in which women speak of land. Women tend to say, 'I hold (*mardirni*) that country from my *pimirdi* (father's sister) or *warringiyi* (father's father) or *kirdana* (father)' and thereby stress the relationship to their living teachers and role models.

As we can also see from Figure 7 a woman is *kurdungurlu* for the country her mother holds from her father. Thus a woman will say, 'I hold that country from my *jamirdi* (mother's father)'. She shares her responsibility with her own sibling set, her 'mothers' sisters' children', her 'mothers' fathers' sisters' children' and her 'mothers' brothers' daughters' children'.

Thus for a woman *kirda*, her actual daughter may play the role of *kurdungurlu* in ritual performances. This is possible because the age difference may be as little as sixteen years. For male *kirda* of a country, the primary *kurdungurlu* will be his sister's children, that is, his nephews. The persons who together act as *kirda* are related by patrilineal descent, which for women entails an aunt-niece pair, while for men a father-son pair. The former use a reciprocal term, *pimirdi*, and the relationship is an egalitarian one. The father-son relationship is one marked by authority and respect and perhaps an age difference of thirty-five years. Although male and female *kirda* differ in their kin inter-relationships, the unity of these agnatically-tied sibling sets is emphasized in the sign/gesture language. *Pimirdi*, and son to father, are indicated by a gentle tap with the outstretched finger on the chin.

On Figure 7 I have also indicated a further descent-based relation to land which, following Koch,[7] I have called 'second generation *kurdungurlu*'. People such as the Wakulpu Nungarrayi, who follow their father as *kurdungurlu*, belong to this category. Not all persons who trace their *kurdungurlu*-ship in this way will be considered *kurdungurlu*: they must also have the necessary knowledge and ritual skill. Because the Nungarrayi have lived near Wakulpu, learnt of its significance from their father, and celebrated its rituals with the Nampijinpa who are *kirda*, their status as *kurdungurlu* is well founded. However, without knowledge of life histories their claims appear to be an exception to the rule that *kurdungurlu* are the children of women *kirda*.

The fourth category of descent-based relationship to land – which I have traced on Figure 7 – is that of one's *jaja* country. This is often spoken of as 'granny country' on the mother's side (that is, maternal grandmother), but most commonly it is presented as a relation between countries rather than between persons. Granny countries belong to the same patrimoiety, and thus in ceremonies where there is the division into *kirda* and *kurdungurlu*, as the reciprocal halves of the spiritual universe, those who call each other *jaja* unite in the same moiety. This constitutes a company relation of a kind and one that is apparent in a section system where the groupings of kin locate ego and mother's mother in the same section: reference to one's granny country is only available through distinctions within the kin system. I return to this below in my discussion of marriage and land.

Within a four-section system, such as the Alyawarra, the relation between the patrimoieties appears as one of direct reciprocity. In Figure 8 we can see by following the arrows that moiety 1 is *kurdungurlu* for moiety 2 when the *kirda* are Kngwarriya and Pitjarra (as for Jarrajarra), and that moiety 2 may be *kurdungurlu* for 1 when, for example, the *kirda* are from Purla and Kimarra (as for Wurrulju).

Within an eight-subsection system (Figure 9) the reciprocity is more difficult to represent: it is necessary to merge certain categories of kin, but if one speaks at the level of patrimoiety, then the reciprocity is clear (Figure 10).

Appendix 2

FIGURE 8

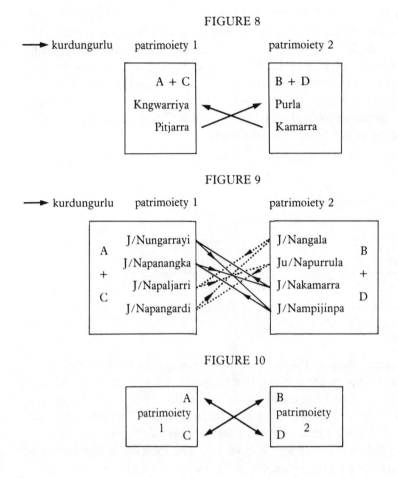

→ kurdungurlu   patrimoiety 1   patrimoiety 2

A + C	B + D
Kngwarriya	Purla
Pitjarra	Kamarra

FIGURE 9

→ kurdungurlu   patrimoiety 1   patrimoiety 2

A + C
- J/Nungarrayi
- J/Napanangka
- J/Napaljarri
- J/Napangardi

B + D
- J/Nangala
- Ju/Napurrula
- J/Nakamarra
- J/Nampijinpa

FIGURE 10

A patrimoiety 1
C

B patrimoiety 2
D

MARRIAGE

When we look at the way in which marriages are contracted, we find that the reciprocity between countries is stated in terms of ties of affinity and descent. In the Aranda system, the preference appears to be to find spouses in adjacent countries. In Figure 11 I have set out the reciprocity which would occur if *kirda* from country A found their spouses in country B and vice versa, that is, if a woman of country A – say a Nampijinpa – married a Japangardi of B, and a Napangardi of B married a Jampijinpa of A. But in country A there are also

267

J/Nangala who will marry the N/Jungarrayi of a third country, say C and the N/Japanangka of B who will marry Ju/Napurrula of another, say D. The pattern thus widens to resemble the overlapping checkerboard of Figure 12. Within this system there is always the possibility of incorporating yet another country and the potential for spreading knowledge further afield. At the borders of Kaytej we find intermarriage with Warlpiri, Anmatjirra and Warumungu and thus 'countries' which have dual affiliations.

FIGURE 11

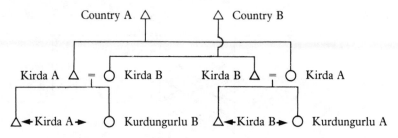

Looking again at Figure 11, we see that the *kirda* of A will draw their *kurdungurlu* from B and that the *kirda* of B will draw theirs from A. The reciprocity is clear. In a four-section system the Purla and Kimarra turn to Kngwarriya and Pitjarra as *kurdungurlu* and vice versa. But in a subsection system the *kurdungurlu* for A will be found in two different countries: in B and C. The location of *kurdungurlu* is determined by marriage, and thus the way in which marriages are contracted underwrites the alliances between countries.

FIGURE 12

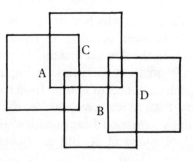

Appendix 2

How marriages are contracted then becomes an important factor in understanding the ritual maintenance of land.

RITUAL RECIPROCITY

Let me now indicate how marriage alliances, descent-based relations to land and the subsection system may be shown to be an interacting whole, underwritten by the notion of ritual reciprocity. If we consider each of the patricouples (pairs) as an entity, that is, as an estate or country, wherein

W is J/Nakamarra + Ju/Napurrula
X is J/Nungarrayi + J/Napaljarri
Y is N/Japanangka + J/Napangardi
Z is N/Jampijinpa + J/Nangala

we see that tracing affinal ties between countries produces the following pattern:

FIGURE 13

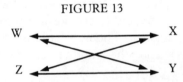

If we then trace the *kirda* to *kurdungurlu* tie, we find the same pattern. Viewed in this way, we can see that the relations of people to land is a web of circulating relationships wherein reciprocity is indeed achieved. It is not a system of isolated patriclans each maintaining and jealously guarding a discretely owned territory. Without the links established through marriage, without the ritual reciprocity of *kirda* to *kurdungurlu*, patriclans would exist in total isolation, unable to paint themselves for ritual, unable to visit their own sites, unable to maintain their own country or to reproduce the next generation.

To explain how this is played out, let me describe two cases which occurred in 1980. In case 1 (Figure 14), a Japangardi was being initiated, and in case 2, a Jungarrayi. As a Nakamarra I was given

FIGURE 14

Initiation Relationships

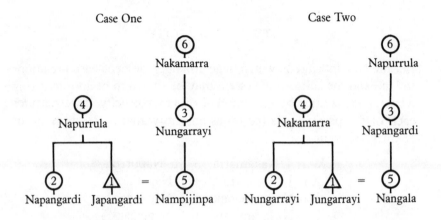

instructions in both sets of negotiations: as the mother in Case 2 and the mother of the mother-in-law in Case 1. In Case 1 it was the duty of the Napangardi (2), sister of the initiate, to 'pick up' the mother-in-law, a Nungarrayi (3), for the Napurrula (4) mother. The Nungarrayi mother-in-law then contracted to provide a Nampijinpa (5) daughter as a wife for the Japangardi. The negotiations occurred between the mother (Napurrula) and the mother of the mother-in-law, a Nakamarra (6).

In Case 2, the sister of the Jungarrayi (1) initiate, Nungarrayi (2) (the mother-in-law in the previous sequence), 'picked up' Napangardi (3) (the sister in Case 1) and took her to her mother, Nakamarra (the mother of the mother-in-law of Case 1). The Napangardi mother-in-law was then obliged to provide a Nangala daughter for the Jungarrayi initiate. Negotiations occurred between the Nakamarra mother of the initiate and the Napurrula mother of the mother-in-law. This pair are, of course, classificatory joint *kirda* for the *kurdungurlu* country of the boy and in some cases are the acting *kurdungurlu*. In the painting up which occurs in the women's ceremonies, an opportunity is taken to extend the knowledge and rights of such classificatory relationships so that they achieve a new ritual status.

These cases were a squaring of the ledgers between families because, as women said, 'The Jungarrayi who gets our Napangardi,

FIGURE 15

Initiation and Marriage

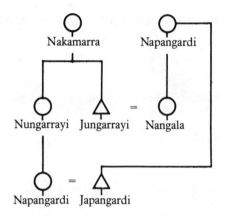

gives us back his sister for Japangardi in business.' Genealogically, this exchange implicates three generations with Japangardi and Napangardi appearing two generations apart (Figure 15). This can be accommodated within Warlpiri and Aranda kinship systems which tend to classify grandchild and paternal grandfather as siblings. They are of course in the same generation moiety and have the same 'skin' name.

In the model of marriage which I have generated in the exchanges of mothers-in-law, initiates and sisters, we see clearly that initiation is indeed a multipurpose ritual which serves to realign relationships, 'to turn people around', and to provide a forum within which alliances between countries may be established and maintained.

Although in this discussion I am not concerned to discuss at length differences between 'MMBDD' and 'ZSD' marriage,[8] it is worth noting that in Figure 15, with the sister and brother two generations apart, a 'ZSD' marriage is easily generated. Laughren (personal communication) suggests a man ideally marries two generations below to the daughter of a maternal nephew who is older than he is. Thus for a man, marriage is to his 'ZSD', while for a woman it is to her 'FMB'. Once again this is easily demonstrated in Figure 15.

Meggitt[9] notes that 'In a structural sense intermarriage between a pair of Warlpiri matrilines involves men in the exchange of sisters' but he prefers to focus on lines rather than groups. The topic of marriage is vexatious because of the asymmetry between a male and female model of a first-choice marriage. For a man this is ideally said to be with his 'MMBDD', but this must be seen as a category of cousin, rather than as an actual genealogically-traced relationship.

NOTES

1.   See Meggitt 1962:82-4; Wafer 1982. I am grateful to Jim Wafer for allowing me to draw freely on his excellent material.

2.   After Wafer 1982:22.

3.   *Ibid.*:23.

4.   *Ibid.*:24. From an idea of David Nash and Alan Wechsler of M.I.T., Cambridge, Mass. U.S.A.

5.   Meggitt 1962:168.

6.   *Ibid.*:169.

7.   Kock *et al.* 1981:5.

8.   Meggitt 1962:199.

9.   Meggitt 1962:196.

BIBLIOGRAPHY

Ardener, Edwin
  1975 'Belief and the problem of women', in *Perceiving Women*, Ardener, Shirley (ed.), London, Malaby, 1-18.

Ashwin, Arthur C.
  1927 *From South Australia to Port Darwin with Sheep and Horses in 1870-71.* (ms. copy, Canberra, Australian Institute of Aboriginal Studies.)
  1970 'And the lubras are ladies now', in *Woman's Role in Aboriginal Society*, Gale, Fay (ed.), Canberra, A.I.A.S., 31-8.

Bates, Daisy M.
  1938 *The Passing of the Aborigines*, London, John Murray.

Baume, F. E.
  1933 *Tragedy Track: the story of the Granites*, Sydney, F. C. Johnson.

Beckett, J. T.
  1914-15 'Report on Aborigines to the Chief Protector of Aborigines, Darwin', *Report of the Northern Territory*, The Parliament of the Commonwealth of Australia, 26-8.

Begler, Elsie B.
  1978 'Sex, status and authority in egalitarian society', *American Anthropologist* 80 (3), 571-88.

Bell, Diane
  1978 'For our families: the Kurundi walk off and the Ngurrantiji venture', *Aboriginal History*, 2 (1), 32-62.
  1979a 'The Pawurrinji puzzle', a report to Central Land Council, Alice Springs. 40 1. (ms. copy A.I.A.S.)
  1979b 'Statement to the Utopia land claim hearing', Exhibit 57 to the Anmatjirra and Alyawarra land claim to the Utopia Pastoral Lease. 37 1. (ms. copy A.I.A.S.)
  1979c 'Women and the land', *Identity*, 3 (11), 22-30.
  1980a 'Desert politics: choices in the "marriage market" ', in *Women and Colonization: anthropological perspectives*, Etienne, Mona and Eleanor Leacock (eds), New York, Praeger, 239-69.
  1980b 'Statement to the Willowra claim hearing', Exhibit 65 to Lander Warlpiri/Anmatjirra Land Claim to Willowra Pastoral Lease. 10 1. (ms. copy A.I.A.S.)
  1981a 'Women's Sites in the Victoria River District', report to the Aboriginal Sacred Sites Protection Authority, Darwin.

1981b 'Daly River (Malak Malak) Land Claim: women's interests', Exhibit 8. Submission on behalf of traditional owners. N.L.C. Darwin, 34 1. (ms. copy A.I.A.S.)

1982a 'Cox River (Alawa-Ngandji) Land Claim: women's interests', Exhibit 13. Submission on behalf of traditional owners. N.L.C. Darwin, 59 1. (ms. copy A.I.A.S.)

1982b 'In the tracks of the Munga-Munga', Exhibit 27, Cox River (Alawa-Ngandji) Land Claim. 33 1. (ms. copy A.I.A.S.)

In press 'Topsy Napurrula: teacher, philosopher and friend', in *Fighters and Singers*, White, Isobel, Diane Barwick & Betty Meehan (eds), Canberra, Australian National University Press.

Bell, Diane & Pam Ditton
1980 *Law: the Old and the New*, Canberra, Aboriginal History for the Central Australian Aboriginal Legal Aid Service.

Bern, J.
1979a 'Politics in the conduct of a secret male ceremony', *Journal of Anthropological Research*, 35 (1), 47-59.

1979b 'Ideological domination', *Oceania*, 50 (2), 118-32.

Berndt, Catherine H.
1950 'Women's changing ceremonies in Northern Australia', *L'Homme*, 1:1-87.

1963 Commentary 'The social position of women', Reay, Marie in *Australian Aboriginal Studies*, Shiels, Helen (ed.), Melbourne, Oxford University Press, 335-42.

1964 'The role of native doctors in Aboriginal Australia', in *Magic, Faith and Healing*, Kiev, Arie (ed.), New York, The Free Press of Glencoe, 264-82.

1965 'Women and the "secret life" ', in *Aboriginal Man in Australia*, Berndt, Ronald M. and Catherine H. Berndt (eds), Sydney, Angus & Robertson, 236-82.

1970 'Digging sticks and spears, or, the two-sex model', in *Woman's Role in Aboriginal Society*, Gale, Fay (ed.), Canberra, A.I.A.S., 39-48.

1979 'Aboriginal women and the notion of "the marginal man" ', in *Aborigines of the West: their past and their present*, Berndt, Ronald & Catherine H. Berndt (eds), Perth, University of Western Australia Press, 28-38.

Berndt, Ronald M.
1957 'In reply to Radcliffe-Brown on Australian local organisation', *American Anthropologist*, 59:346-51.

1976 *Love songs of Arnhem Land*, Melbourne, Nelson.

Berndt, Ronald M. & Catherine H. Berndt

Bibliography

1951 *Sexual Behaviour in Western Arnhem Land*, N.Y., Viking Fund Publishers in Anthropology, No. 16.

1964 *The World of the First Australians*, Sydney, Ure Smith.

Bowen, Elenore Smith
1964 *Return to Laughter*, New York, Doubleday & Co.

Cawte, J.
1974 *Medicine is the Law*, U.S.A., University of Hawaii Press.

Chewings, Charles
1930 'A Journey from Barrow Creek to Victoria River', *Geographical Journal*, 76 (4), 316-38.

1936 *Back in the Stone Age*, Sydney, Angus and Robertson.

Chodorow, Nancy
1974 'Family structure and feminine personality', in *Woman, Culture and Society*, Rosaldo, M. Z. and L. Lamphere (eds), Stanford, Stanford University Press, 43-66.

Collier, Jane F. & Michelle Z. Rosaldo
1981 'Politics and gender in simple societies', in *Sexual Meanings*, Ortner B. Sherry and Harriet Whitehead (eds), Cambridge, Cambridge University Press, 275-329.

Cowlishaw, Gillian K.
1979 'Woman's Realm: a study of socialization, sexuality and reproduction amongst Australian Aborigines', University of Sydney, Ph.D. thesis, 436 l.

Denham, Woodrow Wilson
1978 'Alyawara, ethnographic data base', New Haven, Connecticut, Human Relations Area Files, 137 l.

Edholm, Felicity, Olivia Harris & Kate Young
1977 'Conceptualising women', *Critique of Anthropology*, 3 (9 & 10), 101-30.

Elkin, A. P.
1935 'Anthropology in Australia, past and present', in *Australian and New Zealand Association for the Advancement of Science*, Report, 22:196-207.

1977 *'Aboriginal Men of High Degree'*, St Lucia, University of Queensland Press (2nd ed., first published 1945).

Ellis, Catherine Joan
1970 'The role of the ethnomusicologist in the study of Andagarinja women's ceremonies', in *Miscellanea Musicologica, Adelaide Studies in Musicology*, 5:76-208.

Evans-Pritchard, E. E.
1965 'The position of women in primitive societies and in our own', in

The Position of Women in Primitive Societies and Other Essays in Social Anthropology, Evans-Pritchard, E. E., London, Faber and Faber, 37-58.

Eylmann, Erhard
1908   *Die Eingeborenen der Kolonie Südaustralien*, Berlin, Dietrich Reimer.

Fee, Elizabeth
1974   'The sexual politics of Victorian social anthropology', in *Clio's Consciousness Raised*, Hartman, Mary S. and Lois Banner (eds), New York, Harper and Row.

Firestone, Shulamith
1971   *The Dialectic of Sex*, Great Britain, Jonathan Cape.

Gale, Fay (ed.)
1970   *Woman's Role in Aboriginal Society*, Canberra, A.I.A.S.
1983   *We are all Bosses*, Canberra, A.I.A.S.

Gale, Fay
1972   *Urban Aborigines*, Canberra, Australian National University Press.

Gillen, Francis James
1968   *Gillen's Diary: the camp jottings of F. J. Gillen on the Spencer and Gillen expedition across Australia 1901-2*, Adelaide, Libraries Board of South Australia.

Golde, Peggy (ed.)
1970   *Women in the Field*, Chicago, Aldine.

Goodale, Jane C.
1971   *Tiwi Wives: a study of women of Melville Island, Northern Australia*, Seattle, University of Washington Press.

Gosse, William Christie
1874   'Report and diary of Mr W. C. Gosse's central and western exploring expedition, 1873', Adelaide, Government Printer, Libraries Board of South Australia, 1973.

Gregory, A. C.
1969   *Journal of Australian Explorations*, Brisbane, Government Printer (South Australian State Library facsimile editions, no. 14).

Hagen, Rod & Meredith Rowell
1978   'A claim to areas of traditional land by the Alyawarra and Kaititja', Central Land Council, Alice Springs, 41 l. (ms. copy A.I.A.S).
1979   'The Anmatjirra and Alyawarra land claim to the Utopia pastoral lease: submission on behalf of the traditional owners of the area claimed', Central Land Council, Alice Springs, 53 l. (ms. copy A.I.A.S).

Hagen, R., J. Lloyd & B. Reyburn
1982   'A Warumungu Land Claim to Unalienated Crown Land', a Central Land Council Submission, Alice Springs, 316 l.

276

Bibliography

Hale, Kenneth L.

1974 'Warlpiri-English vocabulary prepared for use in the Yuendumu Warlpiri language programme', M.I.T., Cambridge, Mass, U.S.A. 96 l. (ms. copy A.I.A.S).

1980 'Remarks on the joint land maintenance responsibility of *kirda* and *kurdungurlu*', Exhibit 47 to the Lander Warlpiri/Anmatjirra Land Claim to Willowra Pastoral Lease, 4 l.

Hamilton, Annette

1970 'The role of women in Aboriginal marriage arrangements', in *Woman's Role in Aboriginal Society*, Canberra, A.I.A.S., 17-20.

1975 'Aboriginal women: the means of production', in *The Other Half*, Mercer, Jan (ed.), Harmondsworth, Penguin, 167-79.

1978a 'Descended from father, belonging to country: problems in the constitution of rights to land in the eastern Western Desert', School of Behavioural Sciences, Macquarie University, N.S.W. 19p. (ms. copy A.I.A.S.).

1978b 'Dual social systems: technology, labour and women's secret rites in the eastern Western Desert of Australia', paper presented to the International Conference on Hunters and Gatherers, Paris, June 1978, 17p. (ms. copy A.I.A.S.).

1979 'Timeless transformation, women, men and history in the Australian Western Desert', University of Sydney, Ph.D. thesis.

Hart, C. W. M. & Arnold R. Pilling

1960 *The Tiwi of North Australia*, N.Y., Holt, Rinehart & Winston.

Hartwig, M. C.

1965 'The progress of white settlement in the Alice Springs District and its effects upon the Aboriginal inhabitants 1860-1894', University of Adelaide, Ph.D. thesis, 669pp.

Hiatt, Betty

1970 'Woman the gatherer', in *Woman's Role in Aboriginal Society*, Gale, Fay (ed.), Canberra, A.I.A.S., 2-7.

Hiatt, L. R.

1962 'Local organization amongst the Australian Aborigines', *Oceania*, 32:267-86.

1971 'Secret pseudo-procreative rites among Australian Aborigines', *Anthropology in Oceania*, Hiatt, L. R. and C. Jayawardena (eds), Sydney, Angus and Robertson, 77-88.

Kaberry, Phyllis M.

1939 *Aboriginal Woman, sacred and profane*, London, Routledge.

Koch, Harold, Grace Koch, Petronella Wafer & James Wafer

1981 'A claim to areas of traditional land by the Kaytej, Warlpiri and

Warlmanpa', submitted by the Central Land Council on behalf of the traditional owners of the area claimed, Alice Springs, 82 l.

Kuhn, Thomas S.
1970 *The Structure of Scientific Revolutions*, (second edition), Chicago, University of Chicago Press.

Leacock, Eleanor
1978 'Women's status in egalitarian society: implications for social evolution', *Current Anthropology*, 19 (2), 247-75.

Lévi-Strauss, C.
1949 *Les structures élémentaires de la parenté*, Paris, Presses Universitaires de France.

McConnel, Ursula
1930 'The Wikmunkan tribe of Cape York Peninsula', *Oceania*, 1:181-205.

Maddock, Kenneth
1972 *The Australian Aborigines: a portrait of their society*, London, Allen Lane/Penguin.

1980 *Anthropology, Law and the Definition of Aboriginal Rights to Land*, Nijmegen, Institute of Folk Law.

Mead, Margaret
1977 *Letters From the Field 1925-1975*, New York, Harper and Row.

Meggitt, M. J.
1955 'Djanba among the Walbiri, Central Australia', *Anthrops*, 50:375-403.

1962 *Desert People: a study of the Walbiri Aborigines of Central Australia*, Sydney, Angus and Robertson.

1972 'Understanding Australian Aboriginal society: kinship systems or cultural categories', in *Kinship Studies in the Morgan Centennial Year*, Reining, Priscilla (ed.), Washington, The Anthropological Society of Washington, 64-87.

Mitchell, Juliet
1974 *Psychoanalysis and Feminism*, Ringwood, Penguin.

Mountford, C. P. & Alison Harvey
1941 'Women of the Adnjamatana of the northern Flinders Ranges, South Australia', *Oceania*, 12 (2), 155-62.

Munn, Nancy, D.
1973 *Walbiri Iconography: graphic representations and cultural symbolism in a Central Australian society*, Ithaca and London, Cornell University Press.

Nash, David
1980 'A note on *kurdungurlu*', Exhibit 48 to Lander Warlpiri/

Bibliography

Anmatjirra land claim to the Willowra pastoral lease, 20 l.

(ed.)

1981   *Source Book for Central Australian Languages*, compiled by Kathy Menning, Alice Springs, Institute for Aboriginal Development.

Nash, David & J. Simpson

1981   ' "No-name" in Central Australia', *Chicago Linguistic Society*, Chicago, University of Chicago, Vol. 1-2:165-77.

O'Connell, J. F.

1977   'Room to move: contemporary Alyawarra settlement patterns and their implications for Aboriginal housing patterns', *Mankind*, 11:119-31.

Ortner, Sherry B.

1974   'Is female to male as nature is to culture?' in *Woman, Culture, and Society*, Rosaldo, M. Z. and L. Lamphere (eds), Stanford, Stanford University Press, 67-87.

Parker, Catherine Somerville (Langloh)

1905   *The Evahayi Tribes: a study of Aboriginal life in Australia*, London, Constable.

Peterson, Nicolas

1969   'Secular and ritual links: two basic and opposed principles of Australian social organization as illustrated by Walbiri ethnography', *Mankind*, 7:27-35.

1970a   'Bulawandi: a Central Australian ceremony for the resolution of conflict', in *Australian Aboriginal Anthropology*, Berndt, Ronald M. (ed.), Nedlands, University of Western Australia Press, 200-215.

1970b   'The importance of women in determining the composition of residential groups in Aboriginal Australia', in *Woman's Role in Aboriginal Society*, Gale, Fay (ed.), Canberra, A.I.A.S., 9-16.

Peterson, Nicolas, Patrick McConvell, Steven Wild & Rod Hagen

1978   'A claim to areas of traditional land by the Warlpiri and Kartangarurru - Kurintji', Central Land Council, Alice Springs (ms. copy A.I.A.S.).

Pink, Olive

1936   'The landowners in the Northern division of the Aranda tribe, Central Australia', *Oceania*, 6(3), 275-305.

Radcliffe-Brown, A. R.

1930-31   'Social organization of Australian tribes', *Oceania*, 1:34-63, 206-46, 322-41, 426-56.

1954   'Australian local organization', *American Anthropologist*, 56:105-6.

1956   'On Australian local organization', *American Anthropologist*, 58:363-7.

Reay, Marie

    1963a   'The social position of women', in *Australian Aboriginal Studies*, Sheils, Helen (ed.), Melbourne, Oxford University Press, 319-34.

    1963b   'Aboriginal and white Australian family structure: an inquiry into assimilation trends', *Sociological Review*, n.s., 11(1), 19-47.

Reid, J. C.

    1978   'The role of the *Marnggitj* in contempory health care', *Oceania*, 49(2), 69-109.

Reiter, Rayna R.

    1975   *Toward an Anthropology of Women*, New York and London, Monthly Review Press.

Roheim, Geza

    1933   'Women and their life in Central Australia', *Royal Anthropological Institute Journal*, 63:207-65.

    1974   *Children of the Desert*, New York, Harper and Row.

Rohrlich-Leavitt, Ruby Barbara Sykes & Elizabeth Weatherford

    1975   'Aboriginal woman: male and female anthropological perspectives', in *Toward an Anthropology of Women*, Reiter, Rayna R. (ed.), New York, Monthly Review Press, 110-26.

Rosaldo, Michelle Zimbalist & Louise Lamphere

    1974   'Introduction', in *Woman, Culture, and Society*, Rosaldo, M. Z. and L. Lamphere (eds), Stanford, Stanford University Press, 1-15.

Sheils, Helen (ed.)

    1963   *Australian Aboriginal Studies*, Melbourne, Oxford University Press.

Slocum, Sally

    1975   'Woman the gatherer: male bias in anthropology', in *Toward an Anthropology of Women*, Reiter, Rayna R. (ed.), New York, Monthly Review Press, 36-50.

South Pacific

    1959   'Warrabri Aboriginal settlement', *South Pacific*, 10(4), 75-9.

Spencer, Baldwin & F. J. Gillen

    1899   *The Native Tribes of Central Australia*, London, Macmillan.

    1904   *The Northern Tribes of Central Australia*, London, Macmillan.

    1927   *The Arunta*, London, Macmillan.

Stanner, W. E. H.

    1934   'Report on fieldwork in North Central and North Australia 1934-5', Canberra, A.I.A.S., 102 l. (ms. copy A.I.A.S.). Issued in microfiche 1979, A.I.A.S.

    1959   'Durmugam: a Nangiomeri', in *In the Company of Man*, Casagrande, J. A. (ed.), New York, Harper and Row.

Bibliography

1965 'Aboriginal territorial organization: estate, range, domain and regime', *Oceania*, 36(1), 1-26.

1966 *On Aboriginal Religion*, Oceania Monographs, No. 11, Sydney, University of Sydney.

1968 *After the Dreaming: black and white Australians - an anthropologist's view*, Sydney, Australian Broadcasting Commission.

1979 *White Man Got No Dreaming, Essays 1938-73*, Canberra, Australian National University Press.

Strehlow, T. G. H.

1947 *Aranda Traditions*, Melbourne, Melbourne University Press.

1970 'Geography and the totemic landscape in Central Australia', in *Australian Aboriginal Anthropology*, Berndt, Ronald M. (ed.), Nedlands, University of Western Australia Press, 92-140.

1971 *Songs of Central Australia*, Sydney, Angus and Robertson.

Stuart, John McDouall

1861 'McDouall Stuart's last expedition into the interior of Australia', *Journal of the Royal Geographical Society*, 31:65-145.

Tanner, Nancy & Adrienne Zihlman

1976 'Women in evolution. Part 1: innovation and selection in human origins', *Signs*, 1(3), 585-608.

Terry, M.

1934 *Hidden Wealth and Hiding People*, London, Putman.

Toohey, John

1979a 'Land claim by Alyawarra and Kaititja', Report by the Aboriginal Land Commissioner, Australian Government Printer.

1980a 'Anmatjirra and Alyawarra Land Claim to Utopia Pastoral lease', Report by the Aboriginal Land Commissioner, Australian Government Printer.

1980b 'Lander Warlpiri Anmatjirra Land Claim to Willowra Pastoral lease', Report by the Aboriginal Land Commissioner, Australian Government Printer.

Transcript of Evidence

1980 *Aboriginal Land Rights (N.T.) Act* 1976 re Lander Warlpiri/Anmatjirra land claim to Willowra pastoral lease.

1981 *Aboriginal Land Rights (N.T.) Act*, 1976 re Warlmanpa, Warlpiri, Mudbara and Warumungu Land Claim.

Tuxworth, Hilda

n.d. *Tennant Creek: Yesterday and Today*.

Wafer, J.

1982 'A Simple Introduction to Central Australian Kinship Systems', Alice Springs, Institute for Aboriginal Development.

Wafer, J. & P.
  1983 'The Mount Barkly Land Claim', a C.L.C. Submission on behalf of the traditional owners of the area claimed, Central Land Council, Alice Springs.

Warner, W. L.
  1937 *A Black Civilization*, New York, Harper.

Welfare Report
  1961 'Warrabri Aboriginal reserve, Central Australia', Welfare Branch, Northern Territory Administration, 36pp. (copy A.I.A.S.).

White, Isobel M.
  1970 'Aboriginal women's status: a paradox resolved', in *Woman's Role in Aboriginal Society*, Gale, Fay (ed.), Canberra, A.I.A.S., 21-9.

  1975 'Sexual conquest and submission in Aboriginal myths', in *Australian Aboriginal Mythology*, Hiatt, L. R. (ed.), Canberra, A.I.A.S., 123-42.

Yallop, C. L.
  1969 'The Alyawara and their territory', *Oceania*, 39:187-97.

  1977 *Alyawarra: an Aboriginal language of Central Australia*, Canberra, A.I.A.S.

GLOSSARY

(K = Kaytej W = Warlpiri S = Strehlow's orthography of Aranda)

affines	persons related through marriage. Hence ties of affinity, affinal relations.
Akwerlpe (K)	place and country name, = Wakulpu (W). See map p. 112.
Alekarenge (K)	place name for Warrabri, = Ali-curang, 'belonging to dog'.
altyerre (K)	dreaming, = *aljirra*.
Arnerre (K)	country name, Taylor Crossing. See map p. 112.
churinga	see *tjuringa*.
classificatory kin	within such a system the same term is used for lineal and collateral relatives. For example *kirdana* glosses father, father's brother, father's father's son, See kin diagram Appendix 2.
endogamy	marriage inside one's own group. For example where one marries within one's own generation level we have endogamous generation moieties.
Errwelje (K)	place and country name, = Wurrulju (W). See map p. 112.
Etwerrpe (K)	country name, 'sand-hills', = Uturrpa. See map p. 112.
Jarrajarra (W)	place and country name. See map p. 112.
jaja (W)	kinship term, 'granny', mother's mother, mother's mother's brother, see kinship diagram, Appendix 2.
jilimi (W)	single women's camp.
jukurrpa (W)	dreaming = *djugurba*.
Junkaji (W)	place and country name. Also name of ancestral hero, written *junkaji* to

	distinguish from place. = Jungkaji, see map p. 112.
Karlukarlu (W)	place and country name, Devils' Marbles, 'boulders similar to those at Devils' Marbles. See map p. 112.
kirda (W)	from *kirdana* (W) 'father', all those related to a particular place, country, dreaming on the 'father's side'. See Appendix 2.
kumunjayi (W)	'no name', a replacement term for a term homophonous, or nearly so, with the name of a deceased person. See Nash and Simpson 1981.
kurdungurlu (W)	*kurdu* (W) 'child' (woman speaking), *ngurlu* 'from', all those related to a particular place, country, dreaming on the 'mother's side', complementary to *kirda*. See Appendix 2.
kurduru (W)	women's ritual object, see photograph frontispiece.
Miyikampi (W)	place and country name. See map p. 112.
ngangkayi (W)	traditional healer.
ngapa (W)	water, rain.
Ngapajinpi (W)	place name. Also name of ancestral hero, written *ngapajinpi* to distinguish from place. See map p. 112.
ngarlu (W)	sugar bag, honey.
Ngunulurru (W)	country name, see map p. 112.
njinaŋa (S)	includes all persons of a given 'totemic clan' related – actual and classificatory – as father, son, brother, daughter, sister. See Strehlow 1947: 139-50.
patrilineal	descent traced through male line.
patri-moiety	division of society into halves based on descent reckoned patrilineally.
Pawurrinji (W)	place and country name. See map p. 112.

tjuringa (S)	sacred object, *churinga* (Spencer and Gillen).
Waake (K)	place and country name. See map p. 112.
Wakulpu (W)	place and country name. See map p. 112 = Wakurlpu.
Walapanpa (W)	place and country name, Saddle Hole Dam, Anningie Station. See map p. 112.
wankili (W)	kinship term, 'cousin', mother's brother's daughter, father's sister's daughter. See kinship diagram, Appendix 2.
wardingi (W)	witchetty grub.
Wurrulju (W)	place and country name, = Errwelje (K). See map p. 112.
yawulyu (W)	women's ceremonies and ritual designs, = *awelye* (K).
yungkurru (W)	name of ceremony in which men and women participate, see fn. 4:2.
Yawakiyi (W)	bush berry, *Canthium latifolium*, = *aakeye*, *ahakeye* (K), also *yaakiyi*, *aakiy* (W).
yilpinji (W)	rituals and designs associated with emotional management, 'love rituals'. See fn. 3:26.

INDEX

Aboriginal Benefit Trust Fund, 79
Aboriginal Inland Mission, 123
Aboriginal Land Rights (Northern Territory) Act 1976, 8
    see also, land claims; land trusts
Aboriginal Sacred Sites Protection Authority, 2
Adelaide, 4 (map), 25, 27, 70, 234
adultery, 38, 157
    see also, liaisons; marriage
adze, 91, 99 (photo)
age,
    attraction and, 166
    authority and, 11, 19-20, 29, 35, 45, 52, 81
    knowledge and, 232, 233
Akwerlpe, 114, 138
    see also, Wakulpu
Alice Springs, 3, 4 (map), 18, 123, 150, 163
    see also, towns
alcohol, 31-2, 42, 76, 109 n76, n78, 157, 161
    drunkenness and, 161, 220, 221
    see also, Liquor Act
Ali-Curang (Alekarenge), 4 (map), 8, 72, 112 (map)
    see also, Warrabri
Alyawarra, 7
    change in women's lives, 94-106
    country of, 48, 50, 62, 64, 120
    dreamings, 196-7, 199
    eastsiders, 8, 74-90
    employment of, 78-9
    history of, 62-6
    initiation, 207-26
    jilimi, 81-3
    rituals, 81, 129 (photo), 187 (photo), 188-90
    section system, 196, 261
    orthography, 6

see also, Aranda, eastsiders
Alyawarra and Kaititja land claim, 43, 49 (map)
Ammaroo, 48, 49 (map)
ancestors, see *jukurrpa*
Anmatjirra (Ammatjirri), 120, 186
Aranda (Arrernte),
    Finke Aranda, 214
    initiation, 207-26
    land tenure, 101, 118, 137-9, 179 n13, 240
    orthography, 6, 255
    rituals, 101
    subsections, 261
Ardener, E., 244, 254 n54
Areyonga, 154
Arnhem Land, 40 n9, 250, 252 n2
Ashwin, A., 63-4
assimilation, 70-72, 103
Attack Creek, 60-61, 63, 72
Australian Institute of Aboriginal Studies, 1, 30-31
Australian National University, 1, 3, 250
Australian New Zealand Association of the Advancement of Science (A.N.Z.A.A.S.), 233-5
authority of women, 17, 33, 46, 81, 177, 179
    see also, age; autonomy; ceremonies; independence; *jilimi*; land; social organization; women
autonomy of women,
    decision-making, 35, 51, 59, 106, 212
    economic, 26, 43, 50-51, 84, 96
    in myth, 165, 174
    loss of, 104, 161, 249
    self image of, 230

286

traditional, 150, 152, 231
see also, authority of women;
   independence; *jilimi*; women

Banka Banka, 143
Barrow Creek, 48, 49 (map), 64, 76,
   82
   telegraph station, 58, 62, 66
   massacre, 63, 102
   rations, 45, 54
   wolfram, 69, 111
Barwick, D., 3, 42, 234
Bates, D., 234, 262 n16
Bathurst Island, 236
Beckett, J. T., 66, 100
Bell, D., 181 n49, 227 n12
Bell, G., 3, 10, 31, 38, 52 (photo),
   232
Bell, M., 3, 10, 31, 38, 52 (photo),
   211, 214, 232
Berndt, C. H., 40 n10, 177, 180
   n26, n30, 229, 233, 234, 243,
   250, 252 n8, 253 n52
Berndt, R. M., 178, 181 n41, 250
birth, 22, 103, 151, 161
   see also, initiation
blood, 37-8, 156, 157, 161
boards, *see* sacred boards; *churinga*
body painting, 11-14, 14 (photo),
   111, 125-8, 129 (photo), 154-9
   passim, 187-90, 198, 221
   see also, *kurduru*; *yawulyu*
Bohannan, L., 9, 39 n2
Bonney Well, 61, 118
bosses, *see* independence
Bowen, L., *see* Bohannan
Brooks, F., 67, 69
Brooks' Soak, 69
Bullocky Soak, 71
Burg Wartenstein, 2
bush berry, see *yawakiyi*

camels, 44, 96
camps,
   family, 15, 84, 101-2, 110
   Kaytej, 74, 81-4

spatial relations of, 73-89
special purpose, 220
Warlpiri, 14-17
Warrabri, 7-8
see also, *jilimi*; sorry camps
Canberra, 3, 4 (map), 11, 25, 26, 27,
   30, 34, 38, 41
cattle stations, 45, 49 (map), 64-7,
   79-80, 101-2
   employment, 48, 78, 80, 94-6
   stand down, 80
   see also, eastsiders; pastoral
   frontier
Cawte, J., 180 n22, 242
Central Australia,
   ceremonies of, 126-46, 162-79,
   191-205, 205-26
   exploration of, 60-62
   pastoral frontier and, 64-9
   telegraph lines and, 62
Central Australian Aboriginal
   Legal Aid Service, 9, 29, 36
Central Land Council, 2, 9, 29, 36
Central Mount Stuart, 63, 106 n7
ceremonies,
   crises of life, 81, 151, 161
   east and westside, 79, 101-2
   exchange, 190-205
   men's and women's, 182ff
   structure of, 182, 183, 185, 191
   resolution of conflict, 153, 160,
   193
   see also, initiation; *yawulyu*;
   yilpinji; *yungkurru*
Chalmers family, 66
Chewings, C., 43, 51-2, 58-9, 106
   n7, 180 n33
church, 124
   see also, missions
churinga, 51-2
   see also, *kurduru*; sacred boards
colonization, 42, 44, 45, 76, 78,
   100, 249
colour, 128, 155, 158, 166-9
conception dreaming, 122, 142-3,
   147

Coniston massacre, 49 (map), 67, 69
Councils, 8, 33, 38, 46, 74, 79, 88-9, 149, 185, 192
country,
    desert, 22, 163
    limits of, 130, 132, 202
    relation to, 264-7
    yilipinji, 163, 174, 178-9
    see also, land; land tenure; territories
craftswomen, 83, 95 (photo), 97 (photo), 99 (photo), 111

Daly River, 4 (map), 250
Darwin, 2, 4 (map), 64, 70, 123, 163, 191
Davenport Ranges, 48, 61
death, 84, 115, 123
Department of Aboriginal Affairs, 29, 86, 88-9
Devil's Marbles, 48, 54, 76, 110-11, 163-5, 167, 186, 188, 192-202 *passim*
    see also, Karlukarlu
diamond dove dreaming, 12, 13 (photo), 159
diet,
    bush tucker, 22, 27, 52, 54, 57 (photo), 63 (photo), 105 (photo), 121, 131, 132, 134
    contribution of the sexes, 54, 107 n22
    food distribution, 54-6
    see also, rations
dispute resolution, 124
    see also, ceremonies (resolution of conflicts); fights
Ditton, P., 2, 3, 124
Dixon Creek, 167
dog,
    dreaming, 8, 72, 137, 143, 188
    camps in, 15, 45, 119
    hunting, 26
Dreamtime, 21-2, 52, 76, 91-4, 125, 130, 170, 174-5, 182-3, 191
    see also, jukurrpa; Law

dreaming,
    dogma of, 91
    instances of, 93, 193, 196, 200
    localized and travelling, 134, 136-7
    see also, dog; *jukurrpa*, kangaroo; *ngapa; ngarlu; wardingi; yawakiyi*
drought, 64, 67
Durkheim, E., 236, 242

Eastsiders of Warrabri, 8, 101
    initiation, 207-26
    life-style, 76-89
    see also, Alyawarra; Kaytej
Education Department, 10-11, 27, 184, 188
    see also; schools
Ellis, C., 40 n10, 234
Elkedra Station, 48, 49 (map), 64
Elkin, A. P., 233, 234, 243, 262 n12
employment of Aborigines,
    army-time, 70
    cattle stations, 78, 80, 94-6
    changing patterns, 46, 105-6
    lack of, 8, 96
    settlements, 28, 91
    mining, 70, 96
    missions, 96
Engels, F., 43
Epenarra, 42, 49 (map)
Errwelje, 114, *see* Wurrulju
Erulja, 187 (photo)
Etwerrpe, 112 (map), 138
Evans-Pritchard, E. E., 244
exploration, 60-62
Eylmann, E., 65

family planning, 151-2, 159, 236, 243
family structure, 45, 78, 79-80, 81, 101-2, 151, 161
    household heads, 83, 104
    white families, 87-8
farm (Warrabri), 86, 88-9
fat, 12, 124, 128, 130, 145, 153

(photo), 154-6, 164, 166, 221
fieldwork, 231-2
    advice, 8, 9
    methods, 29-31, 183, 185, 235
fieldworkers, 9, 180 n22, 232
    classification of, 25-30
fights, 37-8, 42, 58, 73, 76, 80, 110,
    134, 158, 161, 172, 198, 235
    see also, violence
fire,
    country in, 22, 51, 68
    dreaming, 130, 136
    ritual, 126, 219
Firestone, S., 245
Frank, -., 63
Freud, S., 244, 245
Frew River, 48, 49 (map)
    attack, 65-6

Gale, F., 234, 253 n17
genealogies, 67, 111, 118, 140, 142
    Kaytej *jilimi*, 117
    shallowness of, 90
gender relations, 23, 170, 193-4
    changes in, 94-106
    complementarity, 23, 206, 244,
        254 n52
    dual systems, 246-7
    evolutionists, 245-6
    feminist analysis, 229, 244-50
    male dominance, 23, 34, 230,
        242, 244, 246, 249
    Marx, F., 242, 244
    models of, 24, 206, 235-6,
        241-50
    sexual asymmetry, 23, 244-6
    universalists, 245-6
    see also, autonomy;
        independence; men;
        paradigms; sexual politics;
        women
gestures, 15, 19 (photo), 44, 128,
    145, 173, 214, 218, 225
    see also, sand drawing; sign
        language
Gillen, F. J., 24, 40 n7, 43, 52, 58,

63, 106 n7, 235
goanna, 27, 54, 124, 154
Golde, P., 39 n3
Goodale, J., 229, 232-3, 234, 236,
    243, 252 n4, 254 n50
Granites, 69, 71
Greenwood Station, 48, 68, 110,
    118, 130, 167, 195
Gunn, Mrs. A., 234

Haasts Bluff, 49 (map), 62
hairstring, 27, 155-6, 198-9, 201,
    218, 224
Hale, K., 10, 39 n4
Hamilton, A., 1, 83, 246-7, 253 n23
Hanlon, -., 66
Hanson River, 48, 61-3, 67, 112
    (map)
Hart, C. W. M. and A. Pilling, 229,
    236, 252 n4, 253 n50
Hartwig, M., 61, 63, 65
Harvey, A., 252 n16
Hatches Creek, 48, 49 (map), 69,
    111
    see also, wolfram mines
health, 21, 130, 145-62
    cases of treatment, 153-60, 153
        (photo)
    changes in, 153
    concept of, 146
    crises of life, 152
    herbal remedies, 151
    kirda and *kurdungurlu*, 152-8
    matriline, 152, 154, 156-7
    troubles, 149
    relation to *yilpinji*, 145-6, 173
    western practice, 151, 159
Health Department, 29, 149-50
health-workers, 85, 149-50
Hermannsburg, 49 (map), 107 n12,
    192-204 *passim*
Hiatt, L., 236, 253 n23
history,
    Central Australia, 41-73
    first contact, 43, 61, 69-70, 120
    see also, exploration; mining; oral

history; Overland Telegraph; pastoral frontier
Hooker Creek (Lajumanu), 4 (map), 42, 50, 71
hospital, 85, 87-8, 124, 149, 159
Hubert River, 61
hunting and gathering society, 8, 26-7
  changes, 41, 47-8, 54-5, 79, 91, 161
  country and, 30
  mythic, 165-6, 168
  women's role, 46
  see also, diet

independence, 33, 55, 212, 247
  bosses, 7, 11, 24, 28, 47
  dependence to, 46, 151, 247
  economic, 43, 50-51, 84, 96
  jilimi and, 84
  liaisons, 58-9, 100
  models of, 230, 248
  self image, 104, 182, 230
initiation, 157, 205-26
  birth symbolism, 222, 227 n8, n16
  circumcision, 207, 223
  difficulty learning about, 207
  east and westside compared, 79, 207-25
  father-in-law nomination, 223
  feeding rituals, 208, 222-3
  'finish-up', 209, 220, 225
  firestick, 209, 217, 220, 223, 224
  'half-night' dancing, 220-23
  location of ceremonies, 214
  mother-in-law nomination, 207, 219-20, 224-5
  structure of, 209-25
  timing of, 17, 79
  women's participation, 207-26
Institute for Aboriginal Development, (I.A.D.), 6, 9
Institute of Aboriginal Studies, *see* Australian Institute of Aboriginal Studies

jaja (mother's mother), 122, 127, 134, 143, 265-6
Jakamarra of Barrow Creek, 154
Jakamarra of Wauchope, 154-5
Jampijinpa of Wakulpu, 194 (fig.), 195-204 *passim*
Jampijinpa of Walapanpa, 192, 194 (fig.), 195-204 *passim*
Jangala of Hermannsburg, 192-205 *passim*
Jangala of Phillip Creek, 148-9
Japangardi of the dream, 92-3
Jarrajarra, 111, 112 (map), 114, 119, 121-2, 134, 136, 141-2
jilimi, 7, 11, 16 (photo), 94
  Alyawarra, 217
  changes in, 37, 84, 145
  east and westside, 81-4
  Kaytej, 82-3, 110-36 *passim*
  residents, 16, 111-36
  structure, 16, 82-4
  Warlpiri, 16-17, 81
jukurrpa, 47, 50, 104, 111, 130, 134, 144, 146-7, 193, 200, 205, 226, 230, 247
  change and continuity, 90-94
  see also, Dreamtime; dreaming; Law
Junkaji, 112 (map), 134, 167, 200, 202, 204
Jupurrula of Wurrulju, 67, 116-17, 185-7, 194 (fig.), 194-5

Kaberry, P., 40 n10, 177, 180 n30, n39, 229, 232, 234, 254 n50
kangaroo dreaming, 134, 136, 217
  and country, 55
Karlukarlu, 97 (photo), 112 (map), 128-37, 153 (photo), 163, 185, 195-202 *passim*
  women of, 110-28, 238
  see also, Devil's Marbles
Kanturrpa, 112 (map), 123
Kaytej,
  changes in women's lives, 94-106
  country, 48, 54, 61, 110-44

passim, 227 n13
eastsiders, 8, 74-89
employment, 48, 80-81
see also, cattle stations
history of, 63-72
initiation, 79, 207-26 *passim*
jilimi, 82-3, 110-36 *passim*
land tenure, 50, 101, 137-44,
    264-72
orthography, 6, 255
rituals, 28, 81-2, 130-6, 145-6,
    153-61, 162-79, 191-205
subsections, 261
Kelly's Well, 62
kinship, 29, 36, 56, 236
Arandic system, 256-7
avoidance, 15, 18, 36
country and, 90, 115, 118, 124,
    127, 134, 137, 140-41
role and status,
    aunts, 21, 25, 35, 91, 209,
        265-6
    brothers, 35, 214, 218
    children, 7, 10, 16, 42, 71, 85,
        100, 147, 152, 156, 189
        and country, 52, 55, 79
        child rearing, 56, 231,
            234, 236
        as teachers, 18
    co-wives, 58, 80
    daughters, 20, 35, 42, 114-15,
        119, 141, 154, 158, 202, 224
    fathers, 20, 35, 56, 69, 71, 90,
        113, 140
    fathers-in-law, 35, 223
    grandparents, 16, 35, 90, 111,
        122, 132
    husbands, 15, 35-6, 42, 121
    mothers, 25, 35, 42, 52, 56,
        90-110, 140, 153 (photo), 155,
        158, 159, 209, 256-9
    mothers-in-law, 110, 157, 209,
        213-14, 218-20, 224-5, 258-9,
        269-72
    mothers' mothers, 152, 217-18
        see also, jaja

siblings, 90, 118, 141
sisters, 25, 27, 35, 53, 119,
    154, 158, 159, 209-21 *passim*,
    in myth, 167
sons, 42, 110, 118, 123, 213-14
sons-in-law, 15, 18, 33, 35-6, 84
uncle, 35
widows, 17, 27, 180 n27
wives, 42, 202
    see also, marital relations
    see also, marriage
Warlpiri kinship terms, 258-9
white families, 87-8
    see also, social organization;
        subsections
kirda,
    country and, 51, 92-3, 111-28,
        138-43, 250 (photo), 253 n29,
        265-71
    health and, 152-8
    initiation and, 221
    ritual structure and, 20-21, 165,
        184-9, 193, 238-40, 247
    see also, jilimi; kurdungurlu; land
        tenure; social organization
Koch *et al.*, 266
Kuhn, T., 241, 244
Kularturlangu, 68, 132
kumunjayi, see speech taboos
kurduru, ii, 95 (photo), 127 (photo),
    132, 196-202 *passim*, 203
    (photo)
    see also, sacred boards
kurdungurlu,
    country and, 93, 111-28, 138-43,
        250 (photo), 253 n29, 265-71
    health and, 152-8
    initiation and, 216-22, 238-40
    ritual and structure, 20-21, 129
        (photo), 165, 184-9, 193,
        238-40, 247
    see also, jilimi; kirda; land tenure;
        social organization
Kurinji (Gurindji), 12
kurinpi myth, 164, 167-9, 171, 188
Kurundi Station, 48, 66

Lake Woods, 123
Lander River, 50, 67, 76, 112
 (map), 138
land,
 marriage and, 267-71
 loss of, 101-2, 103, 151, 168,
  174, 249 (in myth), 167-9,
  171-3
 tenure, 50-51, 110-28, 137-44
 yawulyu and, 128-37
 see also, country; territories
Land Rights,
 see *Aboriginal Land Rights
  (Northern Territory) Act,* 1976
Land Claims, 38, 39 n1, 115, 131,
  133 (photo), 187 (photo)
 Alyawarra and Kaititja claim, 43,
  49 (map) Kaytej, Warlpiri and
  Warlmanpa claim, 49 (map),
  179 n1
 Warlmanpa, Warlpiri, Mudbara
  and Warumungu claim, 49
  (map), 179 n2
Land Trusts, 8, 39 n1
Laughren, M., 3, 179 n1, 213, 227
 n2
Law (Aboriginal), 12, 20, 34, 37,
  47, 62, 76, 92, 94, 152, 170,
  183, 248
 see also, dreaming; *jukurrpa*
Leacock, E., 43, 245
learning styles, 19 (photo), 19-28,
  34-9, 207-17, 231
Lévi-Strauss, L., 242
liaisons,
 Aboriginal, 58, 116, 148
 black/white, 45, 65, 69, 70, 73,
  98, 100-101, 163
 missionaries, 77
 mythic, 168, 173
life history, see oral history
Liquor Act, 109 n76
love, 130, 145, 155, 162
 kin and, 35-6
 magic and, 162, 176
 sex and, 163

local organization, 236-7
 *see also, jilimi; kirda;
  kurdungurlu;* land tenure;
  social organization
Luritja, 232

McConnel, U., 252 n16
Maddock, K., 229, 252 n2
marriage, 32, 42-3, 54, 80, 98, 121,
  180 n27, 236-7
 affines, 35, 238-40
 initiation and, 205, 215, 219,
  223, 271-2
 marital relations, 16, 18, 25, 31,
  36, 121-2, 157, 251 (photo)
 polygyny, 103, 121
 rules, 19, 92, 100
 statistics, 78, 162
 systems, 261-2, 267-72
 see also, kinship; social
  organization
massacres, 41, 51, 60-61, 64, 67, 78,
  116, 119, 144, 189
 see also, Barrow Creek; Coniston;
  Frew River; Powell Creek
Mead, M., 39 n3
meetings, 29, 33
Meggitt, M., 24, 40 n11, 48, 55, 60,
  73, 83, 100 109 n79, 162, 180
  n22, n26, 181 n50, 208, 212,
  226, 237, 238-40, 262
Melbourne, 4 (map), 11, 25, 27
Melville Is., 233
men, 34-8,
 attitudes to children, 56
  to food getting, 56
  to women's ceremonies, 11,
   124, 183-91, 243
 authority, 33
 exclusion of, 37, 124, 190
 meetings, 29
 myth in, 165-72, 183
 political roles, 24, 29, 34, 46, 125
 solidarity, 37
menstruation, 151-2, 161
Milner, Ralph and John, 64

mining, 50,
 employment of Aborigines, 70,
  96
 impact of, 69, 98
Mitchell, J., 245
missions, 45, 50, 68, 70-71, 78, 96,
 100, 120, 123, 192
 see also, Phillip Creek
Miyikampi, 44, 111, 112 (map),
 123, 134
Montagu, A., 243
Morphett Creek, 72
Morton, J., 67
Munn, N., 171, 180 n26, 181 n31,
 n50, 229, 238-40, 242
Murray Constable, 67-8
Murray Downs Station, 49 (map),
 64
myths, 52, 118, 172, 174
 grandmothers, 133-4
 kurinpi, 164, 167, 169, 171-2
 ngapa, 148, 164, 167-9, 171
 Rainbow Men, 130, 167-9
 yawakiyi, 132
 see also, dreaming; *jukurrpa*

Nakamarra,
 author's classification, 18, 20-21
 Karlukarlu of, 3
 Pawurrinji of, 5
names, 6, 18
name taboos, 68, 85, 90, 186
 see also, speech taboos
Nampijinpa (Big), 117 (fig.), 118,
 123, 142
Nampijinpa (health), 159
Nampijinpa (Little), 117 (fig.), 142
Nampijinpa of Wakulpu, 3, 111-18,
 124, 131, 136, 192-202 *passim*,
 194 (fig.)
Nangala of Wakulpu, 117-18, 194
 (fig.), 198-202 *passim*
Napanangka (Warlpiri), 44
Napanangka of Wakulpu, 116, 117
 (fig.), 203 (photo)

Napangardi of Karlukarlu camp,
 123
Napurrula (Warlpiri), 3, 159
Napurrula of Karlukarlu camp, 3,
 27, 52, 53 (photo), 54, 71, 115,
 117 (fig.), 122-3, 124, 127
 (photo), 131, 136, 194 (fig.),
 195-202 *passim*
Napurrula (*ngangkayi*), 156
Nash, D., 5, 255, 262-3
Neutral Junction Station, 82,
 188-90, 198
New Zealand, 27
Ngalia Warlpiri, 78, 238, 239
ngangkayi, 120, 149, 154, 155, 156,
 159, 160-61
Ngapajinpi, 122, 128, 198
ngapa (rain/water), 112 (map), 114,
 127, 128, 130, 134, 148, 154,
 156, 159, 163, 164, 167-9, 180
 n31, 185, 188, 192-202 *passim*
 see also, myth; Rainbow Men
ngarlu (honey/sugar bag), 134
Ngunulurru, 112 (map), 114, 142
Northern Territory, 25, 39, 100,
 162
Nungarrayi (mother of Nampijinpa
 of Wakulpu), 114-15, 117
 (fig.)
Nungarrayi of Wakulpu, 3, 45, 52,
 68-9, 117-22, 124, 131, 135
 (photo), 136, 154, 157,
 192-202 *passim*, 194 (fig.), 204
nurturance, 21, 56, 76,133 (photo),
 144, 146, 160-61, 178, 182-3,
 205, 230, 248
 see also, health; initiation; land;
 yawulyu; yilpinji

ochres, 11, 124-5, 154-5, 198,
 216-17, 221
 see also, health; *yawulyu*
O'Connell, J., 253 n29
oral history (life history), 41, 45,
 67, 81, 113-15, 119, 120-21,
 131-2

orthography, 6, 255
outstations, 73
Overland Telegraph, 62, 66, 98,
    106 n12

pacification, 42, 63, 65, 67, 102,
    119
painting, *see* body painting
Papunya, 77
paradigms, 24
    'anthropology of women', 242,
    244
    'man equals culture', 241-2
    'toward a feminist perspective',
    244-50
Parker, Langloh, 234, 252 n16
parraja (wooden carrier), 17
    (photo), 134
pastoral frontier, 64-9
Pawurrinji, 12, 14 (photo), 44, 112
    (map), 116, 122, 134, 195, 251
    (photo)
pensions, 26, 76, 83-4
    see also, rations; Social Security
Peterson, N., 1, 237
Phillip Creek, 27, 42, 49 (map),
    70-71, 77-8, 86, 96, 123, 148,
    162
Pilling, A., see Hart, C. W. M. and
Pink, O., 234
Pintupi, 77
police, 68, 77, 86, 87-8, 124, 147
Port August, 8
Powell Creek, 72
prostitution, 98
    see also, liaisons
punitive parties, 44, 63, 68, 115
    see also, massacres; pacification

Radcliffe-Brown, A. R., 236, 237
rain, see *ngapa*
rainbows, 130, 158, 164
Rainbow Men, 130, 167-9
rainfall, 22, 83
rape, 150
rations, 45-6, 63, 66, 69, 70-71, 77,
80, 113, 250
Reay, M., 234, 252 n16
red ochre, *see* ochre
religion, studies of, 5, 23
    see also, dreaming; *jukurrpa*, Law
'ring-place', 110-28 *passim*
    see also, ceremonies
Rivers, W. H. R., 236
Roheim, G., 48, 107 n12, 167, 176,
    180 n26, n39, 232, 242-3, 254
    n50
Roper River, 250
Ross, —., 61
Roth, W. E., 235

sacred boards, 11-14, 41, 62, 123,
    127-8, 130, 187 (photo),
    187-9, 198-204 *passim*, 250
sand drawing, 19 (photo), 20
    see also, gesture; sign language
Sandover River, 48, 49 (map), 64
sanctions,
    of women, 37, 55, 80, 124, 164,
    206
    of men, 37
schools, 10, 77, 85-7, 121, 124, 148,
    151, 213-14
    and teaching assistants, 85, 184
secrecy, 10, 27, 30-31, 33, 36, 102,
    131, 142, 184-5, 207, 246
    and fieldwork, 2-3, 9
settlements, 7-8, 31, 37, 46, 52,
    102, 178, 231
    Warrabri, 72-90
    see also, Papunya; Warrabri;
    Yuendumu
sex segregation, 45, 59, 206, 226,
    241, 246, 248, 250
    camps of, 17, 94
    ceremonies and, 183-4, 190
    fieldwork, and, 26-39, 183
    food and, 56
sexual politics, 45-6, 104, 162-3,
    177-8, 183, 193, 206, 226, 242,
    248

Singleton bore, 54
Singleton Station, 49 (map), 120
sign language, 111, 115
  see also, gesture; sand drawing
sites, 38, 93, 115, 122, 126, 137-8,
  183
  access, 30, 37, 163-4
  burial, 115
  conception, 143
  maintenance, 14 (photo)
  visit, 30
  violation, 62-3, 147
  'skins', 18, 208,
  see also, kinship; marriage, social
    organization; subsection
    system
Skull Creek, 63
Slocum, S., 56
snake dreaming (*warnajarra*), 158,
  193, 239
social organization, 260-72
  generation levels, 19, 260, 271
  matriline, 25, 87, 90, 152, 154,
    156-7
  moieties, 156, 260-61
    endogamous generation,
      238-40, 247
    matrimoieties, 19, 29, 260-61
    patrimoieties, 19, 119, 260
  patriclan, 237
  patriline, 51, 90, 141
  see also, jilimi; kinship; local
    organization; marriage
Society Security, 42, 46, 83, 250
  Department of, 83
  see also, pensions; rations
songs, 11, 93, 109 n79, 124, 126,
  128, 143, 145, 155-6, 184-9
  love, 163, 169, 170-71, 173, 175,
    178, 181 n41
sorry camps, 82
  see also, death
speech taboos, 44, 68, 85, 115
  see also, name taboos
Spencer, B., 24, 48, 106 n7, 235
Spencer, B. and F. J. Gillen, 40

  n11, 51, 62, 106 n12, 180 n19,
    191, 204, 212, 214, 226, 227
    n2
Stanner, W. E. H., 5, 92
Stapleton, -., 63
Stirling, E. C., 62
Stirling Station, 48, 49 (map), 132
Stirling Swamp, 48, 164, 186, 188
store-house (ceremonial), 118,
  125-8, 198
store (Warrabri), 73, 76, 86-8, 125
Strehlow, T. G. H., 48, 107 n12,
  171-2, 178, 180 n26, n29, 181
  n50, 212, 226, 227 n2, 237
Stuart Highway, 22, 54, 163
Stuart, McDouall, 60-61, 118
subsections, 6, 18, 91, 94, 117, 134,
  141, 164, 196, 214, 260-64
  names, 261
  classifications, 18, 21, 86
  see also, kinship; land tenure;
    'skins', social organization

Tanami Desert, 116
Tanner, N., 56
Taylor Crossing, 22, 54, 61, 113
Tennant Creek, 4 (map), 43, 62,
  66-7, 69-70, 72, 77, 98, 114,
  123, 148
  see also, towns
territories, 48-50
  see also, country; land tenure
time, dimensions of, 47
Ti-Tree, 113, 148, 188
Tiwi, 233, 236, 243
tobacco, 44-5, 54, 62, 113
towns, 50, 70-72, 79, 98
Tuxworth, H., 43, 60, 100
  see also, Alice Springs; Tennant
    Creek

University of Sydney, 236
Utopia Station, 4 (map), 48

vehicles, 7, 24, 54, 125, 158
Victoria River, 51, 107 n7

Victoria River Downs, 250
violence, 31-2, 37, 63-5, 69, 78
  in myth, 167, 172
  see also, fights

Waake, 112 (map), 113-19, 131,
  133-4, 137, 141, 197-202
  passim
Wafer, J., 5, 258-9, 272 n1
Wakaja, 65
Wakulpu, 68, 112 (map), 111-21,
  127, 128, 130-37, 141, 192,
  202, 203 (photo), 238
Walapanpa, 92, 112 (map), 134,
  197
wardingi (witchetty grub), 112
  (map), 116, 130, 134, 186,
  193-202
Warlmanpa, 7, 21
Warlpiri, 7
  changes in women's lives, 94-106
  communities, 78, 238, 239
  country, 50, 60, 62, 66, 120,
    137-8
  jilimi, 81
  kinship, 256-9
  land tenure, 50, 101, 138, 239
  language, 9, 10, 18
  orthography, 6, 255
  subsections, 261
  teachers, 19-21
  westsiders, 8, 60, 74-89
  yawulyu, 11-15, 12 (photo), 184
Warlukurlangu, 111, 112 (map)
Warner, L., 40 n9, 229, 243, 254
  n50
Warnku, 69, 95 (photo), 112 (map),
  113-14, 120, 131, 137
Warrabri settlement, 4 (map),
  10-11, 42, 47, 54, 72, 143, 145,
  146-7
  history of, 60, 71-3
  spatial relations, 75 (map)
    centre-periphery, 74, 84-90
    east-west, 74-90, 159
  see also, initiation; *jilimi;*

  yawulyu; yilpinji; yungkurru
Warumungu (Warramanga), 7
  at Attack Creek, 60-61
  ceremonies, 123
  history, 50, 166
  territory, 48, 62, 114, 120
  reserve, 72
  as westsiders, 8, 76
water carriers, 97, 99 (photo)
water resources, 22, 67, 69, 77, 131,
  168
  water-holes, 41, 61, 66, 70
  soakages, 113, 121, 136
Wauchope, 48, 49 (map), 54, 69-70,
  110, 120, 127, 131, 155, 195
Wave Hill Station, 50
welfare, 27-8, 72, 78, 100, 113
Western Desert, 246-7
westsiders, 8
  life-style, 76-89
  initiations, 207-225
White, I., 1, 233, 252 n8
Wickham, J., 66
willy-wagtail, 12 (photo), 13, 20-21
Winnecke, C., 62, 64
Willowra Station, 4 (map), 133
  (photo), 157-9, 213, 215
wolfram mining, 48, 69-71, 111,
  113, 120, 155
  see also, Barrow Creek; Hatches
    Creek; Wauchope
women,
  exclusion of, 37, 179
  in myth, 52, 165-73
  knowledge of country, 22,
    113-23, 126, 193
  knowledge of men's ceremonies,
    33, 184-205 *passim*
  responsibility for land, 21, 87,
    95-6, 131, 133 (photo), 251
    (photo)
  solidarity, 17, 33, 37, 46, 56, 58,
    164, 166, 182, 249
  see also, age; authority,
    ceremonies; independence,
    jilimi; kirda; kurdungurlu; land

tenure; marriage; men; social organization
World War Two, 70-71
Wycliffe Well, 62
Wurrulju, 111, 112 (map), 116, 122, 134

Yalata, 233
yandaridji, 171
yawakiyi (bush berry), 112 (map), 116, 130-31, 156, 158, 186, 191-202 *passim*
  red, 196
  black, 197
  ritual, 197
yawulyu, 10, 11-14, 24, 118-19, 112-13, 126-46
  and health, 152-61
  and land, 130-36
  and love, 145-6, 162-79
  see also, initiation; *jilimi; kirda; kurdungurlu;* land tenure; social organization; *yilpinji, yungkurru*
yilpinji, 130, 145-6, 162-79, 180 n26
  care with, 173
  colour, 169-70, 172, 181 n33
  country and, 163, 174, 178-9
  display, 170, 172
  feelings and, 172-3, 176
  health and, 145-6, 173
  magic and, 162, 170, 173, 176-8
  marriage and, 162, 175-7
  myth, 164-9, 171
  power of, 176
  reasons for, 173
  sex and, 163, 172, 173, 180 n30
  songs, 163, 175
  themes of, 163
  see also, ceremonies; health; *jilimi;* love; marriage; *yawulyu*
yirpadirlpadirlpa, 130-32, 201-2
Yuendumu settlement, 4 (map), 42, 50, 71, 77, 96, 213, 215, 239
Yuendumu orthography, 6, 255

yungkurru, 184, 187, 191-205, 227 n2
  boards, 198-205
  common core of knowledge, 191
  dreamings, 192-204
  participants, 192-4
  sex segregation, 184
  sites, 192-204
  songs, 200-201
  structure, 191-205
  young men and, 193
  see also, yawulyu; yilpinji

Zihlman, A., 56